D0312965

FUN WHILE IT LASTED

My Rise and Fall in the Land of Fame and Fortune

FUN WHILE IT LASTED

My Rise and Fall in the Land of Fame and Fortune

BRUCE McNALL
with Michael D'Antonio

NEW YORK

Copyright © 2003 Aureus Ventures, Inc.

All rights reserved. No part of this book may be used or reproduced in any manner whatsoever without the written permission of the Publisher. Printed in the United States of America. For information address: Hyperion, 77 West 66th Street, New York, New York 10023–6298.

Library of Congress Cataloging-in-Publication Data

McNall, Bruce
    Fun while it lasted : my rise and fall in the land of fame and fortune / Bruce McNall with Michael D'Antonio.—1st ed.
        p. cm.
    ISBN 0-7868-6864-3
    1. McNall, Bruce   2. Commercial criminals—California—Biography.   3. Fraud—California—Case studies.   4. Businessmen—California—Biography.   5. Capitalists and financiers—California—Biography.   6. Hockey team owners—California—Biography.   I. D'Antonio, Michael   II. Title.

HV6766.M5 M36 2003
364.16'8'092—dc21
[B]
                                                                                                2002032823

Hyperion books are available for special promotions and premiums. For details contact Hyperion Special Markets, 77 West 66th Street, 11th floor, New York, New York 10023-6298, or call 212-456-0133.

FIRST EDITION
10   9   8   7   6   5   4   3   2   1

ACKNOWLEDGMENTS

~

EVERY WRITER, ESPECIALLY EVERY FIRST-TIME AUTHOR, depends on a host of people for support and encouragement. I can count many people who helped me live through the experiences I recount here. From the jet-setting days to the prison nights, I have been blessed with faithful friends. One who bears special mention is Michael Eisner, who saw the value of my story and, fortunately, kept pushing me to tell it all.

In a more direct way I have received unlimited support from my friend and business partner Robert Geringer. I have borrowed much of his wisdom and humor for these pages. No thank you can fully express my gratitude to him, but I offer it here anyway. I am similarly grateful to Isabel Meyer and Rebecca Aebersold, who were able assistants and first readers as this book was written. They were kind enough to laugh at the funny parts even as they suggested important improvements. I never could have completed such a personal and emotional experience as this without the love and support of my children Katie and PJ, as well as my mate Dayna Hester, with whom I hope to spend the remainder of my life sharing whatever the world has in store for those final chapters.

Among the many people who offered advice and counsel I would offer special thanks to Brian Lipson, who is much more than an A-list agent.

My thanks go also to Robert Miller, Will Schwalbe, and Leslie Wells of Hyperion, whose patience and confidence were always there, even when I sometimes felt lost. Most of all I thank them for suggesting I work with the writer Michael D'Antonio, who guided me from the first word to the last, demanding of me the candor and effort that in the end made this story of my life thus far the truest I could write.

FOREWORD

~

THE FIRST THING EVERYONE WANTS to know is how I did it. How had I turned my intelligence, nerve, and a bit of fraud, into a business empire worth hundreds of millions of dollars? And how had I hidden the truth, while enjoying a jet-setting public life for so many years?

After asking how, the inevitable question is: Why? Why did I push so hard? Why did I take so many risks? Why did I ultimately break the law in pursuit of my ambitions?

Federal prison, especially solitary confinement, gives one ample opportunity to reflect on questions like these. I used my years behind bars to reflect on the mystery of my own life. This book is the product of those years, my attempt to understand and to explain myself to all those who consider me a friend, a partner, a showman, and even a scoundrel.

I have been all of these things and more. Indeed, all my failings and insecurities will be evident here, even as you see me courting presidents and billionaires and trading favors with star athletes and actors. If I can claim all the power, wealth, fame, and achievements of my life, I must also accept responsibility for my failures.

The story I tell here is the truth, as plainly as I can say it. It is supported not just by my memory, but by research, thousands of pages of legal documents, and many corroborative interviews. But even as I offer my best recitation of the facts, I don't expect you to agree with all of my conclusions. However, as my life unfolds before you, try to consider whether you, in the same place and time, would have resisted temptation any better than I.

1

THE COIN I WOULD HAND YOU, if you were with me right now, would be nearly two thousand years old and about the size of a silver dollar. It would be a lustrous bronze sestertius, one of the largest coins minted by the Roman empire. As you felt the weight of both the metal and history in your hand, I'd ask you to look at the obverse, or face side. There you would see the profile of a man with a long nose and a slightly upturned chin. His hair is long and curly. He wears a laurel wreath. Along the circumference of the coin is the message, "NERO CLAUDIUS CAESAR AUG GERM P M TR P IMP P P."

The first few words are easy to understand. They identify Nero, the Caesar who ruled Rome from A.D. 54 to his suicide in A.D. 68. The rest of the letters signify that his empire included Germany, he was the head of religion (*pontifex maximus*) and that he acted with the authority of the tribune (*tribunicia potestate*).

"This is a coin that was minted under the orders of the most powerful man in the world," I would tell you. "It was held and traded by Roman citizens. It may have been in the possession of Nero himself, or his family, or one of his soldiers."

All Roman coins told a story, maybe the news of the day or some propaganda. Look on the reverse side of this one. It shows the Temple of Janus, pieces of which remain today in modern Rome. In ancient times, when temple doors were closed it meant there was peace in the world. It was rare that the doors of the temple would be closed because Rome was almost always at war with someone. But on the coin they are closed. The message was clear: Nero brings peace to Rome.

The coin is a dazzling little artifact, and the story makes it all the more appealing. All ancient coins have this appeal. Take the silver denarius that the Roman general Brutus—yes, *that* Brutus—minted after he murdered Julius Caesar in 44 B.C. It bears the clearest likeness of him we have, showing his fine features and slender neck. On the other side are pictures of two daggers and a liberty cap and the Latin inscription EID MAR. The propaganda message of this coin, which Brutus used to pay his army, was: *I stabbed Caesar on the Ides of March for the cause of freedom.*

Because only a few exist in the world, the Brutus denarius, which is the size of a modern American dime, would probably be valued at more than $100,000. But a Nero sestertius could be had today for as little as $500. More common, but nevertheless ancient, historic coins minted by the Romans, Greeks, or Egyptians can be bought for as little as $10 apiece. Think about it. A coin once clutched in the hands of the people who built the Colosseum or the Parthenon, a truly beautiful work of art, is yours for the price of a hamburger, fries, and a Coke. And, unlike the lunch, it will be around and might even increase in value year, after year, after year.

If the beauty and material value of the coins aren't enough to excite your imagination, then consider one last, romantic fact. Almost every ancient coin has its own story, which almost certainly includes a bit of skullduggery. It is likely that most of the ancient coins in private hands today were literally dug out of the ground somewhere in Europe, the Middle East, or North Africa. Indeed, untold numbers of coins remain buried in those regions, left by those who used the earth as their bank vault and died without telling a soul where their wealth was hidden. History is filled with accounts of people inadvertently finding such treasures. The largest hoard ever discovered was found by children playing in a pasture near Marseilles in 1366, who found some glinting silver in a small hole. As they scraped at the sides of the hole with their hands, coins fell to the bottom. The hole became a pit, and still the coins rained down. Reports from the era recall that twenty mules were needed to carry the more than four million coins from the site. They were eventually melted into silver bullion.

Even today, though most countries ban the practice, prospectors quietly search for such holes-of-gold, and they continue to find them. The coins are sold over and over again and mingled with others, until they are part of the legitimate marketplace. It may have happened six centuries ago, or last week. Either way, if you look hard enough into the story of every coin, you'll find an Indiana Jones. It lends a certain romance to the hobby.

I first saw an ancient coin, and began to learn how to profit by trading them, when I was about fourteen years old. I had a job as a clerk in a small coin-and-stamp shop in the town where I grew up, a Los Angeles suburb called Arcadia. Coins of the World Etc. occupied a storefront in a drab strip mall on Baldwin Avenue. The place had a worn linoleum floor, fluorescent lighting, and a couple of long glass display cases. It smelled of cigarette smoke and beer and body odor.

My boss was the owner, Ed Walthall. When I first started working for him, Ed was in his early sixties. Stout and bald with a scraggly beard, Ed was a chain-smoking, hard-drinking bachelor who wore torn and mismatched clothes and bathed only on Saturday nights. He was so paranoid that he carried a gun with him at all times. But he was also kind to me, and offered more respect and attention than any man I had met up to that point in my life, including my father.

Although Ed's business was concerned mainly with American coins, I was fascinated by the older stuff from ancient Rome and Greece. After a while he was happy to let me buy and sell a few of these items in exchange for minding the place when he went across the avenue for a long, beer-soaked lunch at a bowling alley. One day, while Ed was on his break, a military veteran came in with a metal ammunition box the size of today's desktop computers. It was filled with trays of ancient coins. The man, who was somewhere between forty and fifty years old, said that he had acquired them in Egypt, where he had paid $2,000 for them all. Now he was having trouble getting rid of them.

I took out one tray and saw bronzes struck in Egypt and some large Greek drachmas. One coin was truly rare. It had been minted by Constantine the Great after he had converted to Christianity. Altogether, that single tray was worth $3,000. And there were several more trays. The seller was willing to take $3,000 for the whole lot, if I could pay him soon.

"I'll talk to my boss," I said. "There's got to be something we can do." He left his phone number and took away the coins.

Ed said no, explaining that ancient coins were hard to sell and $3,000 was much more money than he had ever spent on one purchase. But the way I saw it, he just lacked the imagination to see the opportunity in that metal box. That night I pleaded with my mother and father, but they were also unmoved. I went to bed thinking about my last option, the one person in the world who always made me feel loved, and accepted, my grandmother.

The next day I took a bus across Los Angeles to Mar Vista and my grandmother's little two-bedroom cottage. Though I had failed with Ed and my parents, those experiences had taught me something. It's not easy to understand ancient coins and their value. With my grandmother, I tried a simpler approach. I told her the story of how the coins had come to me, making sure to share my passion for the history they represented and my excitement over the possibility for profit. When I finished, I could see she had listened carefully.

"All right," she said. "I'll write you a check."

A few days later, the coins were mine. As I carefully examined and cataloged them, I realized their value was even higher than I first believed. I took a small number of the best to a couple of L.A.'s more prominent coin dealers, who bought them right away. This gave me more than enough money to repay my grandmother. (When I tried to add interest to the payment, she refused it.) Eventually I sold all of the coins. My best guess is that I made more than $10,000 in profit. And it was all because I had been able to talk my way into the deal.

Once I realized the depth and breadth of the obscure world of ancient coins, I read everything I could find, devouring even the most arcane catalogs of information word for word. I discovered that, at their most basic, ancient coins were, like modern money, instruments of exchange. They elevated commerce from simple bartering—my goat for your four chickens—to an orderly process.

The first coins were minted in the seventh century B.C. in Greek states—in what is now Turkey. They were lumps of electrum, a soft local metal, stamped on one side with simple designs. Minting technology and craftsmanship improved steadily. By 290 B.C., a coin from Rhodes, for example, would bear the face of the sun god Helios, the god that was depicted by the Colossus of Rhodes. On the reverse of the coin was a rose, the flower for which the island was named. In Athens all of the coins had, on their obverse side, the goddess Athena. The reverse side was typically an owl, the symbol of wisdom. Almost anyone who looks at these coins and runs a finger over their images, is filled with a sense of awe. Here is a Pegasus, a gorgon, a lion's head. These are the images ancient people lived with every day.

Though the art is breathtaking, in the time when they were merely money, an ancient coin's value depended on its weight and metal. The most valuable pieces were gold and silver. Logically enough, they were minted to be roughly the same weight and size from place to place. Thus, a traveler from one Greek city or state would be able to make purchases in another, though he carried only the coins from home. This kind of exchange was possible even if the two states were at war. Nothing got in the way of money and commerce.

Precious metals such as gold and silver increase a coin's value to modern collectors, but a coin's meaning—the story it tells—and its rarity are far more important. Every collector, whether he or she accumulates coins, cars, or railroad cabooses, wants the items that are hardest to get, and those that have true historical significance. This is why a newspaper from December 8, 1941, reporting the Pearl Harbor attack, is far more valuable than the one published the day before. Of course, the smaller the number of any item, the greater its value. The famous, misprinted Inverted Jenny stamp of 1918, showing a Curtiss biplane upside down, is worth $100,000 because only one hundred exist in the world. I once owned a block of four Jenny stamps, which today would fetch half a million dollars at auction.

Historical significance and rarity fuel a collector's instinct for hunting down certain prizes. As a beginner, I couldn't hope to capture the rarest coins—even in the 1960s they were valued as high as $100,000 apiece—so instead, I tried to build a meaningful collection. I was most fascinated by the Romans, so I sought to have at least one image of as many of the emperors, their wives, and their children, as I could acquire. I was a rather obsessed and probably odd young man, intently pursuing Agrippa, Trajan, and Vespasian the way other boys chased dates with cheerleaders.

After obtaining a coin, I didn't put it on display or gaze at it for days. But I did feel good, as if a terrible itch had finally been scratched. With my collection I felt a sense of order, control, even power.

There's one other significant thing about collecting; it's addictive. I mean that it can become, for some, as consuming and ultimately out of control as a drug habit. Of course the out-of-control part doesn't happen for a long time. First you are swept away by your new passion. You find yourself thinking about it all the time. For me, it was a matter of constantly looking for that next acquisition and maneuvering to get it.

For someone with a true collector's spirit, the whole matter of pursuing and then holding new items is profoundly urgent. If I came across a coin that was rare, I immediately began to worry that if I didn't grab it, someone else would, and it would be off the market. These weren't things you could order like a pair of shoes. They appeared and then were gone. I first felt the drive to have one such special coin when I was fifteen years old and saw one that honored an emperor with the unfortunate name of Pupienus (pronounced *poopy-a-noose*).

Coins of Pupienus—this one was a sestertius—are prized because he was emperor for less than one year and therefore minted relatively few coins of any denomination. The one that caught my eye was offered for sale by Wayne Phillips, a dealer in Los Angeles with far more ancient coins than were held by my old friend Ed Walthall. The sestertius showed the emperor with a great long beard. The coin was a bit worn, with a dark brown patina, and it was priced at $400.

At age fifteen I could have done a lot with $400. My friends would have bought minibikes or saved it for a car. But there was nothing else I wanted, nothing else that mattered. Wayne agreed to let me purchase it over time, with weekly payments. I took on another job as a stock boy at a liquor store to scrape up the cash. Once I took possession of that treasure, I hid it away from my mother, my father, and my sister. I didn't think they would understand its value, or why I had spent so much money on it.

Money is a big problem for most serious collectors. It was for me. So, like many addicts, I became a dealer—a pusher of sorts—who tried to get others hooked so that I could sell them a supply and fund my own, ever-growing, habit. None of this was done consciously. In fact, even now I see the ordinary collecting of ancient coins as a positive, educational activity. My fascination with them as art objects was real, and the excitement I showed as I began to sell them to others was genuine. I loved them. I thought everyone else should love them, too.

As a teenager in sleepy Arcadia, I was a little fish among ancient-coin collectors, but we all swam in a very small pond. In the mid-1960s there were probably just a few hundred people in California who cared about centuries-old denars, drachmas, and sestertii. All of the dealers I bought from, save one, handled the ancient items only as a sideline. They were far more interested in American coins, which had to be a hundred times more popular.

The exception was Joel Malter, a junior-high teacher in the beach community of Venice, who was also the most respected ancient-coin expert in Southern California. Everyone who was interested in coins knew of Joel Malter. His knowledge of the field was deep, and even though he operated part-time out of his garage, he was the most active trader around. It was inevitable that once I began looking for coins, I would hop a bus to Venice to see his stock. It was also natural for me to turn to Joel to sell many of the coins I had acquired, including those that came into Coins of the World Etc. in that ammo box.

More than six feet tall, with a kind face and friendly blue eyes, Joel must have been a very popular teacher. He readily welcomed my interest, and brought me into his life almost as if I were a son. My own family was very introverted. My father was a single-minded scientist who had very little time for me, and offered absolutely no encouragement to me. My mother, chronically ill with arthritis her entire life, was fragile. My only sibling was my sister, Patty, who was a full eight years younger than I. Because of the age difference, we were not particularly close. In contrast with my family, the Malters seemed to be happy and full of life. Joel's wife, Adele, was very beautiful and lively. His son, Michael, about five years younger than me, was funny, energetic, all boy.

I loved the Malters, and I think they loved me back. Joel was certainly pleased, maybe even delighted by my interest in the ancient world and its artifacts. These weren't baseball cards we were dealing with, so how many teenagers were around to share his obsession? He guided my education in the field, exposing me to ever-more sophisticated books and other materials. One of the first things I bought from Joel was the basic guide book to Roman coins, *Roman Coins and Their Values* by David R. Sear, an expert from England. I devoured that book and eagerly sought others. I remember the day that Joel excitedly told me, "I think I'm getting a set of Cohen for you." Cohen, a nineteenth-century Frenchman, had produced an eight-volume set of books that was deemed to be the definitive source of information on the history and relative value of ancient coins. The set cost a couple hundred dollars, but I gladly paid it. Using my high-school French, I pored over my volumes of Cohen, absorbing dates, descriptions, and values the way other boys take in batting averages and team records.

In retrospect, I can see that we were probably geeks of a sort, but we didn't care. We were endlessly fascinated by the coins and what they represented. And we could see that unlike other hobbies, ancient coins represented a real opportunity to make money. This became very clear to me when Joel moved from Venice to Encino and into a bigger, fancier home with a swimming pool. He quit teaching, and began working full time as a coin dealer, opening an office on Ventura Boulevard. His business boomed.

A clever strategy helped Joel sell coins all over the country and, eventually, all over the world, by mail order. His main sales tool was a rudimentary catalog, listing the coins he had to sell with pictures of some of them. When an individual customer ordered from the list, Joel would send along a few selected coins that were tailored to that person's interests. If someone ordered a coin of Nero, for example, he would send something depicting Nero's wife. He'd add a note saying, "I think you might also like this one. If you want to keep it, send payment. If not, just return it."

Joel's clients came from every walk of life. His intuition about them was remarkably good. He knew that once someone had a new, unexpected coin in his hands, it was a lot easier for him to write a check than to let go of his new possession. It was like one of those old record clubs, except better, because the selections Joel mailed out were tailored to fit. Back at Coins of the World Etc., I tried to copy Joel's methods. If a customer was Italian-American or Jewish or Christian, I talked to them about coins that connected with their heritage or interests.

Although I didn't recognize it at the time, it's clear to me now that I had an uncanny ability to relate to adults. I focused on the person I was talking to and figured out what pleased him. Most of the time people wanted to believe

I was smart, clever, mature, capable. So that is what I gave them. I dressed older than my years and talked in a more serious, thoughtful way—at least, I pretended to. Much of the time I was faking it, but I was right often enough. It worked whether I was in school explaining that I understood a subject that I hadn't studied, or at work vamping my way through Roman history for some would-be collector. The most important thing was the confidence and assurance with which I presented myself—regardless of whether or not I actually was confident or self-assured. Strangely enough, these techniques never worked with my peers. They could sense, maybe even smell, that I was a nervous, nerdy, square kind of kid. But adults loved me.

It helped that when it came to coins, I was entirely sincere. Like every addict who can't believe that everyone doesn't love his favorite drug, I couldn't accept that anyone would resist the lure of ancient coins. And I believed that with every sale I was creating new collectors who shared my passion for history. Of course, it didn't hurt that I was making money to plow back into my own habit.

It wasn't long before I outgrew Ed Walthall's little shop, where ancient coins were almost an afterthought amid the stamps, U.S. currency, and bric-a-brac he sold. I started working for Joel just before I left high school for the University of California at Los Angeles. I took with me the few steady customers I had cultivated in Arcadia, and a young man's boundless energy and enthusiasm. That summer, Joel had enough confidence in me to send me to Europe where I toured the world's largest dealers and looked for items to add to his inventory. While the other graduates of my high-school class spent the last summer of childhood on the beach or working at hamburger shops, I began to discover what waited beyond L.A.

Europe is the natural center of the global trade in ancient coins. Records of coin collecting there go back to before the first century A.D., when Romans collected Greek coins as art objects. The hobby became widespread during the Renaissance, as the first books on Roman and Greek coins, complete with line drawings, were written and published. Today Europe remains the center of this passion, and many national governments there have substantial holdings. The French treasure, held by its national library, is especially notable. And many royal families hold priceless collections that have been amassed over centuries. For an American collector, a visit to the great commercial coin houses of Europe is akin to a Catholic's pilgrimage to the Vatican. It is a dream and a thrill approached with both great expectation and more than a little humility. For me to undertake a grand tour "over there" at the tender age of eighteen was truly exhilarating.

I started in London, where I met David Sear, author of my much-studied handbook *Roman Coins and Their Values*. After Sear it was on to the venerable Spink and Sons. Founded in the 1790s, the Spink shop was all polished hardwood and gleaming glass. I felt very intimidated by the place until George Mueller came out, introduced himself, and said that yes, he recalled my name from the mail orders I had sent.

Then in his mid-forties, George was heavyset and about six feet tall. He was dressed formally in a threadbare black jacket, white shirt, and tie. He sported a tiny moustache and spoke with an accent that charmed me. While I waited, he went into a back room and put together a tray of coins. When he brought them out I tried to think of Joel's clients, and mine, and I purchased a few coins that I thought they would want. Because I represented Joel, I didn't need cash or a check. Spink would simply ship what I requested to Los Angeles along with an invoice.

After London, I went on to the Continent and coin houses from Amsterdam to Paris to Vienna. I had a roster of members of the International Association of Professional Numismatists, and I used it to guide me to the best dealers. Most were located in the same part of each city—a coin district, if you will—and as I grew more at ease, I allowed myself to go down the side streets to visit some of the lesser-known sellers. The farther you wander from the most reputable dealers, the closer you get to coins that could have been stolen or smuggled out of a country in spite of the laws prohibiting transport of

national art treasures. As a new face in the coin world, I wasn't shown anything special during my first visits to these places, but just knowing what
might be found gave me a bit of a thrill. As exciting as my side trips were, my
ultimate destination was Zurich and the coin department of Bank Leu (pronounced *loy*) where Professor Leo Mildenberg reigned as one of the world's
great authorities on ancient coins.

I arrived in Zurich by train and found the least expensive room available
at the St. Gotthard, an old hotel on Bahnhofstrasse near the station. It was a
bit run-down, but like every place in Zurich, it was immaculate. Nothing I
had seen in Europe had prepared me for Zurich. In a country where it seems
like everything was cleaned and painted just yesterday, Zurich stands out as
especially well-scrubbed, even sterile. It scared me a little.

After checking in at the hotel, I walked the few blocks to the bank, which
occupied a tall stone building with gargoyles on the roof and guards at the
door. In the lobby, a white-gloved receptionist directed me to the marble stairs
that led to the second floor. Up there I found the numismatic department,
which occupied a simple, modern office decorated with photos of the rarest
coins, enlarged and printed in brilliant color.

I was greeted by a secretary. I said I wanted to look at ancient coins. At a
normal dealer's shop, this request is enough to produce a few trays for you to
scan. This was no ordinary dealer.

"What kind of coins are you interested in?" she asked.

"How about Roman imperial?"

"What period of Roman imperial?"

My God, I thought to myself. What do they have here?

Before I could muster up an answer, an old man, short and slender with
thinning gray hair, emerged from a back office. He wore round, wire-rimmed
glasses and an impeccable dark suit.

"May I help you?"

"I'm Bruce McNall, from Malter and Company in Los Angeles, and I'm looking for some ancient coins."

He answered first with a soft, welcoming smile. Then he spoke with a slight German accent. "I'm Dr. Leo Mildenberg. I'm delighted you came."

He asked me to sit down, and called for a tray of coffee and cookies. He asked me about Joel, and about my special interests. I told him I hadn't seen much from the fourth and fifth century of the Roman Empire. He excused himself and soon returned with the first of what would be many trays of coins from those periods.

For nearly two hours Dr. Mildenberg brought out coins and allowed me to inspect them as closely as I wished. I couldn't afford the very rare, expensive items. But I picked out the coins I recognized as good bargains that would be easy to resell back home.

"I see," said Dr. Mildenberg. "You have quite an eye, don't you?"

That afternoon I cherry-picked those trays, choosing coins that had probably sat in the collection a little too long without being repriced. In Europe they might have been considered just a cut above ordinary, but in America they would be gobbled up by collectors who couldn't frequent a place like Bank Leu, but who were always hungry for important new items. The profit that could be made by a retailer like Joel depended on aggressive hunting. If I could travel around Europe and track down even a few coins for $2,000 apiece that could be retailed for $4,000 each, it would be time and money well invested.

On this particular trip I more than met my quota for acquisitions. The items I picked from Bank Leu's vaults included some fine Byzantine gold pieces. Others were minted by less well-known emperors, and they would have made fine additions to my own collection, if I could have afforded them. But more important than the coins was the relationship I established with Leo Mildenberg.

Leo was the most sophisticated man I had ever met. Born and raised in

Berlin, he had a doctorate in classics and ancient history. He had worked in a bank in Berlin until the Nazis came to power. Somehow he had survived the Holocaust, and afterward married a woman from Switzerland. He been forced to start his career all over again after the war, and had built the Bank Leu coin department with the help of his associate, Silvia Hurter. Through it all, he had maintained an abiding optimism about life and his fellow human beings.

It might have been another case of youth working in my favor, as it had with Joel, or perhaps Dr. Mildenberg had seen me as someone who might become a valued client over the long term. For whatever reason, the most important figure in the world of ancient coins had welcomed me without reservation.

Before we parted, Leo's face took on a mischievous look, and he asked me if I wanted to see some items that were not for sale but would probably delight me. He then began taking out his personal collection of tiny animal sculptures. Made out of brass, marble, ceramic, semiprecious stone, and even wood, the little figures ranged from a stone turtle the size of your thumb to a twenty-four-hundred-year-old Phoenician glass bird as big as your hand. There were carved bears, dogs, cats, frogs, birds, lions, and more. They had been made to serve as decorative art, as toys, or perhaps even as religious talismans. For Dr. Mildenberg, they seemed to confirm a certain beauty and innocence that was as much a part of the human experience as any of the hardships he had experienced in his own life.

After my coin-hunting adventure, I returned home fully expecting to become a serious student at the University of California at Los Angeles, where I would prepare myself to become a professor of ancient history. Given that my father was a Ph.D. and a scientist, I just assumed I would also get a doctorate and then devote myself to a discipline that was highly intellectual and even a bit obscure. The McNall credo called for heavy thinking, not heavy lifting.

At UCLA I played to my strengths. The papers I wrote, even the essays on tests, all drew somehow on the store of esoteric knowledge I had acquired about ancient coins. In a short time I attracted the attention of two star faculty members, Speros Vryonis and Milton Anastos. Both were Harvard-educated, and both were ranked among the top scholars of the Byzantine era.

Byzantium was created by the first Christian emperor, Constantine, as the Eastern half of the Roman Empire. It stood for nearly one thousand years after the West and its capital, Rome, fell to invading Germans. For all that time, the citizens of the region called themselves Romans. And they continued to create coins, which included Christian symbols and a more austere approach to design.

Anastos, who was already in his sixties when I met him, was an avuncular man with a smoothly bald head who peered at you through thick, black-rimmed glasses. He was mainly interested in the artistic history of Byzantium, the sculpture, literature, music, etc. Vryonis was twenty years younger, and had been Anastos's protégé. Vryonis focused mainly on the classical history of the region, the wars, the emperors, and the great events. Slim and darkly handsome, he tended to be more aloof than Anastos. He was very smart, and he wanted you to know it.

It was sometimes difficult to tell what Vryonis and Anastos thought of me, but they must have been impressed by anyone who, as a freshman, announced he wanted to make a career of being a professor of ancient history. In the late 1960s, it seemed as if everyone else at UCLA was either devoted to the counterculture rebellion, or, if they were serious academics, were deep into science and technology.

My independent study of ancient coins had given me such a firm grounding in history that I found it easy to talk with my professors about their specialities, and they treated me like a young peer. Vryonis saw me as an academic protégé, someone he would train for the next generation of scholars. Anastos and Vryonis were both casual coin collectors, and they were intrigued when I told them about my work with Joel Malter. I periodically brought coins into the department. They bought some and even referred friends who became customers.

I was a pretty unusual college student. While my classmates worked in dining halls or coffee shops for minimum wage, my work with Joel netted me enough money to pay for a secondhand Mercedes and a first-rate apartment in the Westwood section of Los Angeles, near the campus. I was able to offer my girlfriend at the time, Cathy Lorber, who was also a classics student, much more than dates at the movies or a meal at a hamburger shop.

During my senior year, Vryonis and Anastos nominated me for a Regents Fellowship and pushed until I got it. The award, one of a handful granted each year, would give me free tuition and a paid teaching position, while I earned a doctorate. It also moved me closer to an equal status with my professors, and my relationship with Vryonis became even closer. In the summer before I began graduate school, he brought up the idea of a partnership. He would join me in a new venture—we'd call it Constantinople Fine Arts—to offer coins to a more prominent, and wealthy, clientele. I would acquire the coins wholesale from Joel Malter and make the sales pitches. Vryonis would use his stature as a scholar to open doors and lend our business credibility.

There was more than a little irony in our setup. In truth, I knew a lot more about ancient coins and their value than Vryonis. But he had the better story to tell, at least about himself, because he was mature, Ivy-educated (a big plus in L.A.), and Greek. His presence would calm the fears of many clients. He also brought another important element to our partnership: a direct line to our first big customer, a media mogul named Sy Weintraub, whom he had met at a party.

Wealthy and well-connected, Weintraub owned Panavision, the company that provided cameras for every motion picture made in Hollywood. He also produced his own films, including the Tarzan series of the late 1950s and 1960s. In addition, Weintraub owned the film rights to the Sherlock Holmes series, and was chairman of the executive board of Columbia Pictures. He knew everyone in Hollywood and entertained the town's elite on a regular basis. We knew if he became an avid collector, the fever would probably spread. And in his circle, there were many men and women who could pick the best from Joel Malter's vault and cover the cost out of their household checkbook. With this in mind, Speros Vryonis arranged for an appointment. Once we were inside, it was up to me.

Out-of-towners tend to assume that L.A.'s best addresses are in Beverly Hills or, perhaps, Bel Air. They are wrong. The most exclusive enclave is tiny Holmby Hills, a place where mansions hide behind graceful brick walls and dense privet hedges tended by armies of gardeners. The Weintraub house was tucked away on Mapleton Drive, a stone's throw from the Playboy Mansion and about a million miles away from any house I had ever entered before.

The driveway leading to the Weintraubs' door sliced across a vast green lawn. As Vryonis and I drove up to the house, a pair of German shepherd dogs ran over to inspect our car. When we got out, I could hear the *thwack* of tennis balls being hit on a private court out back. The house itself was a sprawling, modern, one-story affair that was made for entertaining. We rang the bell and were greeted by a houseman, who let us into a huge room filled with antiques and art. A moment later a slender, balding man wearing tennis gear and sporting a glowing tan and unnaturally white teeth appeared. This was Sy Weintraub.

As Weintraub led us to his private study, I studied the surroundings. Everything in that house, every stick of furniture, every lamp and wall covering, was the most expensive of its type. Original art was hung and lighted so visitors could not mistake its value. Even the colors of the walls and rugs, mostly reds and burgundies, had been selected for their richness.

Still, there was something awkward in the way it was all arranged. Even in the late 1960s, the heavy, flocked wallpaper Weintraub had was considered gauche. The velvet upholstered furniture in his den reflected expensive but bad taste. There seemed to be no organizing concept behind his choices in the art on display. It was a mishmash of paintings and sculptures in a variety of styles drawn from several time periods. The only thing that linked them together was their high cost. Altogether, the parts of the mansion that I saw gave me the impression that its owner wanted to communicate his wealth, with no regard for good taste, and it worked.

In the den Sy introduced us to his wife, Linda Palmer, a young, beautiful photographer. She was a voluptuous blonde who had previously been married to Warner Bros.'s studio chairman Ted Ashley. Sy let Linda know we were there to talk business, and she left us alone.

We sat on two red velvet sofas with an ornate table between us. The houseman brought us iced tea, and I laid out some coins and explained their importance. Sy tried to look interested, but I could see he was only mildly impressed by the stories I told. Then I turned to the matter of the coins' value. He owned some U.S. coins, which he held as investments. I told him that ancient coins were much more rare than old U.S. nickels and dimes, and that the market was international. With the right strategy, he could acquire a collection that would increase in value quite rapidly.

"This is an investment, like buying fine art or gold or silver. People in Europe have used coins as a hedge against inflation for generations," I told him.

Sy didn't show any emotion as I talked. When I finished he said nothing for a long minute. Then he asked a single question. "What would it take to build one of the greatest collections in the world?"

My heart just about stopped. I had never thought about such a project. I told him I wasn't sure at all.

"Well, would it be $50 thousand or $50 million?" he said. "What are we talking about?"

The truth was, I didn't know. Certainly it would be impossible, at any price, to match the holdings of Europe's royal families and governments. But I guessed that with careful selection, an impressive private collection, if not the best in the world, could be created for a few million dollars.

"Okay," he said as he rose to his feet, and signaling that the meeting was over. "Let me think about it."

Sy led us to the door himself. It closed behind us with a *clank*, and Vryonis and I said nothing until we were in the car. He then turned to me and smiled. "He's interested," he said. "He's very interested."

It took Sy just a few days to summon us again to his house. This time, before driving over to Holmby Hills, I went through Malter and Company's inventory and grabbed every high-end coin I could find. I took the most beautiful Greek and Roman pieces. Many were worth $10,000 or more, but even the less expensive ones were of pristine quality. Quite a few were from Bank Leu and were being held by Joel on consignment. The most dramatic coin in the bunch was a gold octadrachm of Ptolemy IV. About the size of a half dollar and twice as thick, it was the largest gold coin of the ancient Greek world. It bore the profile of Ptolemy on one side and a cornucopia on the other. Ptolemy IV was a descendant of Ptolemy the Great and a forefather of Cleopatra. If that didn't impress Sy Weintraub, nothing would.

Once I had selected the coins I found a beautiful wood-framed box, typed out labels, and carefully arranged the coins. When I finished I had more than two hundred coins, and the invoice I wrote set their total value at a little more than $500,000. Joel was flabbergasted. "You're just going to drive this over to this guy's house?" he asked. "What if you get hit by a truck?" I promised to drive very carefully and reminded Joel that Sy Weintraub represented more than a single sale. He could become a major, long-term client.

In Sy's den I made an elaborate presentation, picking out the best coins and noting their factors—rarity, historical significance, condition—that made each one special. After each little spiel Sy would ask, "What will it be worth in three years? How about five years?"

It was disappointing to find that Sy was completely blind to the romance of the coins. He didn't see collecting as an intellectual thrill, or as a way to connect to history. For him the coins were an investment vehicle. Instinctively, I played to that interest, telling him that over time, coins had always appreciated well. I told him about coins I had bought for $100 that had tripled in value in five years. Like a stockbroker, who cannot promise gains, I was careful to avoid predicting actual future increases in value. But I could speak authoritatively about what I had seen in the marketplace. In my mind, a person of means who didn't include ancient coins in his investment portfolio was missing an opportunity.

My pitch concluded with the very best coin in the lot, the gold octadrachm of Ptolemy IV. When I finished, Sy was quiet for a moment and then asked, "Okay, how much?"

I estimated that the octadrachm was about $20,000.

"No," he said. "How much for the whole box?"

I told him they were worth a little more than a half million dollars, but that if he wanted the whole collection we could just round it off at $500,000. He said, "Great," as if he were buying a pair of shoes, and went to his desk. He took out a large, ledger-style checkbook and quickly wrote out payment. He tore the check from the book and handed it to me as casually as he might tip a parking valet.

As he gave me the check, Sy asked me if we had made a good start on building the finest collection in the world. I said yes. Then he asked me what the next step toward that goal would be.

"I would literally have to search the world for you, if that's what you want."

"I do," he said.

2

A FEW MONTHS AFTER THE BIG SALE to Sy Weintraub, I was back at UCLA to begin my graduate studies in ancient history under the Regents Fellowship. I started to teach freshman classes, which was required. And I began to think about a dissertation. But I also began to feel doubts about the course I was following: a path leading to a lifetime in academia.

It was a gradual awakening. First I had to admit that while I loved standing in front of a classroom and sharing my excitement about the ancient world, the rest of teaching—paperwork, meetings, grading—left me cold. My girlfriend Cathy seemed happy to handle much of it for me, but the truth was that I was using her. I was also fooling myself, fooling everybody, about the level of my scholarship. Serious students of the ancient world must have command of Greek, Latin, French, and perhaps Arabic. I could fake most of those languages, but I was far from fluent. Worse, I just wasn't that interested in academic research and writing. My mind didn't work that way.

Ironically, Cathy was a far superior academic, and would have put a Regents Fellowship to better use. She was highly intellectual, gifted in languages, and far more interested in the whole breadth of the field. Most importantly, she wasn't distracted by the romance, excitement, and fortune that I knew waited in the ancient-coin business. Our little company, Constantinople, had made a $150,000 profit in that one sale to Sy Weintraub. In the early 1970s, this was roughly eleven times the median annual household income in America. Though we put much of it back into the business, I also received big payments. It was more money than I would ever see in academia, no matter how successful I might become.

As much as the money distracted me from my studies, I was even more compelled by the sense of power I felt as I hunted for inventory, found clients, developed a pitch, and made a sale. I was always looking for the next client, the next fish, which I hoped would be a little larger than the one I just ate. The thrill of the chase, and the big payoffs, were intoxicating. And they were all dependent on the very skills and talent—for communicating, judging value, selling—that I had been developing for years. It all felt right, like an extension of my core self, in a way that studying and teaching history did not.

Once I recognized this, I knew I had to drop out of graduate school. And in the end my choice was probably more traumatic for my mentors—Vryonis and Anastos—than it was for me. After all, I had known all along that I had been a kind of counterfeit academic. It was actually a relief to get out before I was found out.

After leaving UCLA, my main concern was finding great coins to build a first-rate collection for a customer—Sy Weintraub—who didn't know a denarius from a button and didn't seem to care. Because I knew he didn't love the coins, I didn't expect Sy to stay interested for very long. For that reason I wanted to sell him as much as I could, as fast as I could. To do that, I had to appeal to both his ego and his wallet.

To feed Sy's ego, I had to find a way for the coins to become a truly visible status symbol. The trouble was, unlike a house or a car or even a painting, a coin makes a poor display. To solve this problem, I had photos taken of each one. I had the photos enlarged and printed along with little text blocks noting each coin's history. When the text and picture were framed with the coin, Sy had something he could put on a wall, or a table, and show off to his friends.

Sy's friends were like him: rich, famous, and hard to impress. I was drafted into the effort. Every few weeks Sy would throw a big party or have just a few good friends over for dinner, and I would be the entertainment. Though I was barely an adult, and a complete stranger to their world, a word from Sy was enough for me to be accepted by the likes of Berry Gordy, Richard Zanuck, Leonard Goldberg, and Aaron Spelling. He also introduced me to some of Hollywood's younger power players like David Geffen and Peter Guber. We would enjoy our drinks and hors d'oeuvres, and then Sy would trot me out like a trick pony to dazzle them with tales of Caesars and senators, soldiers and traitors. I always had a couple of coins in my pocket. Putting a twenty-five-hundred-year-old coin in someone's palm, as casually as you might hand them a quarter, inspires a certain awe.

As always, I tried to tailor the story to my audience. My approach to David Geffen, then a major record company owner, was typical. A regular at Sy's parties—in those days he wasn't "out" as a gay man, so he often came with Cher as his date—Geffen was obsessed with music. I showed him coins decorated with instruments. One in particular was a Nero dupondius showing a lyre. (Though it is highly improbable that Nero actually fiddled while Rome burned, he was a musician and loved to play.) Geffen was an avid collector of modern art, but only mildly impressed by the coins as objects. As I would find with all the others, he wanted an investment. When Sy told him he could make 20 percent or more per year, he signed up for $100,000 in coins.

Geffen's order was relayed by Sy, who, as this stream of business began to flow, made himself my invisible, if not-so-silent partner. It was a brilliant move. He would hand me the clients, help me woo them, but maintain the appearance of detached objectivity when, in fact, he was a partner taking half the profits on every sale. In Geffen's case, for example, I spent about $80,000 on the coins that he bought for $100,000. When the sale closed, Sy and I each took $10,000 profit.

The same kind of thing happened over and over again. Gordon McClendon, who owned TV and radio stations around the country, put up more than $5 million. Leonard Goldberg went for $1 million. Others, like movie producer David Begelman's wife Gladys, took smaller bites, buying $100,000 worth of coins here, another $100,000 there. Pretty soon I was in receipt of orders for so many ancient coins that I was hard-pressed to come up with the stock. I would fly to Europe and find some new ones, bearing the expense of the hunt. I didn't mind, as long as Sy was buying, too.

With a heavy checkbook, I became a welcome face in coin shops and banks around Europe. I was also able to enjoy better hotels and better restaurants. On one memorable trip I brought along Joel Malter's son, Michael, sixteen at the time, to show him a bit of the world and one key element of the family business. We went to London first, and then Zurich to visit Leo Mildenberg. I picked up several significant items at Bank Leu, but Leo gave me something very exciting to anticipate for some future trip. In a few months' time, he said, he was to conduct the sale of one of the greatest collections in the world, which was held by a French family named Gilet.

Leo practically danced as he led us to his vault to show me some of those coins. They were all beautiful Roman and Greek specimens. In an almost reverent voice I quietly asked him which was the best. He reached for a tray that held one single silver coin.

"This, my good friend, is the greatest coin in the world."

Resting in the center of the velvet lined tray was a silver decadrachm of Athens. It met every criterion for value. First, the relief and finish of the coin suggested it was practically in mint condition. The front of the coin showed Athena, the goddess of war; the reverse bore the image of an owl with its wings spread and an olive branch. Besides being beautiful, the decadrachm was incredibly rare. Just seven and a half were known to exist, and the others were in museums. (The Louvre owned the half coin.) Third, and most importantly, it was of supreme historic importance. It is widely accepted that it was struck to commemorate the Greek defeat of Persia in 465 B.C. That victory, over a fearsome adversary with a much larger army, had assured the ultimate ascension of Western civilization. If the war had gone the other way, the culture and history of Europe and America would be very different indeed.

Leo was right. The silver decadrachm on that tray *was* the greatest coin in the world, at least the greatest one not held by a museum or a national government. And I had an idea about who might like to possess it.

From Bank Leu, we headed to our main destination for that trip, an auction to be conducted in Bern by a dealer called Munzen und Medaillen. Hundreds of ancient coins and other antiquities owned by Pierre Straus and Herbert Cahn, two well-known dealers, were going on the block. The auction was held in the ballroom at a premier hotel, the Schweizerhof. Following the standard practice, tables were arranged in a large square, with an auctioneer at the center of the head table and major traders seated all around. The tables were covered with white cloths. Dishes of candy and bottles of water were distributed around. Lesser players, individuals who might make just a few bids, were consigned the rows of chairs set up behind the tables. They didn't get any candy or water.

My place was at one of the tables. I bid vigorously, picking up some rare coins—the kind that usually don't come on the market—as well as a number of excellent but more ordinary items. Michael, who watched from the chairs, was mesmerized by the auctioneer's language skills. As each coin was walked around the table by a pretty young woman holding a velvet tray, the auctioneer described it in both German and English. Then, as the bids got rolling, he switched from English to German to French and Italian, depending on who raised a hand.

After the auction I was working my way out of the room, Michael in tow, when a thin, aristocratic-looking American stopped me. "Mr. McNall," he said. "I'm Bob Hecht. If you like antiquities and coins I have some items you might like. Why don't you come up to my room?"

Although he had occupied one of the cheap seats in the back of the room,

Robert Hecht was one of the most important figures in the entire antiquities business. In his early fifties at the time, he had thinning gray hair, and wore wire-rimmed glasses. He looked like somebody's nice old grandpa, but he was in fact one of the most mysterious figures in the field of ancient art. Though Bob was rumored to have been a spy in World War II, he admitted only to serving in the war and choosing to settle in Europe afterward. Whatever his past, he had become the world's largest single source of recently discovered antiquities, which he somehow managed to locate and sell despite the strict laws limiting the movement of these treasures around the world. Heir to the wealth of the Hecht's department store chain on the East Coast, Bob had the money and the connections to deal at a very high level. What everyone knew, and no one mentioned, was that his connections included many of the grave robbers, smugglers, and go-betweens who evaded the authorities to bring items to market.

Smuggled antiquities have to be laundered, much like the cash acquired by crime syndicates, before they can be circulated in the open market. At the time, this was often done by passing an item through Beirut or Zurich, where there were no export controls, and then on to a middleman like Bob. Once Bob acquired a vase, an urn, or a coin, and sold it to a collector or a retail house, it was considered legal.

The business of selling ancient art had worked that way, outside of public view for decades, until one of the biggest deals Bob ever made exploded in the press. It happened in the early 1970s, when The Metropolitan Museum of Art in New York announced the million-dollar purchase of a previously unknown, twenty-five-hundred-year-old Greek vase that was more beautiful than any in the world. The archaeologists' term for this type of vase is calyx krater, which describes handled vases huge enough to hold six or seven gallons, which were used to mix water and wine. This particular piece was signed by the artist Euphronius, who was probably the most gifted artist in the ancient Greek world. He had decorated it with the most vivid painting ever seen on a krater. It showed a dead Sarpedon, mythological son of Zeus, being carried from the field of battle by the winged figures of Death (Thanatos) and Sleep (Hypnos).

The Euphronius krater was, and is, a breathtaking sight. The rust-colored figures are painted on a black surface that gleams almost like new. The details of the figures—muscles, hair, clothing, wings—are crisply accurate. Unlike so much ancient Greek art, the work on the krater flows with genuine emotion, and the use of decoration serves to both beautify the overall work and to direct the eye to the key scene.

The sale of the spectacular krater was soon accompanied by controversy. First the museum's director, Thomas Hoving, was criticized for selling too many valuable ancient coins to raise the money to acquire it. Then the Italian government stunned the arts world by charging that the krater had recently been unearthed by thieves digging in a tomb north of Rome and had been illegally smuggled to Hecht in Switzerland. The authorities intended to investigate, prosecute, and recover what they firmly believed was a national treasure.

In a yearlong struggle that was played out in the worldwide press, Bob Hecht's original claims about the origins of the krater unraveled. It was not, as he stated, the long-held property of a Lebanese family. Nor had the vase been held in a private home for fifty years. The truth was most likely as the Italian police had stated it. According to them, Hecht had purchased the krater, then in pieces, from a shady middleman for $100,000. It had then been put back together by Swiss restoration expert Fritz Buerki, whom Hecht used often, so that the Met's trustees could see it and approve its purchase. For their part, Hoving and others at the museum had simply chosen not to ask too many questions.

Despite the best efforts of the police and press, especially the *New York Times*, the Met never acknowledged the validity of the Italian claims. Nor did they accept that they had violated the spirit of international agreements prohibiting trade in stolen works. The Met stubbornly refused to relinquish the vase, and holds it still today. Though he was never convicted of a crime in this case, Hecht's name became synonymous with the underside of art dealing.

Even so, the market for ancient art was so constricted and heated that buyers were willing to deal with him if it meant obtaining a rare and valuable piece. It didn't hurt that his reputation made him an exciting character, and dealing with him brought on a rush of adrenaline. At least, that was how I felt as I walked down the hallway to his hotel room.

Hecht himself answered my knock on the door. He brought me inside where the pieces of an ancient vase were arranged on the bed on top of the wrinkled newspaper that had been used for its protection. Bob had obviously just acquired it; there was still dirt on some of the pieces. He was no doubt intending to have Fritz Buerki—the same restorer who had handled the Euphronius krater—fit it back together. "Isn't it splendid?" he asked, pointing at the pieces.

All around the room were men—Turks, Italians, Greeks—talking and smoking and haggling over the bits and pieces of history that they pulled out of their pockets and briefcases. I recognized a few of the men from the crowd at the auction, where they had obviously been studying the buyers and the market prices. These were the fellows who pulled you aside during a break, reached into their pockets and brought out a few glittery prizes for you to buy at a special price. Some of them were tough guys. One, an Italian named Giacomo, always had a big man named Ugo with him. Ugo wore lizard-skin boots and bright shirts. He never had anything but junk coins to sell, but if you bought the good stuff from Giacomo you had to buy something from Ugo, too. It was understood.

I was shown a few dozen coins. I bought some—mostly Greek silver from Asia Minor—and picked up a Greek wine cup, called a kylix, for my own collection. It cost $2,500, and I bought it not as an investment, but because it was a beautiful piece of art. It was kiln-fired clay, black with red figures. It would make a fine decoration, and conversation piece, in my apartment back in Westwood.

Everything Hecht showed me was first quality, but what impressed me most was the casual way he treated those objects. To him they were ordinary, almost everyday things. Most were fresh—meaning new to the market—and that added to the excitement. As I left, Bob made sure to tell me he hoped we would do business again. "We really should get to know each other," he said, gripping my hand.

From Bern, Michael and I went on to Rome, where we bought a few things from a dealer named Santamaria, who kept a shop in the Via d'Espagne. Though we had spent almost two weeks abroad, and bought every worthwhile item we could, I realized I hadn't acquired enough coins to satisfy all the buyers I had back home. It was time to search for a new source. As I looked through an international directory of dealers, my eye fell on a listing for a fellow named Evangelistes in Tunis, an hour and a half by air from Leonardo da Vinci Airport. We caught the first available flight.

It was my first visit to the Arab world, and at first I was taken aback by the veils and the robes, the minarets and the date palm trees. Michael and I checked into a little hotel. The next day we went in search of Evangelistes, whose shop was in the very middle of the city's main bazaar.

To my eyes, the bazaar in Tunis was chaotic, confusing, almost impenetrable. Most of the merchants were set up under sheets of tenting, where they sold everything from gold to goats. Here one man waved chickens, soon to be soup, that cackled and screamed as they were swung by their bound feet. A few yards away goats bleated and camels spit at the shoppers who wandered too close. Every kind of food, clothing, and household product was sold. You could pick up jewelry, chickpeas, a radio, and a doorknob without walking more than twenty or thirty feet.

As we explored the bazaar, I saw a few vendors who offered broken pieces of Greek pottery and bits of Roman glass. None of it was worth much. It was discouraging. I was expecting treasures. What I found was little better than trash. Finally I arrived at Evangelistes's shop, which was one of the few that occupied an actual building. Inside we saw a young man, a boy really, who kept watch over a few insignificant pots and battered marble sculptures. The place was dark, musty, and reeked of incense. With my bad French and his bad English we talked about the few items on display.

"Do you have anything else? Anything better?" I asked. Then I explained that I represented Joel Malter, that I had come all the way from Los Angeles, and that I wanted to see Mr. Evangelistes.

The boy disappeared through a veil of heavy beads into a back room. After a long minute he returned with an older man dressed in a frayed suit. This was Evangelistes. He said he had heard of Joel, and he asked me to go with him to the back. There we entered a large space, twice the size of the showroom, lit by oil lamps. The floor was covered by a colorful Persian carpet and as I scanned the items all around I recognized some more important pieces of sculpture and pottery. Evangelistes sent the boy for tea, and motioned Michael and me toward a rickety table. He then turned toward a cabinet in the far corner of the room. The boy returned with little glasses of sugary tea, and set them on the table. Evangelistes told the boy to leave, then he pulled a heavy bag out of the cabinet and lugged it over to us.

"Now, I'm going to show you something," he said as he slung the bag onto the table. He smiled, took a sip of the tea, and then dumped the contents of the bag onto the wool cloth.

Gold, silver, and bronze coins spilled out like grain from a punctured sack. Evangelistes picked up a Byzantine gold piece about the size of a nickel and put it into my hand. It was a solidus showing the bust of Constantine and had been minted in Carthage between A.D. 654 and 685. I hadn't seen one before, and I knew it would be highly valuable on the retail market. He had a couple dozen of them, and we settled on a price of about $300 each. I figured I could double that on the open market.

Evangelistes obviously believed that the Byzantine gold was the prize in his collection, and after making his pitch for them, he allowed me to sift through the rest of the piles of coins he regarded as secondary.

Most were folles, the most common Roman coins of the third and fourth century A.D., but they were hardly common specimens. They were beautifully preserved, and bore the image of Emperor Maxentius. I picked one up and held it close to the lamp and saw the mint mark "OST," for Ostia.

The first port city for ancient Rome, Ostia was founded in the seventh century as a military base but grew into a commercial center. By Maxentius's time, however, it had been eclipsed by the nearby harbor town of Portus. The emperor's decision to establish a mint there restored a bit of Ostia's status.

Maxentius was a vain and irritable man. Because he reigned for just six years, and the mint at Ostia operated only during his time on the throne, his coins are rare. But they are not nearly as significant as the additional folles I saw as Evangelistes dumped another bag on the table. Here were coins of Romulus, the son of Maxentius, who died at a very young age, and other coins bearing the image of Alexander of Carthage, who had claimed to be emperor after Maxentius drowned.

In modern times, Ostia's past had been unearthed first by Pope Pius VII, in the first half of the nineteenth century. At the time, the Vatican controlled the land where the city lay, and many of its exhumed treasures were taken to the Vatican Museums. In more recent history, Mussolini ordered extensive excavations at Ostia, and the site became a major archaeological and tourist center. It was also, for decades after World War II, a hotbed of thievery and smuggling. Some of the crime was done on a truly outrageous scale, with items as big as columns and sarcophagi being stolen.

I could only guess at the tale that might lie behind the treasure that had emerged from Evangelistes's cabinet. The very beginning of the story is probably the easiest to surmise. Since the coins were from only two places, Ostia and Carthage, it's safe to assume that they had been held by a trader of sorts, someone who had come to Carthage from Ostia to do business. He might have secreted his cash somewhere, wandered off, and met a terrible fate. The coins could have then lain undisturbed for centuries. I would never know who eventually found them, or how they made their way to Evangelistes. That information he would never share, and I didn't really want to know.

With all the mystery and potential gain that magnificent pile of coins represented, I had to struggle to stay calm. By the time Evangelistes finished emptying the cabinet, there were more than one thousand pieces on the table. Most were the Maxentius folles, worth between $50 and $100 each. About fifty were Romulus, and they would fetch at least $500 apiece retail. The half dozen Alexanders were worth $5,000 each or more.

"I could sell these for $20,000," said Evangelistes. "If you want everything, $50,000."

I sipped the tea and thought for a moment. The six Alexanders alone were worth $30,000, and I had customers who would take them—who *needed* them—right away. The rest of the cache was worth another $60,000, minimum—more if I took time selling them. I didn't try to haggle with Evangelistes. I just wrote him a $50,000 check for the entire collection. He said I could come back the next day for the coins, and in the interim he would make sure the check was good. Twenty-four hours later, Michael and I were back in the shop, collecting our purchase.

"I am hopeful we will do such business in the future," said Evangelistes. "Come all the time."

We left the sweet-smelling darkness of Evengelistes's shop and found ourselves again in the sun-blasted bazaar, where crowds of people pressed against us and the shouts of merchants and sounds of various animals swirled like the dust in the air. I was suddenly aware of the fact that we would have to get our new possessions out of Tunisia via an airport where signs were posted on every wall warning that the removal of antiquities was punishable by a twenty-year prison term.

Fortunately for us, this was before metal detectors were ubiquitous at the world's airports. And, in most countries, customs officials were reluctant to strip-search American tourists. That meant Michael and I could carry as many coins as possible on our persons and be confident they would not be discovered. We selected the most valuable ones and put them in our pockets, in our shoes, even in the cuffs of our pants. The rest, all Maxentius folles, were parcelled into socks and wrapped in shirts and distributed in our luggage. To minimize the chance of our being interfered with at the other end of the flight, I bought tickets on a plane that went directly to Zurich. All Swiss cities were free ports, meaning that anything could be brought in without a duty being paid.

A taxi dropped us at the Tunis airport where we were mobbed by beggars. We dragged our suitcases inside, where masses of people waited under the watch of security men armed with rifles. The terminal was not anything like what you imagine a modern airport to be. It was a cramped place with low ceilings and long check-in lines for the airlines, clearing customs, and immigration. When we got to the head of the line to have our passports stamped, the clerk asked us, in a bored way, if we were transporting any national treasure. "No," we both answered, and that was it. We were allowed to pass to a waiting area and later boarded the plane.

Nearly all the coins I had picked up at Bank Leu, at the Munzen und Medaillen auction, in Tunis, and elsewhere, were sold within a few weeks of my return to Los Angeles. Sy Weintraub was pleased by the profits he made on my sales to his friends, which he promptly invested in his own collection. Just as I had created other addicts when I dealt coins out of old Ed Walthall's shop in Arcadia, Sy had found a way to use his friends' money to feed his own habit.

As always, Sy pressed me to tell him whether the coins I had brought were the world's best. His fixation on his goal never wavered. I said I had found the best of what was available, and then I told him the news about the upcoming auction of the silver decadrachm. Sy was an avid jogger, so as I told him the story of the Greek victory over Persia, I made sure to mention the messenger who ran from Marathon to Sparta to warn of the Persians' strategies. He was enthralled, and when I finished the only thing he asked was, "How much?"

I had no doubt that the coin would go for a price higher than the one hundred thousand dollars paid for the then record holder—a 1907 twenty-dollar gold piece that had been sold by Stacks of New York. How much higher was a mystery to me. But with so much at stake, Leo Mildenberg was happy to fly to Los Angeles just to answer Sy's questions.

I met Leo at Los Angeles International Airport. Though he had traveled for the better part of a day, he was remarkably fit and alert and wanted to go directly to see my big client. As we rode in my car, my two worlds came together in a strange and beautiful juxtaposition. Outside, palm trees, sun-bleached boulevards, and hamburger stands whizzed by in all their gaudiness. Inside the car, my very cultured friend, his impeccable black suit still unwrinkled and his hands resting on his leather briefcase, spoke to me in his careful, German-accented English about the antiquities that were our shared passion.

We wheeled down Sy's driveway, past the emerald lawn and the sculpted shrubbery. Inside the house, Leo didn't shudder at the artwork on Sy's velvet wallpaper, and he didn't seem to mind that all his host wanted to talk about was the decadrachm's monetary value. Over iced tea he explained the coin's extraordinary qualities, as I had before. Then he estimated that by the time all the bidding was done, the buyer would likely pay more than 300,000 Swiss francs, or more than $125,000. Then there would be a commission of another 10 percent.

As Leo spoke, I realized that despite his distinguished demeanor, despite his graduate degrees and his lofty position at Bank Leu and his worldwide reputation as an expert on antiquities, he was, at bottom, a coin dealer. He was a salesman, and he was there to impress a man who might be worth quite a bit of money to him. After all, even if Sy didn't wind up with the coin, as long as he attended the auction expecting to drop as much as $150,000 or so, his bidding was going to drive the price upward. Which was why Leo had come all that way to talk to him.

The irony was that Sy, the Hollywood dealmaker, a prince in the land of image and story, was buying into Leo's image and story completely. Leo's way of presenting himself, as an authority with impeccable breeding, education, and character, was, in a way, his shtick. By the time Leo left, Sy was firmly committed to flying to Zurich with me and doing whatever was required to get that coin. I loved Leo.

The auction that would include the silver decadrachm was to be held in May of 1974, just after my twenty-fourth birthday. As the date approached, Sy became ever more focused on his goal of seizing the coin. He was so intent that by the time I flew to Zurich, a day or two ahead of him, it was all he wanted to talk about. His obsession was driven first by his competitive nature. He had to have the best, and if someone stood against him, he had to prevail. It was central to his personality. In addition to ego, Sy's pursuit of the decadrachm was also motivated by his hunger for profit. Given what was happening in the world economy at the time, and the state of the ancient-coin market, he had reason to believe that a fantastic profit could be made on that coin, no matter what he paid to get it.

In the early 1970s, ancient coins had become a surprise bright spot in an economic climate that was otherwise stormy. In 1971 and 1972, runaway inflation had led President Nixon to impose wage and price controls. A series of Arab oil embargoes had caused price spikes and severe shortages in the United States. High energy costs were bad for every business, except the oil companies. By 1974, inflation was 11 percent per year, a rate triple what it had been just two years earlier. The Dow fell to 663, a four-year low, and economic growth was near zero.

Under those conditions, the only investments that seemed to increase in value were high-end, hard assets like gold (which increased about 75 percent in 1974), fine art, and rare coins. In fact, between 1970 and 1974, as I was becoming heavily involved in buying and selling, rare coins rose an astounding 348 percent. When you consider that most stocks lost value in that same period, you start to understand why a whole lot of wealthy people became very interested in such an obscure little corner of investing. It was one place where everyone—including me—seemed to make money.

As a collector, I was profiting on the run-up in the market I was helping to create. After all, I was bringing a number of rich investors to that relatively small commodities market, and their presence was driving the value up. Beyond watching my own coins become more valuable, I was also taking commissions on everything I sold. Granted, Sy sliced it in half whenever his friends were involved, but as prices soared and the volume of my business grew, I made more and more money.

As I worked to guarantee the biggest coin sale in history—Sy's purchase of the decadrachm—I faced the very real possibility that I would be pushed aside when the commission was paid. In fact, because it was a Bank Leu auction, Leo Mildenberg had sole claim to the 5 percent fee paid by the buyer *and* would receive as much as 10 percent from the seller. When I arrived in Zurich, the first thing I did was reach an agreement with Leo about that problem. I believed that if Sy bought the decadrachm, I deserved a reward for bringing him to the table. Without hesitating, Leo offered me half the buyer's commission paid to Bank Leu. It was a small cut, but when added to a fee I would get from Sy if the auction went our way, it would be enough. Leo's offer was no act of charity, by the way. He knew that I was going to buy many of the other rare ancient coins that would be offered at the auction. He also knew that by bringing Sy to the auction, I would help him get maximum value for the decadrachm.

It was called the Kunstfreunde, or "art friends" sale. An ornate ballroom at the luxurious Baur au Lac Hotel was set up for the event, with the usual banks of tables and rows of chairs. Sy, who arrived just in time for the auction, posted himself in the back of the room. Worried about being mobbed by the press, and whatever criminal element might prowl the hotel, Sy had insisted on anonymity. That didn't mean he went unnoticed. The ancient-coin world was relatively small, the kind of community where everyone knows everyone else. And a perfectly bronzed newcomer wearing much more expensive clothes than anyone else was going to attract attention. Nevertheless, Sy made me promise to keep his identity secret.

As I took my place behind an engraved nameplate, Sy changed his position to make sure he was in my line of sight. From there he would flash me signals. A pen raised upward near his tanned cheek would mean "go!" An adjustment of his Hermes silk tie would signal "stop!" We had set a limit of 500,000 Swiss francs—about $180,000.

The decadrachm was Lot 147, so Leo had a significant inventory to work through before he reached the main event. *"Attention, s'il vous plaît . . ."* he began and then adroitly moved from language to language and coin to coin, dispatching highly prized items with cool efficiency. As the morning wore on, the crowd grew until every seat was filled and the walls were lined with people willing to stand through the day. At the tables the major dealers, who had brought their own big clients to the auction, were joined by representatives of the French government and of The National Museum in Greece. The Greeks had a special interest in the decadrachm. It was minted in their country, and yet they didn't own one. A special fund had been created, with the help of Aristotle Onassis, to rectify that problem.

I bought several of the more important coins Leo offered. Then came Lot 147. The room literally buzzed, and news photographers rushed to get a shot as a beautiful young woman took up the velvet-lined tray that held the coin and walked around the tables to give us a final, close look. Leo spoke in English, for Sy's sake. "This may be the most important coin to come to auction in the history of the world," he said, "the famous decadrachm of Athens."

The bidding began at 300,000 Swiss francs (about $100,000 U.S.) and thirty seconds later blew past 500,000 francs. I hadn't opened my mouth. I glanced at Sy who, having abandoned our signal system, was shaking his head up and down and mouthing the words, "Go on!"

The bidding slowed considerably after 500,000 francs, which had obviously been a cutoff point for many of the potential buyers. When it reached

600,000 francs, there seemed to be only two serious contestants, the Greek and the French. That's when I jumped in. There was a lot of oohing and ahing as I raised my hand and Leo said, "The bid is 610,000 francs from the young American from Los Angeles, Mr. McNall." We were now over $200,000, U.S.

At that moment, we entered what might be called Act III of the auction. A truly successful and dramatic auction will follow the pattern of a stage play. In the first act there's a burst of excitement as the players are all introduced. In the second act, the characters reveal their strengths and weaknesses as the plot, driven by the conflict over the prize, is crystallized. Everyone in the audience knows that Act III will bring a resolution. Just as someone always gets the girl in a romance, someone always gets the coin at an auction. Of course the play, and the auction, will be all the more satisfying and exciting if the ending comes with a surprising twist.

I represented the exciting plot turn at the decadrachm auction. Arriving just at the moment when it seemed certain that one of two institutional bidders would prevail, I presented the possibility that a brash newcomer might take the prize. A murmur of excitement went through the room as I joined the fight. I could feel my stomach churn and my shirt become drenched with perspiration.

In increments of 10,000 francs, the bidding went past 750,000. At that point the record for a coin sale was thoroughly shattered, and we were approaching the levels paid for extraordinary paintings, sculptures, and ancient vases. At 770,000 francs—almost $280,000—the Greek muttered, "Enough," and slammed his catalog closed on the table. By the look on his face, it seemed he would rather get a shovel and go looking for his own decadrachm than bid any higher. It was down to me and the French government.

Certain that the whole thing was spinning out of control, and beyond his bank account, I kept looking at Sy. No longer calm and steady, he was waving his hand and mouthing, "Go, Bruce, go!"

I bid 780,000 francs.

The Frenchman bid 800,000 Swiss francs.

Sy nodded his head up and down.

I bid 820,000 francs. Then I forced myself to look relaxed, calm, as if I was prepared to go on like this indefinitely.

"The bid is 820,000 francs. Are there any more bids?"

Leo repeated the call a few times. My lone opponent kept his hands on the table and then finally shook his head to signal he was through.

"Sold to the American for 820,000 francs!"

The crowd burst into applause and the auction was immediately suspended. Leo and the lovely young woman brought the coin to me, and we posed for photographs. The reporters in the room asked me to reveal the buyer I represented. I could see Sy beaming with pride over his $280,000 purchase, but I kept my promise. "He is a private American collector," I said. "That's all I can tell you."

In the crush around me, the Greek came and shook my hand. He was followed by the Frenchman. He introduced himself as Valery Giscard d'Estaing. He was then his country's finance minister, but within months he would become France's president. He told me that he had been bidding for Bibliothèque Nationale, the French national library. "If I had known you were going so high," he said, "I would have printed more money."

When Sy finally made it over to me, I told him I was sorry that the auction had been so expensive. "I didn't have any idea it would have gone to this price," I said. He wasn't fazed. "I would have gone as far as a million francs," he said. "I'm almost disappointed it didn't go that high. The publicity for you would have been terrific."

The high that came from the decadrachm auction lasted through the summer. In the fall I married Cathy Lorber. I can admit now that it was not the kind of marriage that follows a torrid love affair. Instead, we were good friends, and good colleagues, and it just seemed like the thing to do. We moved into a house in Encino, not far from Joel, where we had a nice pool and landscaped grounds behind a tall fence and gate.

At about the same time, it became clear to me that I was ready to go it alone in business. First I arranged a happy parting with Speros Vryonis, and then I set about separating from Joel Malter. Joel had reasons to feel conflicted about the end of our arrangement. He had contributed greatly to my education, and in turn, I had brought him the kind of high-roller clients he had never seen before. My salesmanship had led the Malter gallery to its first million-dollar year, and he had to be worried about losing the revenue I brought.

Despite the emotions we both felt, we worked amicably to divide our stock and our liabilities in a fair way. It was amicable, that is, until we discovered that one of our jointly held coins was missing. It wasn't just any coin. It was a Greek stater from the seventh century B.C. Made of soft electrum, it was one of the oldest coins in the world, and was worth about $70,000 at that time. I had held it on consignment from Bank Leu, and had anticipated selling it to Sy or one of his friends.

We spent more than three hours looking for that coin, checking every square inch of the safe, every drawer, every envelope, every box. Eventually I began to wonder if Joel was really looking, or putting on an act to cover a theft. He must have wondered the same thing about me. When we finally ran out of places to search, we sat down to discuss what might be done. It was a cold conversation. Joel insisted that since I had acquired the coin, I was responsible for it, and the burden of paying off Bank Leu would be mine alone. I could have argued the point, but I didn't have the heart. Three or four months later the coin turned up in Joel's shop. Though the mystery was solved, the fact that Joel and I had each been willing to suspect the other of stealing it strained our relationship for many years.

When we separated, Joel allowed me to take possession of the name of a competing business we had acquired a few months before our breakup. Numismatic Fine Arts had been a venerable company, one of the first to offer rare ancient coins in America. I liked the firm's reputation for quality and fairness, and I also liked the ring of its name. "Numismatic Fine Arts" communicated precisely what I believed about ancient coins, that they were genuine fine art objects worthy of collecting.

At Sy's urging I decided to open a gallery on Rodeo Drive, and I expanded my interests to include ancient art items such as vases, glass, some jewelry, and ceramics. The stock for the new gallery would be supplied mainly by Bob Hecht. In fact, I hardly ever acquired pieces from anyone else. Our arrangement allowed me to bring in pieces for display, sell them, and then split the proceeds with him. Gradually we created a market for ancient art where none had existed before.

The ancient art operation would be called the Summa Gallery, *summa* meaning "highest" in Latin. Our neighbors included Hermes and Fred Hayman and Cartier. We put a half million dollars into remodeling and furnishings, making it the kind of place where the fabulously wealthy might feel comfortable dropping $10,000 on impulse.

Almost immediately after we opened, a rumor began that linked me and my gallery to the mysterious Howard Hughes and his Summa Corporation. I made no effort to dispel the myth, because it was a great story. And in Los Angeles, a great story is worth money, whether it's true or not.

3

IN A TIME AND PLACE where good stories mean money, it helps to make yourself into a character—perhaps even a caricature—whom people can readily understand, accept, even love. This isn't a matter of merely exploiting others. The fact is, people want you to give them a performance, to be a recognizable type, because it spares them the hard work of understanding a real person. They feel secure when they can fit you into a category and declare that they really know you. Of course, they don't know you, and deep down they understand it's all a game. But admitting this would make life too hard. They would have to think too much.

With Sy's help, and my own nerve, I had developed a reputation as a wunderkind character. I was known as the exceptional young man who used his knowledge of the mysterious and obscure world of antiquities to make himself and everyone around him rich. People who knew Bruce McNall described him to their friends as an adventurer who brought back great tales and great profits for them to share. What a wonderful role.

But as effective and believable as my character was, it paled when placed next to Jiri Frel. A little over six feet tall, with a craggy face and a shock of ruffled white hair, Frel exuded the disheveled brilliance of a professor whose mind was always on fire. His suits were always slightly rumpled. His tie was always askew. His way of speaking—English flavored with a heavy Czech accent—was blunt and uncompromising. Everything about him communicated that the ordinary was beneath his consideration, and that if you got close enough and listened carefully, you might be transported into the higher realms of his wondrous mind.

"Just look at the work on this!" he would command, holding an ancient Greek vase up to the light. "Can you believe the skill it shows? Can you believe that it survives to this day?" If you didn't like it, he would make you like it. And you would feel grateful to have been persuaded, as if he had lifted the scales from your eyes.

When we met, Frel was acknowledged as one of the world's leading experts on Greek vase painting. He had worked at the Louvre and at The Metropolitan Museum of Art in New York. In the early 1970s, on a trip to Europe paid for by the Met, Jiri had visited with J. Paul Getty and accepted the billionaire's offer of a post at the museum he was creating in Malibu. The richest man in the world, Getty was building one of the greatest museums in the world, and was delighted to spend hundreds of millions of dollars doing it.

In 1974, as I entered the ancient art business with the Summa Gallery, the J. Paul Getty Museum opened in a $17 million building that resembled an ancient villa that had been buried at Pompeii. On its first day it boasted a top-level collection of Renaissance and Baroque paintings, as well as Roman and Greek antiquities. The money that the museum had spent on its holdings had caused wholesale inflation in the worldwide art market.

As the Getty's antiquities curator, Frel controlled the largest acquisitions war chest in the world. He represented to me access to the highest levels of sales for ancient art. When it came to truly valuable works, museums were the only buyers with the expertise to acknowledge lasting historical value and the resources to make a deal. Once I expanded beyond coins to deal in all sorts of antiquities, I believed I would have to break in to their exclusive little universe. Instead, Jiri Frel, whom I met at one of the museum's first parties, would come to the back door and just let me in.

"You know, Bruce, we actually need these kinds of things."

Jiri Frel was sniffing around my gallery, picking up an amber carving here, a fragment of a marble statue there. At the time I was frustrated with him. A few months earlier, I had shown him pictures of a sixth-century B.C. terracotta sarcophagus from Clazomenae, a little-known excavation site in Greece. It was a rare piece that Bob had obtained via a Turkish dealer who had probably smuggled it out through Munich and then to Zurich. Though Frel had some trouble getting along with Bob—they were both aging alpha males—he seemed to like the shady side of the street, where Bob did his work. After Frel had seen the pictures, he asked me to ship the sarcophagus straight to the museum. But when it arrived, he claimed the board wouldn't approve the purchase.

The Getty board wanted only big, expensive items. The problem was that a museum collection cannot be truly great if it lacks a full range of pieces, from the everyday to the extraordinary. Items that are relatively inexpensive and even commonplace must be displayed with great works to provide context and historical perspective. Lesser pieces are also required for research purposes. And no serious museum antiquities department can neglect research.

The great irony in this situation was that Frel had no trouble buying a million-dollar statue, but he couldn't acquire the little vases and bits of jewelry he pored over at Summa Gallery. Of course, anyone who had ever met Jiri understood that when he wanted something, he eventually got it. And as he traced his finger over a pottery fragment, he explained how I could solve his problem while making myself and my clients a little bit richer.

It was an ingenious idea. As he identified smaller items he desired—things at Summa Gallery, in Bob Hecht's holdings, or elsewhere—Jiri would notify me. If the object wasn't in my control, I would acquire it, usually on consignment. Then I would find a client to purchase it, at a most reasonable price. The buyer would then turn around and donate it to the Getty. Here, the arrangement turned tricky. Once the donation was made, Frel would arrange for an appraisal that was much higher than it had cost. The end result was a large tax break for the donor, which covered more than the original price of the piece.

A typical deal might involve three fragments of a Greek vase that I had acquired through Bob Hecht for, say, $100,000. A customer would buy them from me for $200,000. Frel would have them appraised as if they had been restored, which would make them worth $500,000. Done correctly—and it was always done correctly—I would profit on the sale. My customer would get more money back from the Internal Revenue Service in taxes than he or she had laid out for the purchase. And Jiri would add something to the Getty's collection.

Although that basic formula worked well, variations were often needed. In one, Jiri would travel to Europe and buy large pieces, worth $1 million and more. Then he would pay a little extra to have a bunch of small items—pottery fragments, kylixes, glass—thrown in. I would then have my customers purchase those smaller items and donate them for the tax benefits.

Over time, my relationship with Jiri and the Getty grew so close that I was treated like a curator. I could drive my car right up to the loading dock and walk straight into the curatorial area without so much as a blink from the guards. I had some of Summa's stock displayed as "on loan" at the Getty and would then bring potential customers in to view it. Think about how that affected someone new to the world of ancient art. I was showing them pieces on display at a world-renowned museum, which they could then buy for themselves.

Now divorced, in the midst of my coming and going at the museum I began dating, and eventually fell in love with, Gaye Richards, who was assistant to the curator of the museum's antique furniture department. Pretty and sensitive, Gaye was extraordinarily fun to be around. She laughed easily, and was always open to new experiences. We began dating, but I'm not the kind of man who likes dating per se. I prefer real relationships, and Gaye and I fell into one very quickly. We moved into a rented house in Malibu, right on the Pacific Coast Highway, and fell into a comfortable routine. Through Gaye, I became even more accepted as part of the Getty family, and I learned more and more about Jiri. For example, I discovered that he was a terrible snob who talked about the trustees and scholars he met on the West Coast as uneducated boors.

In ways big and small, Jiri always seemed to test the rules. He hated to pay for anything, so meals, travel, even postage would be squeezed out of Getty accounts. Visitors to his house would find it decorated with art bought for the museum, and as he walked through storage areas he would sometimes just pick up something small—a coin, a little artifact—and slip it into his pocket. Where these items ended up was a mystery that was never solved.

Despite his shady deals, his quirks, and his annoying habits, Frel was exciting to be around. And though I was vastly more experienced in the ways of the world than most of my peers, I was still only twenty-four years old when I met him. I was impressionable, and Jiri's way of doing business— wrong as it was—made a big impression. He got things done, and made big deals by bending, if not breaking, the rules. It wasn't so different, in my mind, from smuggling coins out of Algeria. If nobody got hurt, if nobody got caught, where was the harm?

Where Jiri and I did part company was on the matter of fakes. For as long as there has been valuable art, there have been craftsmen and dealers willing to traffic in counterfeits. The Phoenicians sold the Romans fake Syrian and Egyptian art, complete with gobbledygook hieroglyphs. The Romans, in turn, excelled at copying Greek sculpture. During the "Egyptomania" that swept Europe in the 1800s, prices for artifacts exploded. Eventually there were undoubtedly more fakes floating around than genuine articles. The Met displayed a gold Egyptian headdress for more than fifty years before it was discovered to be a fabrication containing just a few bits of ancient gold.

Forgers and thieves thrive whenever the market heats up, and this occurs on a regular basis, as every few years a new group of wealthy buyers—typically people with little knowledge and even less experience—begin buying. Because the wealthy constitute a fairly close-knit community, word spreads. A trend becomes a fad and then a craze as the climbing prices make people believe they will realize big returns. In such conditions, it's much easier to pass fake and stolen goods. Indeed, there are always plenty of people willing to ignore the possibility that an item is tainted because they are betting that they can pass it on, like a bad dollar bill, to the next guy.

However, for a dealer trying to build a reputation, getting caught in the middle of a transaction involving a fake or a piece that was quite obviously stolen could be a disaster. I tried hard to avoid it, but I didn't always succeed. For example, not long after I became an active dealer for museums, Bob Hecht acquired a large fragment of a beautiful marble sarcophagus from the second century A.D. The carving on it showed the Labors of Hercules. Based on a photo, I paid $100,000 for it. But before I even took possession, The Cleveland Museum of Art bought it from me for $160,000. The piece was shipped from Europe to Cleveland, and it was quickly prepared for display.

The stone had just been uncrated in Cleveland when Interpol issued a report on items that had been stolen from museums and archaeological digs around Europe. High on the list was a marble sarcophagus that had been swiped from a small museum at Ostia. At the time, such thefts were common at small museums. Usually they involved a bribe to a guard and a visit to a loading dock in the dark of night. But two things about this particular theft were uncommon. First, the item that had been stolen was especially large, and second, it was missing a piece which, according to the photograph, was exactly the size and shape of the marble I had sold to The Cleveland Museum of Art.

"Look, obviously this piece fits the sarcophagus from Ostia," I told the museum's curators. "We have to get this thing back to them. You can't display something that's just been stolen. We made a mistake. I'll give you your money back."

I expected them to say something like, "Oh, my goodness. Thanks very much for bringing this to our attention." Instead they said, "Wait a minute.

How do we know it is our piece? It looks like it, but there are a lot of marble fragments around. We can't be sure this is where ours originated."

After a bit of a battle, I managed to give them their money back and arrange to have the stone returned to Ostia. Hecht, who was always under suspicion and had been briefly banned from Italy for alleged smuggling, repaid me. He was always scrupulously honest with me in that way. Only he knows whether his lost sale was eventually covered by his supplier, but in the network of art thieves that serves the trade, a certain code of honor would require that Bob be made whole.

Decades later I would come to understand that the Ostia marble incident, and Bob Hecht's whole way of doing business, represented something more risky, even dangerous, than I had been ready to admit. The people who smuggle artifacts are quite similar to those who traffic in drugs. Sometimes they are the *same* people. Every once in a while one of them is arrested, prosecuted, and sent to prison. Every once in a while one of them is murdered for trespassing on another's turf—an offense as serious in their business as it is in the gangs of urban America. But as a young man, with a young man's sense of invulnerability, I didn't focus on the hazards. Instead, I saw in Hecht another powerful man who moved in rarefied circles and made his fortune with his ambition, intelligence, and personality.

In Los Angeles, fortune awaits in the movie business, and the city is filled with seekers. Most want to be creative stars—actors, directors, writers. But the odds against their success are enormous. The surer path, as Sy Weintraub's life showed, lay in the business part of the movie industry. For every leading man in Hollywood, there are a hundred executives and major stockholders getting rich on their talents. In fact, as the creative people come and go, burning brightly and then flaming out, the businesspeople keep on going, making deals and wielding power over the next big project and the next and the next.

With that in mind, I listened carefully when, in late 1977, Sy began talking to me about getting involved in The Business with him. It didn't matter that I knew nothing about how movies were made. What did he know about ancient coins before he started investing? What mattered was that I knew how deals were made, and that he could trust me.

Sy had his eye on author Joseph Wambaugh, who had revolutionized the art of crime writing with *The New Centurions*, a brazenly graphic and honest novel that had been turned into a hit movie by Columbia TriStar. Wambaugh was about to sell the rights to another book, *The Choirboys*. Word was that he was unhappy with how his previous books had been translated onto the screen. I was to offer him Sy's help—*our* help—in doing something more to his liking with the next film. Sy knew that Wambaugh's books were bankable, that he would have no problem getting financing for a film if he had the rights to one of them. It was the most direct way to turn words into money.

We met just before noon in a cop bar in Arcadia, my old hometown. A run-down place called The Other Ball, it was dark, dank, and reeked of cigarettes and beer. Wambaugh sat in a booth with the owner of the place, a black-haired, craggy-faced, Johnny Cash look-alike named Bill Coleman. We shook hands, I sat down, and Wambaugh immediately started explaining why he hated Hollywood people, hated the product they produced, and held serious doubts that I was going to do anything to make him feel better. We were fifteen minutes into his rant before I noticed that all the waitresses in the place were naked.

I had been authorized to offer Wambaugh $300,000 for the rights to make a film based on *The Choirboys*, and I had been further instructed to argue that Sy Weintraub would treat him better than all those insensitive studio heads ever could. He only backed the occasional picture, and when he did, he put his heart and soul into it—or so I was supposed to say. Wambaugh wouldn't hear any of it. He spat out a firm "No thanks," and I was left silent, staring across the table at Bill Coleman.

With the pressure of making a deal gone, the three of us could take a deep breath and relax. Coleman said something about getting over to nearby Santa

Anita Racetrack. He wanted to watch a couple of horses, his own horses, run. As he talked, Coleman waved at a man who sat across the room. The man, six feet one and dressed like a cowboy, got to his feet and walked over to our table.

"This is my trainer, Lin Wheeler," said Coleman. "If you want to talk horses, he's the one. He set me up, and I don't think there's anyone who knows more."

Wheeler didn't have to talk much to keep my interest. The track had always been a lure for me. In high school, I would join a group of kids who often caught the last few races of the day after classes had ended. We always managed to talk some old timer into placing bets for us. I admired the horses, but was allergic to them, so that admiration was expressed from afar. Besides, I was more interested in the potential payoff for an intelligent bet. At the track a few dollars could become a few thousand if you knew what you were doing. I liked the fact that it wasn't just a matter of dumb luck. In that way, it was sort of like ancient coins. If you studied and searched long and hard enough, your effort would be rewarded.

Lin helped me understand that as with everything, the real winners at the track were the insiders. Smart and experienced owners, trainers, and jockeys could carefully prepare their horses to run in cash-rich races against competitors they were likely to beat. But purse money was only the beginning. A successful horse could quickly increase in value and be sold at a windfall profit. Even more money, millions of dollars per year, can be made by leasing a retired racer for stud purposes. Even a so-so filly could become a brood mare and return a nice profit on her purchase price.

Those facts, and more, spilled out of Lin as we left The Other Ball and went to spend a few hours at the track. There, in the afternoon sunshine, with hoofbeats and cheers ringing in my ears, I fell in love with the sport. I had a little money (actually I had just recently reached the millionaire mark) and decided on the spot that it was a good moment to buy a racehorse.

"There's no hurry," said Lin. "There's an auction at Hollywood Park in a couple months. We'll go take a look."

Like all athletes, Thoroughbred horses have agents. At Hollywood Park, Lin introduced me to one of the more colorful ones, a white-haired veteran named Albert Yank. Yank did everything with a certain flair. For example, he had a trademark color—purple—that he used on everything from business cards to jockey silks. On the day we met—in March 1978—he was dressed all in purple, from his shirt to his shoes. Fortunately there was substance behind the style. Albert Yank knew horses.

The Thoroughbreds for sale that day were all two-year-olds in training. "In training" meant that they hadn't yet started racing. Since buyers have no track records to consider, only bloodlines and appearance, prices for such untested horses tend to be lower than those charged for battle-proven mounts. But Yank had one, a big, muscular chestnut colt with a white blaze on his face, that he considered a sure thing. His name was Ruggedness, and his daddy was Executioner, a great racehorse of the early 1970s.

After we made a deal for Ruggedness, Yank and I walked around the stables, considering several other horses. Yank was patient, more patient than I, and he didn't recommend any of them. But he insisted on leading me over to meet a heavyset man who stood alone watching the parade of buyers, sellers, and horseflesh. He was over six feet tall, weighed in excess of three hundred pounds, and had a face as wide as a dinner plate. His dark hair was slicked back in the style of a 1950s executive, and he peered at me through a pair of huge, square-lensed glasses.

"Bruce, I want you to meet the consigner of the horse you just bought," said Yank. "This is Nelson Bunker Hunt."

"You've got a nahs horse there mah friend," he said, Texas dripping all over his voice.

We shook hands. I told him it was my first purchase, but that I was excited about Thoroughbreds and intended to get more deeply involved. He said I was off to a good start with Ruggedness, that I wouldn't be disappointed.

Ruggedness would be trained by Lin Wheeler, who thought the horse would be ready to race by June. I couldn't wait that long. I wanted action, so I asked if there was any way to get into racing right away. Lin had another client selling a four-year-old named Maheras. He was a sprinter, running distances under a mile. Though his pedigree wasn't great, he was a ready-to-run horse with a good record.

I bought 50 percent interest in Maheras for $200,000, and he began winning back my investment right way. Over the next year, I bought several more horses, including Native Prancer and National Flag, both of whom proved to be regular winners at Hollywood Park and Santa Anita. Lin trained them all, found the right jockeys, and carefully matched the horses against fields they could beat. In a sport where wily veterans often endure long losing streaks, we were able to pay all our expenses and pocket net winnings in our very first year.

In some ways, the thrill of watching my horses win was similar to the feeling I got when I made a big coin sale, or snatched a prized bit of ancient art for a bargain price. It wasn't the money that was most important. It was the victory. Winning confirms your judgment about horse, rider, and trainer. But there's more. Unlike a business deal, which is savored privately, a win at the track comes with all kinds of whooping and hollering and public attention. That's the difference between sport, any sport, and business. When you get to the winner's circle, the crowd cheers.

The cheers are joined by the quieter, and more meaningful admiration of others in the sport. A year into my life in Thoroughbred racing, I was sitting in an owner's box at Santa Anita when a familiar face appeared. By this time I knew that Bunker Hunt, oil baron, horseman, and political maverick, was one of the richest men in the world; a genuine billionaire at a time when they were rare.

"You've been winning a lot of races around here, and I haven't been winning anything," said Hunt. "And I've got a lot of horses."

He had wandered over alone—no entourage, lackeys, or courtiers—and he spoke in an easy, comfortable way. Everything about him, from his off-the-rack clothes to his 1950s haircut, communicated that he was a very regular person. And as we talked, I discovered that he was genuinely interested in me. Someone had told him that I was an ancient-coin and art dealer, and he asked me question after question about gold and silver and the relationship between the values of coins and raw metals.

At that time—mid-1979—America was gripped by a terrible economic recession and the worst run-up in interest rates since the Great Depression. The rich saw their ordinary investments decline in value, and the middle class was struck by massive layoffs. Arab oil embargoes and the hostage crisis at the American embassy in Iran had made America seem more vulnerable than at any time in the twentieth century.

For Bunker Hunt, whose political views tilted toward the extreme right, these were all signs of impending doom. As we watched horses run, he told me that he was worried about a communist takeover of the United States, which could be aided by a "Jewish conspiracy" inside the government. If this worst-case scenario didn't occur, he added, we were surely facing an economic collapse that could lead to civil unrest and even martial law. Paper money would be worthless, he said, and the only financial safe haven would be in hard assets. For that reason, he was putting his billions into precious metals, especially silver bullion.

Little—perhaps nothing—in Bunker Hunt's political analysis rang true to me. I'm highly skeptical of conspiracy theories. I didn't believe communism was a true threat to America. And I had confidence in the stability of our economy. But we weren't having a political debate. It was a friendly conversation, and I could see that it might be headed in a direction that could be very profitable. Coins and art are, like silver bullion, hard assets that tend to hold their value in good times and bad. If a billionaire seemed ready to buy ancient coins and art as a hedge against disaster, who was I to try to talk him out of it?

"If you'd like, I can show you some Roman and Greek coins," I offered.

"Why don't you come to Dallas?" he answered. "We'll talk about it."

In Nelson Bunker Hunt, I saw a man who might become hooked—addicted really—to ancient coins. He was driven by a fear of the future, and had a deep emotional need for the protection coins promised. A sixth sense inside me knew that once he made his first purchase, he would probably go on and on until he had amassed a stupendous collection. When Sy heard of my new friend, he thought he had a way to instantly cash out his $4 million investment at a price that would match the astronomical projections he had forced me to agree to with clients like David Geffen. (He had grown bored with the coins, and, I guessed, wanted to invest their value in something else.)

With Sy eager to sell, and Bunker willing to buy, I was in the position of representing both sides of a very big deal. On one side was a seller whose wildly inflated asking price—$16 million—reflected simple, unvarnished greed. On the other side was a buyer who wouldn't know if the Weintraub collection was worth $16 million or 16 cents. Bunker was in the weaker position because his knowledge was limited to what I told him. But my best interest lay in a long-term relationship, and that would depend on me playing the role of honest broker.

When the price—$16 million—came out of Sy's mouth I immediately balked. It wasn't fair. No large collection of ancient coins could increase four times in value in less than seven years. I might have been able to raise half that amount, or a bit more, if I had sold them one by one, or offered them at a hyped-up auction. But there was no way that an individual with any sense of the market would relieve Sy of his entire investment at the price he was asking.

Unfortunately, no amount of talking on my part could move Sy off of his price. As he dug in his heels, I gradually lost respect for him. This was not a matter of wise business practice. It was foolish greed. When he insisted I find out if Bunker would pay it, I faked him out. I told him that Bunker wouldn't make the deal. I had decided to protect Bunker and not even suggest it. And Sy never asked me point-blank if Bunker had made the decision.

Though Sy was disappointed, he still wanted to divest himself of his coins and there were few people in the world able to buy such a collection intact. I flew down to Dallas with all the photos and text I had produced for Weintraub, and a few samples of the coins.

At that moment, I was caught between an old loyal customer and mentor of sorts—Sy—and a new one who represented the opportunity to leap into the very highest realms of wealth and power. Given my growing sense that Sy had manipulated me, and structured our relationship for his own personal gain, I was eager to move away from him. But to keep all my options open, I didn't intend to sever our ties. The question was: How could I make both men happy? How could I hook the whale without letting go of the big fish I already had on the line? The answer could be seen trotting around a stud farm in Lexington, Kentucky.

Every year Nelson Bunker Hunt's Bluegrass Farm produced as many as two hundred Thoroughbred foals that had to be sold to make way for the next generation. Since all those horses were not yet in training, and were at least a year or more away from running, the prices Bunker could get for them were low.

Still, the yearlings had value, especially if you were able to buy a large number of them and wait for a few to become winners. Sy had been intrigued by my involvement in racing, and had said he wanted in. So, I proposed a trade. In exchange for all of the Weintraub coins, Bunker would give Sy $8 million in cash, and an $8 million credit at his next horse auction.

The most ingenious aspect of the deal was the effect that the $8 million would have on the value of all the horses Bunker put up for sale. Auctions work like any other marketplace where the supply of available goods is limited. When a river of cash flows in, it lifts the price of every item that's for sale. Sy's $8 million, even though it was a credit, had to be spent. As a result, every other buyer would have to compete harder—paying more—for those horses that had real value. And no one but Sy, Bunker, and me would know that the most aggressive bidder in the room was playing with house money.

To make things easier on Sy, I agreed to be his partner in the horse business, sharing in the costs of purchasing and maintaining the animals. (Eventually, when he wanted to get out, I would partner with Bunker in taking full control of all the horses. Sy would get his $8 million.) Our babies would be raised, trained, and run under the banner of Summa Stables, which I had formed to manage my own growing number of Thoroughbreds.

It's easy to see how Sy and Bunker each benefited from that deal. Bunker acquired a great coin collection by paying half the asking price in cash, and the rest in horses that he would have had trouble getting rid of anyway. Sy cashed in his coins at a huge profit, and in the process, became a sportsman with a huge stable of racehorses.

Sy, in typical fashion, didn't pay me a penny in commission for his sale. Still, I gained something far more valuable—Bunker's confidence. Add to that the fact that I was relieved of the stress associated with Sy's obsession over the value of his coins, and I felt like the clear winner in the transaction.

The crop we harvested at Bunker's auction was mixed. Most of the horses had extraordinary but untested bloodlines. One was a filly whose papa was Bold Forbes, a Kentucky Derby winner who had recently gone to stud. Her mother was named Goofed, and she had already produced at least one very important offspring, a horse call Lyphard, who had won a number of important races. We paid $1.45 million, the highest ever bid for an unproven horse at auction. Sy named her Barb's Bold, in honor of Barbara Walters, who had become his girlfriend following his recent divorce.

Barb's Bold never lived up to her bloodlines, but Summa Stables had so many horses, and so many surprising successes, that even a million-dollar disappointment was easily absorbed. Argument, a horse I bought in partnership with Berry Gordy, is a good example. Argument cost $1.2 million, but before Gordy's check had cleared, he won the D.C. International. We then sold him for almost $10 million as a stud horse. Later I bought a bargain colt named Lomalad—a two-year-old—and he immediately won the $100,000 Hollywood Juvenile Championship. A few days after, I bought a filly named Sisterhood. I ran her in the Beverly Hills Handicap on grass and she won a purse of about $400,000.

The success came because I had gathered some very good people to run the Summa operation. The real genius in those early racing days was Lin Wheeler, who knew how to find great horses and get them to win. A perfect example was a chestnut filly he found at a little track in Santa Fe. When he first saw her she was dirty and skinny and standing knee-deep in mud. But she had been winning a lot of little races. He put down $120,000, which was probably more money than anyone had ever seen at that track, and brought her to California.

At first, Track Robbery didn't run well at all, even though we entered her in sprints that were the same distance she had run in New Mexico. In fact, she didn't even match the times she had posted before we acquired her. Lin was experienced enough to know she had probably been intimidated by the conditions and the stronger fields at the premier tracks where we had her running. It happens all the time. Horses are emotional creatures. Lin decided that for some reason, she hadn't been comfortable enough in those races to unleash her speed.

"Let's try her at a little longer distance—say a mile and an eighth—and see if she settles in and runs," he suggested. There was nothing to lose, so we tried it. Just as Lin hoped, the very first time she ran at that distance Track Robbery eased herself into the lead and just outran the field. After that she won race after race, taking more than $1.2 million in purses, and earning the Eclipse Award as the best mare in the country.

Very young horses sometimes need to be trained, and have to be housed in a more permanent way. Beginning with the first herd acquired from Bunker's farm, I used a training center in Chantilly, France, just outside Paris. Though it might have seemed extravagant to other Americans, training fillies and colts in Europe was not much more expensive than doing it at home—including the cost of shipping them over and back. The benefits were substantial. First, Chantilly offered soft turf for the horses to run on, which meant they were unlikely to suffer the injuries common in the United States, where tracks are made hard to promote speed. Second, the quality of the French trainers was exceptional. Third, once the horses began to race, the competition at the elite level was not as intense as it was in America.

Europe was also a great place to buy horses, and in my travels there I soon connected with Emmanuel de Seroux, an agent who had an uncanny eye for horseflesh. He was buying and selling for Arab sheiks, American billionaires, Japanese corporations, and the royal families of Europe. In 1981, I hired Emmanuel to work exclusively for Summa, and he began to make us one of the top racing syndicates in the world.

With the help of Emmanuel de Seroux, I would buy, sell, and race horses and manage to make a profit at it, for more than a decade. Racing moved me into a social circle I would never have entered in any other way—opening the door to experiences ranging from sheer excitement to utter absurdity. The excitement came from cheering a horse to a victory that netted a huge purse and raised a Thoroughbred's value. The absurdities arose in the most unexpected, and sometimes embarrassing, ways.

One incident I am by no means proud to mention illustrates the rarefied environment enjoyed by the mega rich at racing's highest level. It occurred the night after a Kentucky Derby at a party hosted by Preston Madden, owner of a stable called Hamburg Place, which was home of the first Triple Crown winner, Sir Barton. Preston was an extraordinary character whose Derby parties were infamous for drunken debauchery.

At one of those parties, Preston led me into his private office where a stunning antique desk dominated the decor. To prove the desk's quality, he poured a couple of shots of bourbon on its top and lit it on fire. When the blaze went out, the desk remained unmarked. With the smell of burnt alcohol hanging in the air, Preston charmed me into buying one of his horses. Then he led me outside to a secluded swimming pool that had been filled with bubbles—as well as naked young women, who had been recruited from the University of Kentucky. I was drunk enough to willingly accommodate one of them, who was determined to have sex on the diving board. For years, Preston would tease me with his memories of that party, which I admit were more vivid than my own. The horse he sold me, by the way, didn't run worth a damn.

As profitable and exciting as horse racing was, the most important thing it did for me was bond me to Bunker Hunt and, to a lesser degree, to his brother, Herbert. The Hunts loved horses more than anything in the world. My involvement, and especially my ability to help them sell their Thoroughbreds, brought me their friendship. Though they were immensely wealthy, and courted by an endless parade of sycophants and supplicants, the Hunts did not seem to have many true friends. The few who gained that status quickly learned that Bunker and Herbert were complex and often contradictory, and rarely the men you would expect them to be.

To the outside world, the Hunts were the often-bumbling inheritors of an enormous fortune—once valued as high as $16 billion—that they had managed to reduce by more than half. Along with their myriad businesses, the family was heavily involved in ultra–right wing activities from the John Birch Society to Campus Crusade for Christ. They sometimes mouthed anti-Semitic rhetoric, and they regarded President Carter and most Democrats as near-communists.

All of these views were troubling to me, but they were balanced by what I saw in the Hunts' personal lives. They were surrounded by Jewish lawyers and accountants, and always treated them with respect—even affection. I once took Berry Gordy to visit Bunker at his office in Dallas, and we had lunch at an all-white social club where Bunker insisted that Berry be seated and served. In countless hours spent together, in hundreds of settings, they never treated any person rudely. Given what they often said about minority groups as a whole, it was a startling contrast.

The Hunts were full of surprises. For one thing, they were incredibly cheap about personal expenses. For as long as I knew him, Herbert mowed his own lawn. And Bunker truly detested paying top dollar for travel. More than once I would leave him at the airport, only to learn he had chosen to cash in his ticket in order to get a cheaper fare on a flight that wouldn't leave for hours. When we were in New York, he rode the subways and complained about the fare. When we were in Paris, he always took the cheapest hotel room available.

During one visit to France, to tend to horse business, we all stayed at the Georges Cinq Hotel in Paris. I had a very nice suite, and we visited with an associate of his who had booked what looked like a palace-sized apartment. Bunker took a room on the top floor that was formerly a maid's quarters. It was barely big enough for a bed. One evening, as the three of us walked back from dinner, Bunker pointed to a flag that was waving from the top of the hotel.

"You know what I'm thinking of doing?" he said. "I'm thinking of putting my underwear out there on that flagpole. My room's right there, and you know what they charge for a load of laundry at that hotel? Twelve dollars."

Bunker's practicality was matched with a kind of down-to-earth social attitude that was charming in its own way. By my third or fourth visit to his Texas office, Bunker began insisting that I forgo hotels and stay in a spare bedroom at his home. He would pick me up at the airport himself, usually in a plain American-made sedan decorated with a "Go SMU Mustangs" bumper sticker. His house was not a mansion, just a very nice colonial on a modest piece of property on Lakeside Drive. Inside, the art was Western—equine. The furniture was solid, but plain. Caroline, Bunker's pretty wife, would make us dinner, or we'd go out to a family-style restaurant, and the conversation would most likely revolve around horses or silver. Bunker was truly obsessed with the fear that the Russians would soon be coming across the Rockies, and he was utterly certain that only silver would make his billions safe.

A child's made-over bedroom and chicken and biscuits at a noisy suburban restaurant were not my style. For that matter, neither were Bunker's conspiracy theories and political views. But all that stuff was beside the point. My purpose was to forge a relationship with Bunker that would allow me to sell him millions of dollars worth of coins and antiquities and put me in a position to make other business deals, should opportunities arise. If that meant sleeping in a tiny guest room and eating biscuits till the gravy came out of my ears, I was prepared to do it.

4

BY 1980, I HAD BECOME the modern-day version of an ancient nobleman, a lord surrounded with dependents—scores of employees and partners—and I reigned over varied and growing enterprises. Numismatic Fine Arts, which generated millions of dollars in commissions each year, remained at the center of my empire. Summa Gallery, aided by Bob Hecht and Jiri Frel, continued to sell investment art and tax breaks for an expanding network of rich clients. Summa Stables provided both a heady distraction, and periodic infusions of cash when a horse won big or could be sold at a huge markup. I had become a multimillionaire, and I enjoyed playing the part, dashing around the world to make business deals and to watch my horses run.

In my personal life I had gone through a fairly friendly breakup with Gaye Richards, which included me allowing her to stay in the house we were sharing and covering her expenses. I felt guilty about falling for another woman, a University of Southern California professor of classics named Jane Cody. They were very different women. Where Gaye had been bright and bubbly, Jane was truly brilliant, and almost as driven as I was. I bonded immediately with her children from a previous marriage, seven-year-old Tommy and ten-year-old Erin. We all grew very close, very fast, and almost before I knew it, we were buying a $5 million house together in Holmby Hills.

The new house, and a more serious relationship, provided balance to my business life, which was moving faster and faster toward more varied and complicated deals and ever-bigger payoffs. I'm not sure what drove me. Some entrepreneurs have lofty goals. They might want to revolutionize technology, create cures for disease, change the world. I had started with a love of ancient history and coins. But that simple passion had been overwhelmed by the excitement I felt when making deals, and by my deep-seated need to win the confidence and favor of the rich and powerful. My most valuable talent was in creating, not valuable works of art, but relationships. I could make people like me, and that was worth money. Succeeding at that drew me, like an addict, to want more and more and more.

As successful as I may have seemed to some people, particularly those who worked for me, every nobleman serves a king and by that time my allegiance was firmly pledged to Bunker Hunt. As billionaires, Bunker and his brother, Herbert, operated at a level known by perhaps two dozen people in the entire world. People who held their kind of wealth were not likely to stand around waiting for you to walk up, shake their hands, and sell them something. Bunker Hunt was the eccentric exception. He kept just a few close advisers. He made important decisions on his own. And he wandered racetracks unguarded.

Bunker wanted friendship. In fact, he often seemed lonely. As one of the richest men in the Western world, he could never tell if someone was a true friend, or just another sycophant angling for his money. I tried to overcome whatever skepticism he felt by sharing his interest in horses, and by listening to his theories about politics and economics. We weren't equals in those conversations. I didn't tell him my liberal ideas about politics, or point out the flaws in his conspiracy theories. But I did tease him in friendly ways about his penchant for cheap air fares and home cooking.

In business, I continuously tried to show the Hunts that I was reliable, scrupulously honest, and that the cash could flow both ways. I bought their horses, and when called upon, I helped them out with silver. On one particular New Year's Eve I was startled by their request that I put down 10 percent on $30 million worth of silver bullion to help them post a loss on their tax returns. I did it, and lost $650,000 on the deal. But I never asked them to fulfill their pledge to cover my deficit.

A $650,000 loss was easy to accept because I was making millions in commissions on the Hunts' purchases of ancient coins. After buying Sy Weintraub's hoard, Bunker and Herbert embarked on a long campaign of acquiring coins as a hedge against the economic disasters that loomed in their imaginations. Together the Hunts became the most powerful force in the worldwide ancient-coin market. Their vast wealth and desire to buy as many valuable coins as possible became common knowledge among dealers, who contacted me from every corner of the globe whenever they came upon a coin they deemed worthy.

Like every other retailer in the world, I wasn't much concerned with the coins' origins. If you investigate thoroughly you will discover that at some point, virtually every ancient coin on the market was smuggled, stolen, or otherwise the subject of shady dealing. (This should have made me more cautious than I was.) It's a state of affairs that is widely accepted, even by law-enforcement authorities, and only leads to problems when questions about a sale become public. That is just what happened when I acquired a rare decadrachm and sold it to the Hunts for $1 million, setting a new record for the highest price ever paid for an ancient coin.

That particular decadrachm, the seventh known to exist in the world, had not been seen until it was offered for sale by a dealer in Europe. It was a beautiful work of art commemorating the Olympic victory of an athlete named Exantus. It was also, to my dismay, eventually proven to have been recently excavated in Turkey and smuggled out. That wasn't a complete surprise, of course. Diggers by the thousands work the countryside in Turkey, often fanning out to isolated spots after rainstorms soften the ground. The Olympic decadrachm had been unearthed in just this way by two men with a homemade metal detector. The hoard they found one dark night would be considered the discovery of the century. It included more than two thousand pieces, with a total weight of nearly sixty pounds. The diggers had a local woman wash their treasure and tossed her a few coins as payment. The bulk of their find then moved through the Turkish Mafia to the legitimate market. The one I bought had been among the few paid to the washerwoman, who had quietly sold it.

That was one of those rare cases where it could be shown that crimes were committed in the discovery and sale of a coin. The Hunts and I eventually turned it over to the Turkish government. Others who bought coins from that hoard fought the authorities for more than a decade, but they too would ultimately relent. While the Hunts greeted their loss of the coin as a business setback, I saw it as a serious blow to a magnificent art collection. I was disappointed that they didn't feel the same way.

I still nursed the dream that Bunker and Herbert would one day become avid, even passionate collectors rather than speculators. Toward that end, I took them on trips to Europe, hoping to excite them with the drama and history behind their acquisitions. At times those trips could seem like package tours for the culturally resistant. One memorable month abroad included a week on a Greek yacht called the *Spalmatore*. We drifted from island to island, with me nudging Bunker and Herbert off the boat to explore ruins and landmarks. At night they were treated to some of the best meals in the Mediterranean, only to complain—"Fish, again?"

I had pretty much lost all hope of turning the Hunt brothers into art lovers when we went to Zurich to see the offerings at Bank Leu. Leo Mildenberg, who was keenly aware of the Hunts' money, began our meeting by telling the Hunts I was perhaps the greatest coin dealer in the world, and that they were in expert hands. He then brought out tray after tray of coins, at least a million dollars' worth.

Bunker picked up one coin and then another, and used an eyepiece to get a closer look. "Yeah, that's nice," he said, in a matter-of-fact way. "That's a pretty lookin' thing."

"What about gold coins?" asked Herbert. "And what can you show us that is undervalued?"

Gold coins, especially Byzantine gold, were undervalued at that time. As I explained that to Herbert, Leo brought out a couple of trays filled with nickel-size coins. They were valued, on average, at about $400 apiece. This was just a couple hundred dollars more than a typical U.S. gold piece, but they were so much rarer, and so much more beautiful, that Herbert instantly appreciated their value.

After he looked at the trays, and quizzed me about prices, Herbert said, "Okay, what would it take to buy all the Byzantine gold coins?"

"You mean all the coins right here?" I asked.

"No," he said, "I mean all the coins there are, in the world. Everything."

I looked at Leo, and his face was as blank as my mind. Together we guessed that there were several hundred thousand Byzantine gold coins circulating in the world, but we could only estimate that buying them all would cost hundreds of millions of dollars. Herbert decided he would start with the lot that was laid before him, paying about $200,000 for them, and then investigate cornering the entire world supply over time.

As Leo wrote up the sale, I indulged in a little small talk, noting that Bunker had become interested in Greek vases and that both of the Hunt men were avid collectors of bronze statues, especially the Western pieces of Remington. Though he would hardly have been a fan of such works, Leo knew what they were and he quickly said, "If you like bronzes, I have something very special to show you."

Leo ducked into the back room and then returned with two bronze pieces. One was a candelabra with a figure of a satyr from about the sixth century B.C. The other was a statue that looked like Alexander the Great from the second or third century. They each glowed with a dark-hued patina. Bunker looked at them and didn't seem impressed, but Herbert thought they would fit nicely with his Remington bronzes.

"How much are these things?" he asked.

"One is $300,000," said Leo, converting francs to dollars in his head. "The other is about $350,000."

"Well, I'll take 'em," said Herbert. He then reached for a newspaper that he had brought with him, the *International Herald Tribune*. He intended to wrap the art pieces in it and take them away, one in each hand. We managed to convince him that the statues were too precious to carry out, and that we would help him avoid paying customs by handling their transport to Texas. He was disappointed. He wanted to take them home and display them right away. But he accepted our advice, and departed happily, after reminding us to start gathering up more Byzantine gold for him to buy. He liked the idea of owning it all.

The idea that someone would even contemplate buying every bit of Byzantine gold in the world would have been downright bizarre if that someone had been anyone but a Hunt. But at the time we were touring Europe, Bunker and Herbert were in the midst of a very serious effort to corner the worldwide market in raw silver. According to some press reports the Hunts, together with a few Saudi royals and an Arab living in Brazil named Naji Nahas, already controlled roughly half the global supply.

That was possible because at the time, a so-called "futures contract" to buy or sell silver at a set price some months away, could be had for a cash payment of just 10 percent of the amount the silver was worth. Under a typical contract, I could put down $10,000 to buy $100,000 worth of silver at, say, $10 an ounce, in ninety days. If the actual price rose to $15, then my contract became quite valuable. In fact, my $10,000 down payment would have become a contract worth $140,000 or more. There were plenty of companies that actually needed the metal, who would pay that amount to beat the market price.

Though the leverage of a futures contract provided stupendous possibilities for profit, the risk was enormous as well. If silver fell to $5, no one would want a $10 contract. At the end of the ninety days I could either take delivery of the bullion at the higher price I had agreed to, or pay someone else to take the contract off my hands. The cost would be the difference between the market price, and my contract price. In the case of my fictional example, I would be out $50,000.

The Hunts managed to be on the right side of futures contracts for nearly a decade, as their cartel pushed the price of silver sky-high. By January of 1980, it had increased to $50 per ounce, roughly five times its value six months earlier. Although other investors holding silver benefited along with the Hunts, the manufacturing companies that needed the metal for everything from photo film to drugs to dinnerware found their operations squeezed and their profit margins shrinking.

Unlike most investors, the Hunts had not just traded options, but had actually taken delivery of millions of ounces of real silver. They hired cargo planes and paid off-duty Texas Rangers to guard shipments of silver to vaults in New York, Switzerland, and other major cities. That practice created a real shortage of silver. Alarmed investors and manufacturing companies began pressuring regulators to do something about it. They responded by changing the rules. Restrictions were placed on the amount of silver any single investor could trade in a day. More importantly, the proportion of cash that had to be put up to secure a futures contract was raised significantly. The days when a comparatively tiny investment could control millions of ounces were ended.

The price of silver began to slide as soon as the new rules took hold. By early spring, Bunker and Herbert were committed to buy vast quantities of silver at $35 an ounce in a market where it was worth about $12. Their futures contracts had become enormous liabilities. When they announced that they lacked the cash to cover the gap, the responsibility for the debt fell to their Wall Street brokers, who had borrowed hundreds of millions from banks to

finance the Hunts' dealings. If the debt couldn't be restructured, the broker-
ages and the banks could be sunk by their losses.

The more federal authorities learned about the magnitude of the Hunt
debt, the more worried they became. Some economists believed that their
default, and the subsequent burden on financial institutions, would harm
the country. America was already in economic crisis. Interest rates were
approaching 20 percent. Unemployment was higher than at any time since
World War II, and entire industries such as steel and heavy manufacturing
were being overwhelmed by foreign competition.

As often happens when a debtor obligation is so big that lenders cannot
afford to see him fail, the solution lay in offering him even more credit. In the
Hunts' case, a consortium of banks put up more than $1.3 billion to bail them
out and save the others who would have been hurt by a bankruptcy. There
was only one catch. Before they could make the deal, the banks needed the
permission of the Federal Reserve bank, which barred loans to cover com-
modity contract losses.

Throughout the silver crisis I listened to Bunker's worries about the market and his paranoid theories about the conspirators—mostly Jews, of
course—who undid his brilliant plans. He had legitimate complaints about
the way trading rules had been changed to cap the amount of silver he could
move in a day, and to require much bigger cash outlays for contracts. Those
moves, designed to protect industries that needed silver, began the decline in
prices that eventually sunk his campaign.

There was little I could offer, save for sympathy, until Bunker told me he
needed political backing for the huge loan that would cover his losses. Bunker
explained to me that he had no friends at the Fed, or on the congressional
committee that oversaw its actions. Indeed, his wild-eyed politics made him
the object of ridicule among most Democrats and quite a few Republicans as
well. In the midst of the crisis he was even cited for contempt when he failed
to answer a subpoena to testify before the committee.

Fortunately for him, and for me, I had a way to help. One of my ancient-coin clients had recently been defeated after a long stay in the U.S. Senate. John Tunney, a Democrat, was very interested in making money. When I asked him if he'd be interested in lobbying on Bunker's behalf, he was surprisingly receptive. "I know this is bizarre," I told John. "I know politically you hate him. But trust me, he's not a bad guy and he really is getting screwed."

When we discussed the fees we'd receive if the loan was approved—more than $5 million for each of us—Tunney became downright agreeable. Bunker, whose views couldn't have been more different than Tunney's, was flabbergasted by the idea. As bright as he was in some areas, Bunker was wholly ignorant in the ways of Washington. But once I explained the advantage of having someone from the opposite side of politics on his team, he quickly adopted the idea.

In the weeks that followed, John Tunney met with the Fed chairman, Paul Volker, a number of times. He also sat down with key members of Congress, including his friend Ted Kennedy, who surely thought Bunker Hunt was a Neanderthal of the first order.

Before the deal was done, Congress held hearings at which Bunker testified. It was there that he issued his now-famous explanation for not knowing his own net worth. "People who know how much they are worth"—he snorted—"generally aren't worth that much."

Despite that kind of bragging, and the suggestion that the Hunts could cover their losses with their own assets, the Fed approved the loan and Congress did nothing to halt it. Bunker got his $1.3 billion. John and I pocketed commissions exceeding $6 million each.

Remarkably, throughout the silver crisis, Bunker and Herbert continued to spend literally tens of millions of dollars on coins and antiquities gathered by me via Bob Hecht, Jiri Frel, and a worldwide network of sources. The Hunts trusted me so completely that all I had to do was find the object, write an invoice, and they paid. In that way I got them thousands of coins along with antiquities ranging from Greek helmets and vases to furnishings and bronzes. They even bought their own pieces by Euphronius; a krater and a kylix. Both were obtained through Bob Hecht and bore the shadows that all of Hecht's items carried.

For me, watching the Hunts conduct a whirlwind of deals was exciting and inspiring. I was especially close to Bunker and saw clearly that he was not the caricature he sometimes pretended. He was not the unsophisticated good ol' boy. Nor was he the impractical rich kid, whose only worth came via accident of birth. The Bunker Hunt I knew was shrewd, intelligent, and highly competitive. Granted, he was a victim of the politics and paranoia he inherited from his father, but he was not out of touch with reality. And while he might have exploited the cracks and seams in the rules and laws that governed business, he had never been prosecuted. He took big, exciting risks, but things always seemed to work out all right.

That didn't mean Bunker always found an easy way out. The collapse of the silver market had created two long-term problems. The first was taken care of by the $1.3 billion loan. The second involved the limits that had been placed on the sale of silver contracts. Those new regulations made it extremely difficult for Bunker to sell all the silver he needed to sell to avert even greater future losses. In 1982, as I presented him with a list of ancient coins I thought he should buy, Bunker suggested a bit of creative financing that would help him shed more silver than the law allowed. Instead of paying cash for the coins, he would give me, in private, $20 million worth of silver that he had in storage in New York or Zurich. I could sell it right away or hold it. Either way, Bunker would have the coins, and the commodities regulators would never know he had shed the silver.

At the time, silver was about $10 per ounce. Bunker was working with Naji Nahas and the Arabs to try to make the price go back up. He was sure that the market was just in a short-term dip. I had an important choice to make. What Bunker didn't know was that I didn't yet possess the coins I offered to sell him. I knew where I could get them, but they were scattered at dealers across Europe. I could convert the metal to cash and buy his coins. But

I could also hold on to the silver, delay actual acquisition of the coins, and gamble with the price of silver. If, as he said, the price of silver was sure to rise, I could make millions of dollars, and he would never know.

He would never know because, like most top-level investors, Bunker Hunt did not actually take possession of his ancient coins and keep them close at hand. In the same way that he used bank vaults in New York and Zurich to hold his silver, he depended on me to secure his collection. He might see pictures, review receipts, or stop by my gallery to see them from time to time, but he held such a vast number of coins that he would have very little idea of what he was viewing. And it would have been ridiculous for him to just keep them around the house.

I took the risk with Bunker's investment because my relationship with him had grown so close, so familiar. I also felt comfortable doing it because I was making lots of money for him, especially with horses. Beginning with the deal I arranged for Sy to buy Bunker's young Thoroughbreds, I had become a key agent for the annual output at Bluegrass Farm. I did it by constructing some of the largest and most complex horse syndicates the sport had ever seen, and the first ever to buy yearlings that had never run.

As each year's foals came of age, I put together groups of wealthy people—coin clients, Hollywood types, even doctors and lawyers—who bought shares in a hundred or more horses. I tried to value the horses based on pedigree, and considered the prices that similar horses were fetching at auction. The first time, I figured the one hundred fillies and colts were worth a total of $24 million. I let Bunker retain half interest in them, and then sold shares in the other half for $12 million. I bought $3 million in shares myself, so I would be the second biggest shareholder.

In those days, tax laws allowed for substantial depreciation on horses. The benefits were so great that some investors covered their first year's cost with the taxes they saved. By the time the horses were two years old they were running and the income flow from their winnings, plus revenue from those we sold, kept the whole thing going.

Though I made no commissions on the syndicates, I truly loved being involved with the sport. Few things are more thrilling than the sound of a dozen or so horses making the final turn on a track and straining for home as a big crowd cheers.

I also enjoyed the challenge of managing the syndicates. To control our horse-keeping expenses we bought a farm east of Los Angeles to house and train many of them. I hired professionals to manage the whole thing. One of the most important jobs involved weeding out the long shots and selling them for the best prices. After all, the bums eat just as much as the champions.

Tax savings aside, many of the members of the syndicates lost a little money on their ponies. However, few complained. It wasn't the type of thing people did for profit. They did it to get involved in the sport, to say, "I own a few horses." The only one who did come out way ahead, in the end, was Bunker Hunt. Each year he unloaded all of his young horses, including many that no one else would have bought, and made $12 million. And he didn't even have to form the syndicate and find the investors. I did all of that for him.

The millions of dollars I had shoveled to Bunker for horses; the Tunney-brokered bailout; the $650,000 I lost on that New Year's Eve silver deal; all of that was in my mind as I continued to lie to Bunker about the coins I had supposedly bought for him after he gave me all that silver. As weeks, and then months passed, the weight of the debt got heavier. I watched the price of silver slide to $6 per ounce and just stay there. Nearly half my value was gone. Even if I wanted to do the right thing and acquire those coins for Bunker, I couldn't. The money wasn't there. But as long as he never asked, I could bide my time and pray for the market to change. Then, without warning, I got a desperate call from Bunker.

"Bruce? Bunker. Listen, I've got a little problem."

"Problem?"

"We have to have an audit of my coins. We're doin' some financin', and the banks want a look at all our assets."

"Okay, Bunker," I said. "But I'll need a little time."

"Fine. They won't come out until next week. I told them that wouldn't be a problem. They'll have our receipts. You just gotta show 'em the stuff."

"Uhhh. Okay, Bunker."

"Great. Bah now."

My stomach began churning even before I hung up the phone. In a week's time the auditors would be in my office looking for $20 million worth of coins that simply didn't exist. To make matters worse, I didn't have the cash that was supposed to pay for the collection. Bunker's silver had lost so much value that even if I liquidated all of it, immediately, I wouldn't get half the money I needed. I could have told him the truth, but I wanted to be Mr. Big. My ego wouldn't let me.

For the first time in my life, I faced a business crisis—of my own making—that was so big I couldn't fix it alone. I would have to tell my staff the whole truth about it, no matter how embarrassing it was. One by one I called them into my office, described the situation, and explained how they might help save me and the company. I was pleasantly surprised when not one person hesitated to help. But I was astounded when, in the end, not one pointed out that I had been reckless, even fraudulent, in my dealings. Later I would realize that they were all too dependent on me to see any other course.

I knew what we had to do. In one short week, we would have to make a $20 million collection appear, and certify that it was the property of Bunker Hunt. Once we got through the audit, we would put everything back in order and begin to slowly make things right.

Several key factors worked in our favor. First, the $20 million figure was a retail number. On a wholesale level, we were talking about something closer to $10 million. Second, the auditors would have no way of determining whether the coins we showed them, tagged with Bunker Hunt's name, actually belonged to him. Ancient coins don't come with serial numbers. If I was holding a denarius for another collector, it was a simple matter to re-label it, temporarily, to show it belonged to Bunker. Finally, we had the advantage of being able to obtain coins from certain sources on consignment. Leo Mildenberg, for example, only needed to hear that I had a potential buyer and he would send me almost anything he had.

The original inventory I had sent Bunker listed three hundred specific coins. The auditors would be checking for each one. It turned out that I had only a few dozen of the right items in house. Some were being held for another big client, Gordon McClendon. Others were in the small inventory I kept for the occasional off-the-street customer who wanted a retail item. I had my staff set to work locating those, matching them against the list, and labeling them for the Hunt collection. Of course, I was still about 270 coins short.

The morning after my fateful telephone call with Bunker, the man I had hired to manage NFA, Steve Rubinger, boarded a flight for Zurich. I had met Steve more than a decade earlier, during a trip to Minnesota to visit a girl-friend's family. I had been startled to find, in that Midwestern city, someone my age who shared my interest in the ancient world. I had hired him when NFA was created, and he had become expert in the trade. But Steve was not exactly suave and charming. He didn't cultivate the kinds of friendships I had made in Europe and around the Mediterranean. And I knew that as he went out to capture the coins on our list, no one was going to do him any favors.

With the list in hand, Steve went city to city, acquiring coins as fast as he could. He tried to get as much as he could on credit, or consignment, but many of the dealers could tell from the way that he acted that he was in no position to bargain. Many squeezed him for top dollar, and demanded to be paid in full, in advance. One exception was Leo Mildenberg. Grateful for every dollar I had spent with Bank Leu, and mindful of how my clients had contributed to the huge increase in coin prices worldwide, Leo allowed Steve to take scores of coins without paying a penny.

After each stop at a European source, Steve called to report his results. We went down the list, checking off the coins he had hunted down and noting those that were still at large. This was not the kind of job Steve was cut out to perform. He was not a natural traveler. He didn't share my delight in other cultures and languages. Nevertheless, he dutifully trekked from Zurich to Basel, Munich, Paris, and London. With two days to spare, we had gotten our hands on everything we needed, and Steve flew home. I didn't care about the cost, because once the coins were checked in the audit, they could be returned.

The scene Steve came upon as he got to the office must have shocked him. Half a dozen of us were poring over coins and lists, and hastily making up labels. Steve dumped out his haul and we fell on it, determined to finish the job. We worked all through the night, checking coins off the list one by one, slipping them into envelopes and arranging them on trays. Morning came and we were still working. We were finishing the last few when the auditors trooped up the stairs and came in the door.

Three auditors, who were joined by one of Bunker's accountants, set up shop in our conference room. I tried to stay out of the way as the trays were brought to them and they peered at each and every coin. It took the better part of a week, but in the end they accounted for every item on Bunker's receipts. The lead auditor came to my office to announce that everything had gone well. In fact, he had never done a more trouble-free inspection of assets.

"I'm so glad it went well," I said, hiding the wave of relief that passed through my body.

"And we'll handle having the coins shipped to Dallas," he added.

My face must have turned white, because he quickly tried to reassure me. "Don't worry," he said, "we'll have Brinks handle it. And we'll insure it for the full amount."

The armored car arrived the next day. The driver and his pistol-packing guard checked off every item as it was loaded. As they pulled away from the curb on Rodeo Drive, they took all the coins I was supposed to return for refunds, and all my hope for an easy fix to the Hunt collection crisis. Bunker would not know about my sleight of hand with his silver, but there would be no escaping the debt I racked up in Steve's buying spree.

To deal with that burden, I sold as much inventory as I could, gathered as much cash as was available, and satisfied everyone who demanded immediate payment. Leo at Bank Leu was the biggest creditor by far, and he willingly agreed to let me chip away at my debt over the course of a couple of years. The most difficult moment in reconciling my debts came when I had to tell my big client, Gordon McClendon, the truth. I called him and in a halting conversation filled with uncomfortable pauses, admitted that I had taken his coins and didn't have the money to pay him. He was disappointed, but not especially angry. In fact, he was more understanding than I, had our positions been switched.

"Well, okay, Bruce," he said. "I understand what happened. You got yourself in a bind and tried to get yourself out." I promised to pay him back, over time, with interest. I did just that, and he ended up doubling his initial investment in the coins. But we never did business again.

My closest associates—Steve Rubinger, Cathy Lorber, the staff at NFA— knew that the Hunt collection crisis had shaken me like an earthquake. But outside the office, no one seemed to notice that I was any different. The only outward change I showed anyone was the weight I gained in that time period. I had always been heavy, a fact I attributed to my passion for fine food and a tendency to eat more when I was under stress. The fact that I had gained ten or twenty extra pounds didn't even alarm Jane. After all, my weight was always going up and down.

Looking back, I would have to say that Jane had a right to know what had gone on because, a year before the audit, we had been married.

My proposal to Jane was made over the phone during a trip to New York. At first she laughed a little—in truth, I wanted the marriage more than she— but then she agreed. Jane got a dress while I arranged for the license. New York required blood tests, but I was terribly phobic about needles. Someone in the wedding party contacted a doctor she knew, and he sneaked us a blood sample from one of his patients. Our friends hustled up rings and flowers. David Dinkins, who would become mayor of New York a few years later, was enlisted to perform the ceremony. Two days after my proposal, Jane and I became man and wife before a dozen friends in a private room at the famous New York "21" restaurant.

Jane gave birth to our daughter, Katie, just as I was frantically trying to satisfy the auditors. I managed to celebrate Katie's arrival and care for Jane, even though my empire was teetering. When it was all over, the lesson I took from the experience was probably the wrong one. Rather than feeling chastened and humbled, I felt as if I had made a great escape. I had taken a risk, and survived.

In some ways, I not only survived, I thrived. In both coins and horses I continued to find big new clients. One of the most important was Allen Paulson, founder of Gulfstream Aerospace Corporation. I met him at Hollywood Park, at a time when he was considering a big investment in the horse business. We were introduced by Marge Everett, chairwoman of the track. While I sold him some shares of horses, we also began buying them as partners.

Allen was the most unassuming and humble rich man I had ever met. He was confident in my judgment and a perfect partner. We won a great many races with horses such as Strawberry Road, Jade Hunter, and Corridor Key. Allen bought the stallion Palace Music from Bunker and me. The horse went on to finish second in the Breeders' Cup Mile, and to sire what might have been the greatest horse of the century: Cigar. Brookside Farm, the huge stable he opened in Kentucky, became one of the most important centers for breeding in America.

Besides doing all the horse business with me, Allen became a major client for coins and rare art. He put several million dollars into art for his homes in Los Angeles and near San Diego. His holdings eventually included everything from small bronze statues and Greek vases to large marble sculptures, all Greek and Roman.

5

IN TEXAS, A MAN WITH MONEY and ambition inevitably finds himself in the oil business. In Iowa, I suppose he starts buying cornfields and grain elevators. In New York, it's Wall Street. In Los Angeles, he becomes a movie mogul, or at the very least an executive producer.

It is an open secret in the movie and TV business that while it takes certain talents and expertise to grab writing, acting, or directing credits, all it takes to become an executive producer is money. Of course, money is the difference between a film that gets made and distributed, and an idea that never gets past talk. That is why L.A. is full of creative people who dedicate their lives to luring guys with money—dry cleaners, real-estate operators, hoteliers, even coin dealers—into the business. Check The Palm or The Grill at lunchtime. Most of the best tables are occupied, not by beautiful actors, but by wide-bellied businessmen enjoying their moment of glamour.

It is impossible to understate glamour's appeal to the man who made his fortune in an ordinary way. For a million dollars or so, he gets to trade his regular life for dinner with the stars, visits to a set, and seeing his name up on the screen. If the ego boost isn't enough to get him involved, there's always the tantalizing prospect of backing a blockbuster.

The late 1970s and early 1980s saw an astounding leap in the box-office haul for big movies. If you take the gross receipts for all the films ever released, and adjust them for inflation, you see that two of the top four—*Star Wars* and *E.T.*—came out in that time period. Those were only the super-mega hits. In a five-year period from 1977 to 1982, seven movies made more than $300 million in today's dollars. While the adventure action genre dominated, among the seven were also the musical *Grease* and the comedy *National Lampoon's Animal House*. A sweet, inexpensive movie like *Tootsie*, released in 1982, pulled in the equivalent of $270 million. Some truly bad movies still made sizable sums. A Chevy Chase movie called *Modern Problems*, which critics described with words such as "dreadful" and "awful," nevertheless raked in $24 million.

With so much money raining down on Hollywood, it was natural to ignore the unshakable central truths of filmmaking: Most movies barely meet their production costs, and a great many lose money. As immutable as that fact might be, no one lives by it. Every project, in its backers' eyes, has the potential for great commercial success, if not an Academy Award. If there's no big star, then the script is terrific. If the script is only so-so, then a Mel Gibson or a Julia Roberts will pull in an audience. There's always an angle from which every film looks like a winner. Even if it's got a ghastly title like, say, *Brimstone & Treacle*.

Brimstone & Treacle might have had an awful title, but it had singing sensation Sting—a big name to play the lead role. The script was pretty good, too. Written by veteran English playwright Dennis Potter, it was the story of a young man who weasels his way into the lives of a British couple with a daughter rendered comatose after a car hit her. The interloper discovers the daughter had been struck when she ran into the street after seeing her father having sex with his secretary. Besides the compelling story, and an intriguing star, the movie would feature Joan Plowright, the great British actress, and an accomplished director, Richard Loncraine. The soundtrack would include solos by Sting, as well as pieces by his group The Police, and the Go-Go's.

The music, the stars, the script, and the director were all part of the package that was put in front of me, like a shiny Christmas present, by Alan Salke. I had been introduced to Alan by Berry Gordy. He had once been Berry's business manager and a top financial official at Motown. His management company handled business affairs of a long list of top bands and solo acts, everyone from Seals & Crofts to Fleetwood Mac. Alan had been around for Berry's adventures in movies—*Lady Sings the Blues* and *The Bingo Long Traveling All-Stars & Motor Kings*—and he had fallen in love with the idea of making films.

I liked Alan. He was very energetic, fun to be around, and very smart about the business side of creative endeavors. And in his work with musicians he had proven his ability to handle the kind of craziness that comes with the entertainment business. Just being around Alan had proven to me that you don't know what chaos is until you tried to manage the affairs of the kind of half-educated, ego-obsessed, and drug-altered characters who dominate the music business.

It's difficult to offer a good example of the kind of lunacy Alan dealt with, because he is so ethical that long after he closed his management company, he maintained the confidentiality that governed those relationships. But I can tell you that one incident he once described as a run-of-the-mill event involved a temperamental rock diva who abandoned her brand-new Rolls-Royce in the middle of Sunset Boulevard because it ran out of gas. Though such events were daily occurrences, somehow Alan was able to prevent most of his clients from squandering every last penny, and in a field where everyone gets fired, or sued, all the time, his roster was remarkably stable. And he and his clients made a lot of money.

With all his previous success, his many contacts in entertainment, and his engaging personality, I found it easy to believe in Alan's plan to start a company that would make movies and TV projects. It looked even better when he told me that his partner was going to be Herb Solow. Herb had produced a bunch of TV movies, but his strong point was series television. He had been in charge of making some spectacularly successful series, including *Star Trek* and *Mission: Impossible*.

With Herb, Alan seemed to have someone who could actually make products that studios and networks would buy and distribute. When he told me I could own the company for a $1 million investment that would be financed by a major East Coast bank, I found the idea almost irresistible. All I had to do was sign for the loan, posting coins and other assets as collateral, and Sherwood Productions—the name came from the street Alan lived on—would be born. *Brimstone & Treacle* would be our first film.

I fell comfortably into my role as a film backer. Like almost everybody, I love movies. My taste runs toward historical epics, smart thrillers, and intense dramas. Ask me to watch *The Caine Mutiny* or *The Deer Hunter*, and I'll make the popcorn. Although I'm not interested in sitting through *Terms of Endearment*, *When Harry Met Sally*, or *Die Hard*, that doesn't mean I discount their value. There are all kinds of movies that make money.

Which brings us back to *Brimstone & Treacle*. As a small company, Sherwood would never be able to compete with big-budget, major-studio projects. We had to be content with small-budget endeavors that might fit neatly into a niche that appealed to a good-size audience. Though it was rather dark, the movie turned out to be pretty good, and the sound track was even better. Before it was released, Sting came to Los Angeles, and I hosted a small party for him. Without being asked, he sat down at the piano and sang several songs. That experience alone was almost worth the price of making the film.

In the end, *Brimstone & Treacle* didn't make much of a splash. We had only limited distribution, and while it won a film festival award in Canada, it didn't generate the kind of excitement among the people who did see it to build a real audience. But when the sales of the sound track and video rentals were added to the balance sheet, we didn't lose a penny. In the peculiar calcu-

lus of moviemaking, that made *Brimstone & Treacle* a success. And it made
Sherwood a real production house. Our financiers, European American Bank
of Long Island, made it clear that they were ready to give us more money for
more movies.

The EAB executives I dealt with were new to Hollywood and, as far as I
could tell, they had been happily seduced by the aura of The Business. It made
sense. What would you rather do, arrange a line of credit for a dentist in Great
Neck, or jet out to the coast to finance a movie? Of course they wanted to do
business in Hollywood. It was fun, and bankers hardly ever have fun.

With EAB's backing, we began looking for scripts we could try to develop.
Development is always difficult. It requires you to buy an option on the material—a book, treatment, or finished script—and then run around looking for
both talent and a distribution deal. In America, distribution, which gets a film
into theaters, was being done by a handful of big studios: Fox, Paramount,
MGM, and others. Foreign distribution, which was often even more valuable,
was done through an even smaller number of firms. In a typical arrangement,
those companies would agree to distribute a movie based on the script and talent you bring to them. If they want the film, they'll put up almost all the
money you need to make it. The rest—called the gap—you pay yourself or
finance. EAB was willing to lend us our gap money, and the cost of running
our little production company.

In those early days, it often seemed like every agent in town was ringing
our phone and throwing scripts at us. Our judgment wasn't always the best.
Alan loved a script called *Risky Business*, which was about a kid who gets in
all kinds of trouble while his parents are away. Herb hated it so we turned it
down. Instead we bought the script for a movie called *Get Crazy*. It was a
spoof of a rock-and-roll movie, and it was trouble from the start. We rented
out a big empty theater, where we did most of the filming, and hired a competent, if not sterling, cast that included Malcolm McDowell, Daniel Stern,
and Ed Begley, Jr. When shooting was completed the director had five hundred thousand feet of film—easily twice what was needed—and his first

assemblage was five hours long. It took nearly a year to edit the mess into something resembling a movie. The audience nationwide wasn't big enough to fill a high-school gym. *Risky Business*, of course, made tens of millions in profits.

Mistakes like choosing *Get Crazy* over *Risky Business* happen to everyone who makes films. In fact, they happen a lot. For example, we had a chance to buy *Back to the Future*, which became a huge franchise movie, but we didn't. Despite our errors, the fact that we actually made some movies that got released was good enough to keep us in business. After all, just proving that you could get an idea onto the screen sets you above a huge number of the so-called producers crawling around L.A. Then we got a big break when a film called *WarGames* practically fell into our laps. It had been funded by MGM, where company president David Begelman had high hopes for it. But instead of riding a fast track into production, *WarGames* had gotten bogged down in petty disagreements. Money ran low. Director Martin Brest was fired. Begelman began looking for a new production company and a financial booster shot. I went to my old friends Bunker and Herbert Hunt and talked them into sharing a $2 million investment in the film and Sherwood Productions got the project.

It wasn't too difficult to get the Hunts into the movie business. First, they trusted me. Second, they believed there was money to be made. And third, they were happy to get a taste of the filmmaking scene. Their only condition was that the movie not be R-rated, or worse, NC-17. They were good Christian men, and they weren't going to be part of anything that damaged the morals of American youth.

There was nothing in *WarGames* that even approached R-rated material. A sci-fi thriller, it starred Matthew Broderick and Ally Sheedy, and told the story of a young genius who manages to hack his way into a military computer system. He gets involved in what is either a stunningly real simulation of the start of World War III or the actual thing. In the climax he and the computer stop short of a cataclysm. To make the computer center seem authentic, we spent $2 million on what was, at the time, the most expensive set ever constructed. The direction, which was taken over by John Badham, was pretty much flawless, and we got very good reviews. *WarGames* grossed $80 million—our profit was $5 million—and Sherwood was suddenly a very successful little production company. It wouldn't be little for long.

David Begelman was a player from the old days of Hollywood, the times when a few major figures could simply order that a move be made, and it was done. The studio-boss system was all but over, having been replaced by committees who were guided by market surveys and audience samplings. But David continued to operate as if the old system was still intact. He relied on gut instinct, which he credited for previous successes including *Close Encounters of the Third Kind*. And he cultivated an arch, auteur image, cruising Beverly Hills in his Rolls-Royce, hosting lavish parties at his home, picking up every check whenever he dined with friends. Tall, tan, and balding, David played his part to the hilt. His speech was impeccable. His wardrobe was just an ascot shy of aristocratic. If you didn't know he was a movie executive, you'd imagine he was a diplomat, or maybe a peer of the realm.

Begelman, who began his career as an agent representing the likes of Judy Garland and Ronald Reagan, was such a polished, successful, and well-connected man that it was hard to imagine he actually committed the crime that had been the beginning of his end as a studio chief. It had happened before we met, when David was president of Columbia Pictures. He had been caught forging actor Cliff Robertson's signature on a check. It was, for him, a piddling amount—$10,000. The only way he could explain it was as some aberrant impulse. He was found guilty of a misdemeanor, but escaped serving jail time.

Columbia fired David when the charges proved true. Prosecutors filed charges, and after pleading guilty David went into psychotherapy. He would eventually blame the crime on his abuse of cocaine and other drugs, and produced an antidrug film as part of his community service. When he had paid his debt, David's lawyer, Frank Rothman, persuaded another of his clients, billionaire Kirk Kerkorian, to hire David to run MGM. When MGM merged with United Artists, Begelman took control of the whole operation. That is the way things are done in Hollywood. If you are good at making movies, and belong to the small club of elite insiders, even a felony does not disqualify you from the game.

But while a studio head can survive a criminal conviction, there's a limit to the amount of bad publicity he can endure. At the time we were working on *WarGames*, a book called *Indecent Exposure* revived the scandal. In what eventually became a bestseller, the author told the story of David's crime in painful detail, and dredged up other nasty items, including the fact that David had lied about earning a diploma at Yale. In fact, he had never graduated from any college, let alone an Ivy League school. The higher-ups at MGM/UA, which was a public, stockholder-owned company, decided that the public relations damage was more than they were willing to accept. Begelman was fired, again.

By a freak coincidence, Alan Salke had been standing in David's office when he got the fateful phone call. He had stood to talk, turning his back on Alan. After listening for a moment, his knees buckled a bit, and he shuddered. He quietly put the phone down and turned, ashen-faced, toward Alan. Tears rolled down his cheek. It was the only time Alan ever saw David demonstrate anything but confidence and poise. He looked like he had been given a death sentence.

"The truth is, I still don't know why I did it," Begelman told Alan that day.

As much as David had been hurt by his crime, the publicity, and his firing, his reputation inside The Business remained remarkably good. People remembered his past generosity, his wonderful parties, and his deal-making skills. Indeed, there are so few people on this entire planet who know how to make a commercially successful film that Begelman's stock, among insiders, was hardly damaged at all. The industry's rich and powerful still loved him, and they all prayed he would be taken in somewhere. That was why, at the urging of Frank Rothman, I hired him to turn Sherwood Productions into a much bigger company.

By throwing him a lifeline, I got myself one of the most competent and best-connected men in Hollywood, and I made myself look like a champion of a wounded favorite son.

(Oddly enough, our other choice for David's job was Larry Gordon. Larry, who jokingly calls himself the "only Jew from Mississippi," started out as Aaron Spelling's driver. He was a major producer by the time we considered hiring him. In the years after my decision he made so many big hits I cannot recount them all, and became president of Twentieth Century Fox.)

David didn't act wounded at all when I sent Alan to negotiate his deal. They met at David's house, a sprawling ranch with a pool on Bedford Drive in Beverly Hills. After little more than a hello, David demanded a $300,000-a-year salary, a big expense account, a huge office, several first-class round-trip tickets to New York each year, and the right to bring along his highly paid yes-man, Michael Nathanson. It was brash talk for a disgraced executive who had just been fired and couldn't be certain he would ever work again. But believing he was worth it, we gave him just about everything he asked for.

Besides granting his compensation demands, I gave David a free hand to run Sherwood. It had always been my style to hire the best people, and then get out of their way. And besides, as my various business interests grew in so many different directions, it was impossible for me to manage them all day-to-day.

With his bank account and pride somewhat restored, David set about transforming Sherwood from a little, boutique-style movie company into a mini-studio. The first thing he did was move us out of our tiny offices and into a huge, lavishly remodeled space, including a private screening room. He eventually occupied the entire ground floor of the MGM producers building and filled it with people—producers, associate producers, script readers, support staff, even a full-time projectionist—all of whom received top-dollar salaries.

I didn't work at the Sherwood offices every day, but I would drive over there from Rodeo Drive a few times each week. When I did it was hard to ignore that David was quickly devouring the profits we had made on *WarGames*. Obviously we would have to double or triple our output of films just to cover the overhead. That could never be done with our old way of doing business: finding material and setting up funding and distribution for each film.

David's answer to the problem was found in his network of friends, which reached to every studio. For several weeks David held meetings with the most powerful executives in town. Just getting in to see those people requires tremendous pull. They will meet with you only if you are a very good friend, or capable of bringing them a whole lot of money. David, the ultimate schmoozer, fit both categories. While he failed to get up-front financing, he did manage to get a commitment from Fox to be our distributor.

The distribution deal meant that our movies would make it into theaters, and that we would get revenue from ticket sales. It was the same as, say, a new candy company getting a commitment from the Southland Corporation to put its chocolate bars on the counters at every 7-Eleven store in the land. The deal gave us enough credibility to convince the bankers at EAB to expand our line of credit to cover day-to-day operations. But before we could start buying stories and film scripts, we needed a little more of our own cash, so the bankers could see we were sharing the risk. For that, we went back to Bunker Hunt.

Since I had just barely avoided being found out in the audit of the Hunt collection, it might seem strange that I immediately went to Bunker for movie money. In fact, it would have been stranger if I hadn't turned to him. After all, Bunker had absolutely no idea that I had played fast and loose with his investment. He knew nothing of my palpitations and sweats, or of the large debt I was working off with the likes of Gordon McClendon and Bank Leu. He believed I was still riding high, getting richer every day as I conquered one business field and then the next. He would have been insulted if I had offered someone else the chance to invest in Sherwood's growth.

. . .

Armed with cash, we put out the word that we were ready to make a lot of deals. Aaron Spelling, probably the most commercially successful television producer of all time, brought us a script called *Mr. Mom*. Spelling's taste— *Charlie's Angels*, *Fantasy Island*, *Starsky and Hutch*—was not mine. But his work had mass appeal. So, even though the script for *Mr. Mom* seemed thin to me, I followed David's advice and we bought it. David then went to work. He hired a young Michael Keaton to play Mr. Mom, and Teri Garr to be his wife. Teri, whom David had hired for *Tootsie*, was in great demand and commanded the bigger salary—$350,000.

The production went very smoothly, but one key element caught me by surprise. The house. *Mr. Mom*'s house. Aaron and David had it specially built, from scratch, on the studio lot where we shot the film. It cost more than a half million dollars, at a time when we could have driven thirty minutes and bought a freestanding building for less. Of course, I didn't understand that a movie house had oversize rooms and removable walls to accommodate cameras, lights, and sound equipment.

Once I understood more of the process, I began to love hanging around the production. I brought friends and our EAB banker, David Berman, to the set. As often as possible I sat in on the "dailies" where the latest footage was viewed for the first time. To me it looked like a TV show, not a piece of cinematic art. But then, it was Aaron's plan that the movie be what's called a "back-door pilot" for a television series. It does happen, occasionally, that a network will create a series based on a movie. When that occurs, a film can grow from a one-time event into a long-running source of ever-increasing revenues.

With *Mr. Mom* in production, David and our growing staff went looking for more projects. Our next buy seemed like a sure thing. Of course, everyone who makes movies talks himself into thinking every project he starts is a sure thing. But this one really was. It was a remake of an old classic called *Blame It on Rio*. The script was written by Larry Gelbart, of *M*A*S*H* fame. The director was the veteran Stanley Donen, who had done *Singin' in the Rain*,

Damn Yankees, Kismet, and *Seven Brides for Seven Brothers.* The male lead would be played by Michael Caine. We planned to shoot it on location, in Brazil, where the exchange rate meant that exquisite scenery came cheap.

With a film like *Rio,* it's easy to talk yourself into feeling very confident. If I had known then what I know now, I would have been a little more cautious. First, though Michael Caine is a wonderful actor, he doesn't always choose a project based on its cinematic merit. As he later told an interviewer, Caine sometimes looks for an Academy Award type of role, but he is also quite fond of being paid piles of money to work in exotic locales. The role, in those cases, is secondary.

Not knowing any of this, I assumed that in accepting his role, Michael Caine was, in effect, confirming that *Rio* was a good idea. I felt the same kind of confidence in the director, Stanley Donen, even after he filled one of the four main roles in a way that should have set off some alarms. Stanley had seen a tiny photo of a girl name Michelle Johnson in the fashion magazine *W.* She was seventeen years old, two months out of high school, and still living in Phoenix with her parents when he arranged for a screen test. Soon afterward, she was signed to play the pivotal role in the film—the young daughter of a best friend, whom Caine's character seduces during a vacation in Brazil. The cast was rounded out by a lesser-known Demi Moore, Joseph Bologna, and Valerie Harper.

I was one of the few in our company who didn't enjoy a trip to Rio de Janeiro as part of our project. I trusted David, even as I heard rumblings about the quality of the work going on down there. Then the success that greeted the release of *Mr. Mom* distracted me from my worries. Although some critics thought, as I had, that the film was barely more than a TV show, audiences loved it. Michael Keaton, in what turned out to be his breakout role, breathed life into some stale bits of comedy—wrestling with a washing machine, being undone by a vacuum cleaner—that were older than Lucille Ball.

Beyond Keaton's charm, audiences found in *Mr. Mom* a story for the times. In the early 1980s much of America, especially the old industrial Mid-

west, was in the grips of a recession characterized by huge layoffs at big factories. Millions of real "Mr. Moms," or at least men who felt like they were
challenged like Keaton's character, were just waiting for that kind of movie.
Joined by their wives, who identified with Teri, they bought $65 million worth
of tickets to view it in theaters and eventually paid another $32 million to see
it on video.

Despite our good studio distribution deal, almost all of the profit from *Mr.
Mom* went to Fox. Still, we made a few million and felt like we were a bunch
of pretty smart fellows as we unleashed *Blame It on Rio* on an unsuspecting
public. Our own advertising should have told us something. The tag line
was, "She's the hottest thing on the beach. She's also his best friend's daughter!" Instead of something playful and coy, the advertising suggested it was a
movie based on a sleazy premise. Unfortunately, Stanley, Michael, and
Michelle managed to guarantee the audience got what it feared, one hundred
minutes of a bloated, middle-aged actor chasing a tan, teenage actress who
grabbed the audience only when she took off her top. (Her breasts would get
us an R-rating, and more trouble down the line.) *Rio* was bad. One critic
wrote, "To say this is an awful movie is like saying air is plentiful." Even the
score was ridiculed.

By the time we finished paying off Michael Caine, covering the cost of
shooting the movie in Brazil, and handing over the cash required by our distributor, *Blame It on Rio* cost us money. And Sherwood itself, despite having great
success with *WarGames* and *Mr. Mom*, was barely solvent. That was because
David was chewing through more than $300,000 a month for overhead.

The one person who tried to keep an eye on David was Alan Salke. It was
not easy. David treated Alan as if he was a competitor, not a colleague, and
he never missed the opportunity to assert that he was a legend in the business
and Alan was a neophyte. But no matter what David said, Alan was a sharp
businessman, and he challenged David's spending. Their tense relationship
exploded when he raised questions about the catering company hired to serve

the cast and crew of *Mr. Mom*. The company was owned by David's wife, Gladys. David saw nothing wrong with the arrangement, even if it paid Gladys more than other companies were paid for similar services. When he lost that battle, Alan left Sherwood.

Alan's departure, the rapid expansion, even the losses associated with *Blame It on Rio*, none of these things were enough to frighten our bankers. In fact, they kept upping our financing, making sure our line of credit grew to accommodate David's spending. Oddly enough, they never sent auditors to confirm my financial condition, even though my personal wealth was ultimately behind the whole operation. If they had checked, they would have discovered that the silver contracts and coins I had listed as collateral were long gone—disposed of to make the Bunker Hunt collection whole—and although my other assets could eventually pay the debt if Sherwood went out of business, they were not liquid.

To my amazement, my signature was enough to keep it all going, and so we plowed our energies, and my money, into the next big thing, a sci-fi adventure comedy called *The Adventures of Buckaroo Banzai Across the 8th Dimension*. The title character, played by Peter Weller, was, believe it or not, a rock star/brain surgeon/samurai who takes up the task of repelling invaders from Planet 10—each of whom is named John—before they take over Earth.

Buckaroo was simply strange. It had a semi-camp, semi-cheesy look and featured special effects and gizmos that resembled what you might see in old Japanese horror flicks. The supporting cast was actually quite impressive. John Lithgow played Dr. Lizardo, the leader of the bad guys. Ellen Barkin was Pretty Penny, the hero's girlfriend. Jeff Goldblum's character, New Jersey, was Buckaroo's pal, and Christopher Lloyd played a villain named John Bigbooty. Years later, Lithgow would insist that he had more fun making *Buckaroo* than he had doing any other acting job in his life. It shows on the screen. He gives a delightful performance, and so do the rest. But the plot and feeling of the film were so bizarre that the general public couldn't accept it. A strong, underground-type following developed, and those people still rent it today on video. But when the movie came out in 1984, it was not a big moneymaker.

In the film business, if big profits ever flow they are generally reserved for the giant studios that finance production and distribute the movies to theaters. Production firms like Sherwood, which typically invest just a few million dollars in each project, almost always settle for a modest profit after they recoup their up-front money. The main goal is to stay in the game, making movie after movie, until you can get better terms on your distribution contracts and then make a hit film.

From *Brimstone* to *Mr. Mom* to *Buckaroo Banzai*, we bumped along. Our debt load grew heavier as our credit line with EAB crept toward $20 million. And while I worried that the loans were based on assets that had melted away, I took comfort in the fact that the Hunts stood beside me. Then Michelle Johnson bared her breasts.

The one condition the Hunts had imposed on their investment was that Sherwood would not make R-rated movies. Michelle's topless scenes had pushed *Blame It on Rio* into the R-rated realm. When Bunker called to tell me he wanted out, that was the first reason he gave.

Bunker spoke in a tone of voice I'd never heard from him before. It was very serious. He said he didn't like the R-rating, and that he and Herbert and their accountant, a guy named Parker, were all coming to Los Angeles and they wanted to meet with me and Begelman. We met on a Saturday, at our offices on the MGM lot.

"Our contract called for no R-rated pictures, mah friend," said Bunker. "We want to be bought out."

That demand made me shudder, because I knew the Hunts represented the cash behind Sherwood's loans. I began thinking of ways to mollify the Hunts, and keep the alliance from breaking apart. David's attitude was more confrontational. He let Bunker have it.

"You can't do this," he said, his voice growing louder with each syllable. "You read the script. You preapproved it! According to the contract, that means you accepted it no matter what the rating was."

He was right, legally speaking. The contract allowed us to make R movies if the Hunts did not object in advance. But that didn't move Bunker and Herbert. They sat there, impassive, like Texas Buddhas. They had already made up their minds. They wanted to be paid half the value of Sherwood, and their posture made it clear they wouldn't leave without us agreeing.

I'm not sure, but I would guess that Bunker and Herbert understood that we would be reluctant to pay the cost associated with taking them to court over their demands. And that was the case. As I thought about their request, I realized that it wasn't about the bare breasts and R-rating. Though they seemed perfectly relaxed, I could see in their eyes that it was about the money. The silver collapse had left them cash poor, and they didn't want to liquidate any assets they might need in the future. Their Sherwood investment had been a frivolous extra, which they could no longer afford. The notion that we had violated the contract was a cover.

I didn't put up much of a fight. I still shared horses with Bunker. I considered both men friends, and I still felt guilty about the coin fiasco, even though they hadn't been harmed. Finally, I wanted to believe that this was a temporary setback. Billionaires might get squeezed, but they are too rich to be toppled. There would come a better day, and the Hunts would be valuable to me again.

"I'll have to figure this out," I told them as the meeting ended. David stayed firm, insisting we wouldn't agree to their demand. I said, "We'll get back to you."

In the days that followed, David fumed and complained. I went to EAB and notified them that the Hunts wanted out. We sat down and tried to figure out what the Hunts' share of Sherwood was worth. We came up with the figure of $4.5 million, which was a little more than the cash they had put in. I made a deal with European American Bank, through Dave Berman, that increased our line of credit enough to pay back the Hunts. I would then own 100 percent of Sherwood without tapping my own money. All EAB wanted was an updated financial statement, approved by outside auditors.

The audit posed a problem, because the coin inventory that had been the core of my personal financial statement had all but evaporated in the Hunt debacle. Of course we could have shown the EAB auditors *some* coins—*any* coins actually. But an easier solution to the problem—one dependent on the odd nature of our business—arose as soon as a new outside accountant, an assertive young woman named Su Waks, arrived in our office. Su noticed that whenever we bought a cache of coins for, say, $100,000, and broke them up to sell at a profit, we didn't pay taxes until that original $100,000 cost was covered. That was despite the fact that we made money on individual coins that had increased in value. This kind of accounting was standard in the coin business, but new to her. As far as she could tell, we might or might not have a tax problem of undetermined proportions. To her mind, that made an accurate audit impossible.

When Waks's superiors at Arthur Andersen heard what she had to say, they agreed. She was told to stop the audit immediately. EAB then decided, to my surprise, to simply forgo their audit and grant me the loan anyway. They accepted the greatly inflated net-worth figure claimed in my personal financial statements, and the movie company had its funding. When it was all over, Su asked for a job. She had previously audited MGM, she explained, and always wanted to work in movies. I hired her, and her assistant, Nora Rothrock, and paid them each double what they had been making at Arthur Andersen.

Su Waks eventually rose to be a top executive in my organization, and she brought Nora up with her. At about the same time I hired Steven Nessenblatt, an attorney, who joined Su at the top of my organization. As an associate at the firm of Gibson, Dunn, and Crutcher, Steve had done some work for Summa Stables. If he worked out, I'd get my legal work done in-house at half the price I was paying his old bosses. If he didn't, I would lose the relatively small amount invested in his salary.

Steve would soon prove himself to be very valuable in negotiations with banks and in structuring deals to my advantage. Not quite thirty years old, he was highly ambitious and yet still impressionable, and a bit insecure. Years later he would say he was vulnerable to the charms of money and power. At the time, I just knew I wanted his talents devoted to my businesses. One evening, as we sat in a restaurant on Rodeo Drive, I took a triangle-shaped ashtray in my hand and told him that the three corners represented my three businesses: coins, horses, and movies. No one person occupied the center, with a grasp of the three. I wanted him in that spot, I said. I then doubled his salary to $100,000, gave him a company Mercedes, and won his complete loyalty.

Having survived the crisis of the coin audit, and then the Hunts pulling out of Sherwood, the burden of EAB's $20 million loan didn't feel heavy. We were going to make more movies, and one of them was bound to produce a big payoff. In the meantime, though the days of stupendous growth were over, the coin and antiquities business continued to produce profits. So did the horse syndicates. If my bankers weren't worrying, why should I?

I was in that fairly calm state of mind when David called me at my Summa Gallery office on Rodeo Drive. "I'm here with Bert Fields," he said. "There's something urgent we want to discuss with you. Now." Bert was David's personal attorney. He was also perhaps the most powerful entertainment lawyer in the country. I grabbed Craig Tompkins, my corporate counsel, and we drove over to the MGM lot. We passed through the gate, parked, and went straight to David's office. He was there with Bert, and as soon as we were seated he got straight to the point.

"I've formed another company," he announced with the same matter-of-fact tone he might use to explain that he was redecorating the office. "I'm prepared to go fifty/fifty with you, if you bring your personal guarantee for the financing as you did with EAB. Otherwise I'll just be leaving Sherwood."

The company David had created would be called Gladden—after his wife, Gladys—Entertainment. To make sure we understood that he was serious, he went on to describe the sweetheart deals he had worked out to finance and distribute his movies. David had gone to his friend Marvin Davis, who owned Fox, and traded the rights to distribute his films in America for an agreement to supply 25 percent of the cost of making each one. He then went to a foreign distribution company called Thorne-EMI, which agreed to pay 55 percent of the costs in exchange for placing the movies in foreign markets. Finally he had put together a video deal with a company called Vestron, which put up another 25 percent. Do the math: He had actually acquired 105 percent financing for the costs of making each film. To cap it all off, the contracts called for ten projects, of David's choosing. His backers would have nothing to say about the scripts, the directors, the stars, or anything else. They would take what he gave them, and pay the bills.

As good as those deals were, and they were better than anything I had ever heard about, they only covered the cost of producing the films. David would still need cash and a line of credit to operate his company day-to-day. That was where I fit in. Given his felonious past, and his lack of personal wealth, no bank would allow David to sign for a big note. And he didn't have the personal reserves to cover the huge overhead that his operating style would require.

As David laid all of this out, anger began boiling inside of me. Here I had been summoned, like a servant, to an office that I owned, to be stabbed in the back by an employee, someone I had rescued from disgrace. I had financed his success with *WarGames* and *Mr. Mom*, only to see him go out and make a wonderful distribution deal, not for Sherwood, but for himself. While he should have been loyally securing the future of my company, he made his own deal while talking on the phones I paid for, and dining on an expense account that I covered. It was a gross betrayal, and I was livid.

Before I could say anything, Craig stood up and announced that we were taking a break to talk. He led me outside, where I vented my outrage. "I'm on the hook for $20 million because of this guy," I said. "I've got all these obligations—like the lease and all the employees—which he created. This is fucking extortion!'"

As I paced and ranted, I realized that I was more hurt than mad. I had considered David the older, wiser friend who would lead me safely through the movie business. I had always depended on such older men—Joe Malter, Leo Mildenberg, Bob Hecht, Sy Weintraub—who had become, in effect, father substitutes. Sure there had been disappointments. Sy Weintraub had proven himself to be hopelessly selfish, and the Hunt brothers seemed hellbent on squandering their fortunes. But none of them had committed such an outright betrayal.

My first impulse was to tell him to get out of Sherwood's offices, and never return. But as I thought about it, I felt a certain fear creep over me. Nothing I did on that day would erase the fact that I was still responsible for that $20 million in debt, which I had accrued with false documentation. And as immoral as he was, David was better at making pictures than anyone I knew. Add to that the extraordinary deals he had made with Fox, Thorne-EMI, and Vestron, and he represented the best option for me getting out from under that burden. By the time I went back into the room, I had accepted that reality.

David did his best to describe our new arrangement as an opportunity, rather than the palace coup it was—despite the fact that he was raising his own salary from $300,000 to $500,000. The new Gladden would assume all of Sherwood's old liabilities, and David would arrange fresh operating funds to come from the Dutch-based division of a French bank—Credit Lyonnais—that was beginning to build a big presence in Hollywood. Based on the distribution contracts David had arranged, they were willing to give Gladden $35 million. With the two banks, EAB and Credit Lyonnais, we might even create the kind of mini-studio that was David's ultimate ambition.

Years later, I would realize that in that confrontation with David Begelman, I had had more options than I recognized. I could have fought David, suing him for bad faith, and for making deals for himself instead of Sherwood. Or I could have called his bluff, refusing to sign for the loans. No bank in the world would have lent to him without a cosigner, and who else would have done it after I told them how Begelman had betrayed me? Finally, I could have just said no and gotten out of the movie business altogether. I might have had to sell a great many assets, but nearly all that I owed would have been paid off. There was a slim chance that EAB would discover the irregularities in my financial reports, but that would have been ignored as long as they were repaid.

The trouble with each of those options was that they all would have produced serious personal conflicts. No matter what, I would have had a major row with David Begelman, which was not something I relished. Then there were all the people dependent on me and my businesses, the dozens and dozens who collected paychecks and found purpose in their lives through their jobs. Not the least of these was my wife, Jane, who would have wanted an explanation for the change in lifestyle that we would have had to accept.

Beyond my loyalties to my family, friends, and employees, and beyond my dread fear of conflict, there was the awful, humiliating prospect of failure. I had become a public figure. The notion that I was someone special was confirmed over and over again in the press. As early as 1981, when *Money* magazine profiled me as one of "Seven Who Made It Big" with small ventures, I had been pumped up by the media. In 1984, the magazine *Spur*, a mainstay of horse racing, went so far as to call me a "genius" and a "modern-day Midas." Maybe it was a matter of carefully choosing my goals, or maybe it was pure luck, but in all my endeavors since those first deals at Coins of the World Etc. I had never suffered an outright failure. Setbacks had always been temporary; losses had always been eclipsed by gains. It might have been a matter of believing my own press, but I found it impossible not to think that with a little more time, and a little more creative energy, I could do it again.

6

EVENTUALLY, EVERY BUSINESS OF ANY SIZE comes to be as much about banking as it is about its true purpose, whether it's making movies or widgets. New film projects or widget factories must be financed through loans, and the care and feeding of the bankers who control those loans becomes a major preoccupation. In our case, they were extremely high-maintenance creatures.

Consider Franz Afman, who was Credit Lyonnais's representative in Hollywood. Franz was a stern-looking, middle-aged man with a completely bald head and a black suit/white shirt, undertaker style of dress. He peered at you through wire-rimmed glasses and spoke with an accent that made you think of Werner Klemperer in the old *Hogan's Heroes* TV series. Afman, whose recommendations meant everything to his bosses in Rotterdam, became a major figure in the movie industry in the early 1980s. Under his guidance, Credit Lyonnais grew into one of the top lenders for film projects. Eventually the bank ended up owning MGM.

We were just one of Franz's clients, and not the biggest at that, so we had to be creative to stay in his good graces. Toward that end, David Begelman arranged for Gladden to pay the rent—more than $10,000 a month—on a Malibu beach house that Franz and his family occupied every summer. Franz was also our frequent guest at the best restaurants in L.A., and on at least one occasion, when we heard his summer vacation fund was running low, we sent him an envelope stuffed with cash.

As time passed, we did similar favors for bankers in all of our various businesses. We paid off personal debts for one officer at Bank of America, and created a sweetheart horse deal for another at First Los Angeles Bank. In that second case, the banker's investment was shifted from losing horses to winners, to make sure he was always in the black. When Ray Dempsey, president of EAB, suggested that his wife could do graphic design work for my coin company, we hired her immediately and paid her far more than the going rate.

The favors we did our bankers often went beyond their personal gain. For example, when our horse bank in Kentucky—Citizens Fidelity—reached its lending limit with a book company owned by then Governor Wallace Wilkenson, I helped them get around the problem. I accepted an $8 million loan from the bank, and then made a personal loan for the same amount to the governor's company. When they repaid me, I sent the money back to Citizens Fidelity. I was happy, the governor was happy, the bank was happy, and the regulations were skirted.

I know those kinds of dealings might sound shocking. Some of them were illegal. But in the world I inhabited, such favors were as commonplace as *baksheesh* in Cairo. Gladden wasn't the only film company making payments to Franz Afman. And you'd be surprised by how many businesses have been built on loans that were approved after a banker's wife got a certain job or his girlfriend was sent on a vacation. Those not-so-little treats are supposed to buy a banker's support for loan applications. But as David knew and I would soon learn, there is a limit to the amount of loyalty you can buy.

By the middle of the 1980s, with our great distribution deals and financing from Credit Lyonnais and EAB, the situation at Gladden was rosy enough that I almost forgot the way David had forced me into our partnership. My respect for him returned, and we were both optimistic about the films we had in development.

They all had their problems. No movie is ever made without a crisis or two, and often I was called in to save the film. Not long after Gladden was formed, I took up a particularly memorable rescue mission when I flew to New York to meet the great agent Sam Cohn. We needed to discuss his client, filmmaker Marshall Brickman, who was directing a film called *The Manhattan Project*, a comic thriller about a kid's science experiment run amok. Brickman was demanding a level of independence akin to that enjoyed by his friend Woody Allen, another Cohn client. David Begelman refused to go along with it.

Sam's "office" was the Russian Tea Room, and we met there. He was a small, older man who exuded both intelligence and street smarts. We got along nicely. I recall telling him, "Marshall is very bright, but he wants the money and to be left alone like Woody Allen. The problem is, he's no Woody Allen." Sam said nothing more than, "It'll be all right." The next day, Marshall accepted that David would share decision-making. As the film was being shot and edited, Marshall periodically came to me to complain, but never made any more demands. The film came out, made a little more than it cost to produce, and we were done with each other.

The troubles with Brickman were nothing compared with what was coming. Our biggest project ever, to be shot on location in the spring and summer of 1986, would be *The Sicilian*, based on a book by Mario Puzo of *Godfather* fame. Given the huge success of *The Godfather*, Puzo's book gave us enough confidence to justify the $1 million we paid him for the movie rights. David then promptly threw a little risk into the project by hiring the industry's most controversial director, Michael Cimino.

Cimino was one part artistic genius and one part infantile egomaniac. Nine years earlier he had been virtually unknown when his Vietnam-era film, *The Deer Hunter*, attracted huge audiences and lavish praise from critics. By the time the film won five Oscars, including one for Cimino himself, he was perhaps the most sought-after director in Los Angeles. At that time, faint rumblings were heard about Cimino's character. He had lied about his age, claiming to be thirty-five when he was forty. He had inflated his academic credentials. And he had led people to believe he was a Vietnam vet, when he was not.

Of course, none of Cimino's transgressions were enough to frighten away the chieftains of Hollywood, who chased after him with bags of money in hopes that he could repeat *The Deer Hunter*'s success. He finally agreed to direct a movie called *Heaven's Gate* for United Artists. Set in turn-of-the-century Montana, *Heaven's Gate* was to be a sprawling masterpiece of Western vistas and shoot-'em-up action. It became a Hollywood synonym for catastrophe. Cimino spent five times the original $7.5 million budget to produce an incoherent, sleep-inducing mess that was almost six hours long. It is widely regarded as the movie that ruined United Artists.

A disaster like *Heaven's Gate* might be enough to put a tottering studio out of business, but wasn't enough to destroy a director who had previous success. It only served to make him a little easier to get. Cimino had followed *Heaven's Gate* with a successful film called *Year of the Dragon*. We considered ourselves fortunate to get him for *The Sicilian*. His eye for landscape and light seemed well-suited for the film's locale. And as an Italian-American, he might be expected to have a certain affinity for the material. Certainly he had the right kind of name.

I met Cimino months before our production began. Though a small man, Cimino was thickly built and his face, dominated by a strong nose, made him seem serious. I liked him, but I could see he could be difficult. We had dinner in Los Angeles, where he complained loudly about the script and David's interference with casting. He wanted to give the lead role to Christopher Lambert, who had just starred in a Tarzan film called *Greystoke*. David was concerned about a French actor starring in a movie about an Italian hero for an English-speaking audience. But as I listened to Cimino, it became clear to me that he would not budge. To get things rolling, we gave him what he wanted, with both the script and casting. But David and I were determined to keep close tabs on him, especially when production began in Sicily.

There are worse things than a spring business trip that begins in Rome, moves to Sicily, and ends on the French Riviera. In late April 1986, that was the route David and I would follow. We planned to visit Cimino in Italy and then attend the annual film festival in Cannes, where the international movie industry does most of the year's business in a few days' time. We would review the available scripts, talk up our own films with foreign distributors, and renew relationships. High on David's agenda was a meeting with Manahem Golan and Yoram Globus, two Israelis whose Cannon Group had bought Thorne-EMI, inheriting our favorable foreign-distribution deal.

In Sicily, we discovered that our movie was, as we expected, over budget and behind schedule, but the problems were nothing of the magnitude that had plagued *Heaven's Gate*. Most of the hang-ups had to do with personnel and equipment. The exception involved the low-level Mafia men who controlled certain locations and union workers. Michael wanted us to meet with them to see if we could overcome the impasse.

We traveled by car along winding country roads to reach a small village that looked as if it hadn't changed in five hundred years. There, in a restaurant off the main piazza, we sat down for dinner with a dozen or so old men in vintage suits. As the wine bottles were emptied and pasta was scraped off the plates, the main sticking point became clear to me. Though they were too shy to come right out and say it, these guys all wanted to appear in the film. They wanted parts. Once we all understood, the fix was easy. There were plenty of little roles for walk-ons and extras. And if a real role didn't exist, we could pretend to involve some of the guys and throw them a day's pay. By the end of the night the problem was solved and Cimino had access to both the countryside and the local labor pool.

From Sicily it was a short flight to Nice, where we rented a car and drove along the coast, to Cannes. We stayed a bit off the beaten track, at the Hotel du Cap, one of the most famous and exclusive oceanside resorts in the region. Built in 1870, the du Cap looks like a French nobleman's summer palace. Made famous by F. Scott Fitzgerald in *Tender Is the Night*, the hotel attracts the Hollywood A-list, and anyone else who might be comfortable paying exorbitant rates, in cash, months ahead of time. Even in the mid-1980s rooms at the height of the festival went for $2,000 per night. For that sum, guests got one of roughly one hundred rooms in a very luxurious and sedate setting—and the very best address.

When you come to the Cannes Festival, you learn that almost anything can happen. The year before, I had been taken on the gambling adventure of my life by Naji Nahas, Bunker Hunt's partner in silver. Naji was a handsome businessman with a bearing that screamed of wealth. He had been involved in *Blame It on Rio*, and when he saw us at the hotel, he greeted David and me like old, dear friends. He insisted we drive with him to Monaco, which was about an hour up the coast, for a visit to the casino.

The casino in Monaco is nothing like Vegas or Atlantic City. There is no neon in Monaco. There are no waitresses in short skirts. You can't get a $4.95 slab of prime rib or a 99¢ shrimp cocktail. It's all very elegant, very serious, and very high stakes. Naji went straight to a table where they were playing the card game *chemin de fer*. It's somewhat like baccarat, but even more dependent on luck. In fact, as far as I could tell, there was no real skill involved at all. The rules governing play are so rigid that you pretty much stand there, take the cards you are dealt, and accept the outcome. *Chemin de fer* means "railroad" in English, and the way the game runs, players often feel like they are, indeed, being railroaded. But because large numbers of players—a dozen or more—crowd around each table, the pots can be huge and a few winning hands can make up for a whole lot of losing ones.

When Naji asked us to go in with him, fifty-fifty, David made it clear he would put up no more than 10 percent of his stake. I agreed to take 40 percent. Naji signaled for what I thought was a half million francs—$80,000—in credit, and set about losing almost all of it. At midnight, when David left, Naji was still losing. I sat in a chair watching him and grew more and more tired. I tried to hide the fact that I was nervous. In that kind of crowd, a loss of $80,000 or $100,000 was nothing.

As much as Naji insisted his luck would change, it didn't. Over and over again the cards were dealt around the table and someone else won. Finally, as Naji ran out of energy, we stumbled over to the cashier's window. It was then that I discovered he had lost 7 million francs, or $1 million.

"Bruce, they need a check," said Naji. "Can you give them one? And don't worry, we'll come back tomorrow, and I'll make it good."

I wrote a personal check for $1 million, which the casino would hold for twenty-four hours. Naji promised to cover it the next day. We drove back to Cannes, and I staggered into my hotel room at about five A.M. Jane's reaction to my tale of the night's adventure was just as angry as you might expect.

The next day David wanted no part of a return to the casino. I went back to make sure Naji covered my check. But before we went to the cashier, Naji said, "Let's sit down, for just a minute, and see if my luck is a little better."

He began losing again, and before I could stop him he had almost doubled our debt. I began to tug at his elbow, but he would not stop playing. Finally, at three A.M., he started winning. Riding the rails of good luck, he quickly got to even for that night and slowly began erasing the debt from the day before. At five A.M., we had a profit. An hour later, we quit. The cashier tore up my check and handed us a bagful of francs worth about $200,000. Back at the hotel I spilled out my share on the bed, which cured Jane's bad mood faster than champagne.

When I returned to Cannes in 1986, Jane stayed home, and Naji was not registered at the Hotel du Cap. There would be no side trips to Monaco. Intent on doing our business, David and I motored into Cannes each morning and then pushed through the crowds to find the people we had made arrangements to meet. Most were ensconced in the grand old hotels that lined the sea.

Behind the hotels, gawkers and tourists jammed the windy little streets lined with restaurants and shops.

On our last day in Cannes, we drove to the Hotel Majestic, where David was to meet with Golan and Globus, our new foreign distributors. Hundred-foot posters of movie stars and banners for films were fluttering on the sides of the buildings along the shore. Paparazzi were everywhere. David, wanting to spare me the hassle of the crowds, left me in the car and dashed inside. He said he'd be back in five minutes.

I waited for ten, fifteen, and then twenty minutes. Then I began to worry. Finally I got out of the car and walked across the street and inside the hotel. Mobs of people filled the lobby. I looked around for David and finally spotted him coming down the big staircase. His face was as white as Italian marble, and he was shaking.

"What's the matter?" I asked.

"Let's go to the car," he muttered. "I'll tell you there."

He didn't say a word as we crossed the street, but once the car door was closed he exploded. "Those motherfuckers. Those bastards. Those fucking Israeli kikes."

Given that David was Jewish himself, I couldn't imagine what had happened to produce that kind of invective. I had to wait while he sputtered and swore until he calmed down enough to tell me. This is what he told me:

David had opened the door to Golan and Globus's room to find the Israelis as well as Franz Afman, our banker, and his boss, Georges Vigon, the head of Credit Lyonnais. There were no pleasantries exchanged, only an order, barked by the upstart Globus, that David—former president of MGM and Hollywood legend—sit down and listen.

"We've reviewed your deal with Thorne-EMI and it's too rich," he told David. "We're not going to honor the contract."

David looked at Vigon, and Vigon looked away. He then turned toward Afman, who just shrugged.

"What do you mean?" asked David. "When you bought the company you bought the assets and liabilities. This contract is legal, in place, and you have to abide by it."

They would hear nothing of it. "You have no deal," they told David.

David then turned to Vigon, reminded him that he was our banker, and that Gladden's viability depended on its distribution deal with Cannon. Vigon, who it turned out was Golan and Globus's banker, too, refused to get involved.

With no options, David huffed about a lawsuit for breach of contract. "This is a very serious matter," he said. As he closed the door behind him, he heard someone call after him in a casual voice, "Do what you have to do."

As I listened to David, I felt both furious and dumbfounded. Cannon's move was bad enough. Practically criminal. But how could our own bankers let it happen? We were their clients, and they were supporting a contract violation that could ruin us. I figured that Vigon would straighten it out. When we got back to the Hotel du Cap, David got Vigon on the phone. In a very cold voice, Vigon said we were now in breach of our agreement with Credit Lyonnais because we had no underlying distribution contracts. "We will not fund you," he said, "until you replace Thorne-EMI with a contract acceptable to us."

"What are you talking about?" I heard David shout. "They breached, not us! How can you support this?"

The truth, which we understood well, was that Credit Lyonnais had a far bigger investment at risk with Cannon than they had with us. And Cannon was having its own problems. They were burdened with nearly $1 billion in debt, and Thorne-EMI's books likely showed a loss on the Gladden projects that had been delivered under our deal. They probably figured that breaking the contract would save them tens of millions of dollars, and that we were so beholden to Credit Lyonnais that we would just take it.

David was not inclined to just take it. He phoned Bert Fields and heard exactly what he wanted to hear. "These guys are acting like thugs," said Bert, "and you've got the best possible grounds for a lender-liability lawsuit against

Credit Lyonnais." Bert suggested we sue everyone, immediately, and hunker down for a legal battle—a war really—that could last for years but that we would ultimately win.

He was right. If we chose to fight we would likely win. But I worried about what might come out in the process. Ever since the Hunt audit, my financial statements had been wrong. In fact, they overstated my personal assets by tens of millions of dollars. In practical terms, I understood that this would likely have no bearing in a claim against Cannon and Credit Lyonnais for what they had done to David and me in Cannes. But I still felt shame about cooking the books, and I feared that the truth would come out in a trial and ruin my reputation. On an emotional level, I didn't feel like I was in a position to point the finger at anyone else. I was a willing player in a game where everyone, including me, routinely broke the rules.

In the end, we filed a halfhearted legal claim against Cannon, which was later withdrawn. David put together a new foreign distribution deal with a company run by Dino DeLaurentiis, which qualified us for renewed funding from Credit Lyonnais. It wasn't the kind of favorable arrangement that we had with Thorne-EMI. In fact, it would drain millions of dollars from our projected earnings. But it was enough for us to keep *The Sicilian* in production, and to keep Gladden Entertainment running. "We should be in the movie business, not the lawsuit business," said David, whose enormous salary depended on us staying in the movie business.

Despite David's argument, Su Waks and Steve Nessenblatt were firmly against my decision to forgo a legal assault on the bank. They knew of the misrepresentations in my bank statements, but insisted that it was not likely that those facts would come out, and even if they did, they wouldn't matter in a suit that focused on the Cannon contract. They were almost as furious at me as they were at Franz Afman when I declined to pursue it. What they didn't fully grasp, but would soon understand, was the fact that as long as my misdeeds were hidden, and the execs at Credit Lyonnais understood their own wrongdoing, I had an important bit of leverage. I was also angry enough to use it. From that point on, I loaded as much debt as possible, from every business I operated, onto that French bank. And I didn't worry much about paying them back.

One person who understood fully the leverage we held against our bankers was Ray Dempsey, president of EAB. From the beginning of Gladden, EAB had played agent for Credit Lyonnais in the financing they provided together. When he heard about the bloodletting at the Hotel Majestic, Dempsey pledged to keep *The Sicilian* afloat. He also recognized the wrongdoing perpetrated by his lending partners, and feared that his bank could share liability. His response was almost immediate. He wanted out.

At the time, EAB's share of our line of credit was worth $20 million, and there was no way that either Gladden, as a company, or I personally could come up with that amount of cash to pay them off. But Dempsey was determined, and motivated. He was in line to receive a big bonus if the bank's books were in good shape. Getting rid of the Gladden loan would move him close to that goal. Over the course of a year, we talked about how it might be done. Finally, I went to New York to meet with another of EAB's top officers, Conrad Gunther. I settled into an apartment I kept at Trump Tower and then went to see him at Gladden's New York office, at Fifty-seventh Street and Fifth Avenue. Gunther took out a yellow legal pad and a red pen and sketched the deal.

With arrows and big circles, Gunther showed how I would create two offshore companies—one to be called Jura, the other to be called Congress. EAB would make two personal loans to me, one for $20 million and one for $5 million. The $20 million would be passed through Jura to Congress, which would be represented by a Swiss lawyer. Congress was then supposed to make a $20 million investment in Gladden. In turn, Gladden would send the $20 million back to EAB, paying off the New York bank's portion of the line of credit. The second loan, for $5 million, was intended to help me make interest payments on the first. Dempsey would later make clear to me that the ultimate repayment of the principal was not a real concern. I could pay it, or not. His goal was to make things look good and then retire with his bonus before the note came due. I took that all to mean that the $25 million did not constitute a real debt. Consequently, I never reported it as a liability on my financial statements when seeking loans from other banks.

If it all went as planned, Credit Lyonnais would be led to believe that Gladden had attracted a big equity investor. The $20 million made our company's books look much better, and would even justify new infusions of cash. I felt good about the deal for a number of reasons. First, it helped Dempsey, who was a friend. Second, it improved Gladden's financial picture. A third benefit came from a caveat we would craft for Congress. The $20 million investment would be contingent on Credit Lyonnais removing my personal guarantee from the credit line it maintained for Gladden.

When I returned to Los Angeles, the only person who opposed the circular transaction with EAB was Steve Nessenblatt. He went ballistic. "No way!" he said. "You can't trust Dempsey. He's putting together a fraud against Credit Lyonnais. Besides, how do you take a bad film loan and turn it into a good personal loan? You're going to wind up getting screwed."

I valued Steve's honesty, because it was expressed out of loyalty. Like so many of my key executives, I had given Steve a great deal of responsibility, and rewarded him with a very high salary, at a time in his life when his peers still struggled to make the slightest progress in their careers. We were bound together, and I knew he had my interest at heart. Even so, I argued with him. "Wouldn't it be wonderful," I said, "if we can use this to fix our problems? If Dempsey is good to his word, I'll no longer have any liability. These businesses will stand on their own."

Su Waks not only agreed with me, but was downright excited about the deal. "It would be great," she said, "if Credit Lyonnais ends up with all the film company loans, and the risk they involve, because after what they did to us in Cannes they deserve it." With Su on my side, it became clear to Steve that we were going to follow the plan hammered out with Gunther. Having made his objections forcefully, Steve acquiesced, and committed himself to making sure we got as much protection as possible as the transactions were crafted. That was Steve's way. He made his case as well as he could, but when a choice was made, he gave it his full support for the good of the team.

In the months that we labored over Gladden's finances, all of our other business activities kept going. Location work on *The Sicilian* was finished and Michael Cimino took his footage into the editing room. He told us almost nothing about his progress as the months passed. Finally he dumped a 150-minute movie on us, declaring it was done. We didn't think so.

Under our contract, Cimino had the right to make the final cuts on the film as long as it was no more than 120 minutes long. He insisted that no more cuts could be made, and pressed us to present it to Fox, our domestic distributor. Even before viewing it, Fox executives said the movie was so long that it limited the number of showings a theater could present each day. It had to be trimmed, or they wouldn't release it. That matter was not negotiable.

When we took Fox's ruling to Cimino, he exploded. "I've been cutting for six months. There's nothing more to take out!" he shouted. We shouted back that there had to be a way to tell the story in 120 minutes. Besides, his contract gave him final say on the movie only if it was 120 minutes or less.

"Fine!" he answered. "You want it shorter, you got it."

This time it took him just a few days to make a new version of the film. When it was delivered, David called me over to the office where we gave it to the projectionist and settled into the screening room to watch it. The shock was immediate. Cimino had cut out every action scene in the picture. In the script a big wedding scene in the mountains is followed by an attack on the wedding party. In what we saw the wedding was followed by a scene at a hospital, where all the people in nice clothes were being treated for their wounds. He had just cut out the battle.

David didn't wait for the end of the film. He got up and went to call Cimino. The conversation didn't go well. Cimino said that his contract had allowed him final cut in a 120-minute film, and that is what he gave us. If we wanted something different, we would have to accept a longer movie. David refused. Cimino stood firm. We went to arbitration.

Every day that passed without the film being complete cost us and our partners—Fox and Dino DeLaurentiis—money. The judge in the arbitration acknowledged that problem and gave us a speedy hearing. We were represented by Bert Fields, and Cimino's lawyers hit us hard with a precedent Bert had established in an earlier case. In that dispute, Bert had aided Warren Beatty against the producers of the movie *Reds*. He had won for Beatty a finding that a contract granting a director final cut was absolutely binding. Our side challenged the claim that Cimino's 120-minute version of the movie was a legitimate piece of work. It was an act of bad faith, no matter what the contract said.

The case attracted a great deal of attention in Hollywood, and as we approached the end of the hearing it seemed as if the judge could reasonably rule for either side. Then we called Dino DeLaurentiis to testify as an expert witness. Dino, a hugely successful producer, had overseen *Year of the Dragon*, Cimino's previous project. After we bought Puzo's book he had vouched for Cimino when we called for a recommendation. Ironically, DeLaurentiis had set the precedent for giving Cimino final cut in the contract for *Year of the Dragon*. Cimino had even shown us the DeLaurentiis contract during our negotiations for *The Sicilian*. But when he took the stand, the dapper, gray-haired little DeLaurentiis had a different tale to tell about the *Year of the Dragon*.

"Final cut? I no give-a him final cut," he declared.

"But we've seen the contract," said Bert.

"Have you seen the side letter?" asked Dino.

The side letter, which was subsequently unearthed, stated that notwithstanding the contract, Michael Cimino did not have the right to a final cut. Field argued that by withholding that side letter, Cimino had defrauded us. The judge agreed. We got back control of the movie, and David personally trimmed it to 115 minutes. Fox released it in the fall of 1987.

When I saw it, I was deeply disappointed. Given that *The Sicilian* was a descendant of Puzo's *The Godfather*, I had expected something with the same beauty, drama, and emotion. Cimino had shown with *The Deer Hunter* that he was capable of making such a movie. But he had failed. I could give you my own take on it, but I'll offer the critic Roger Ebert's words instead: "*The Sicilian* is a dark, gloomy, brooding, and completely confusing melodrama," he wrote. Ebert criticized the cast, the cinematography, the script, even the sound quality. He was right about all of it.

The film was released in fewer than four hundred theaters. It went up against *Fatal Attraction* and *Dirty Dancing* and got thoroughly trounced. Total American gross at the box office was $5.5 million, about a third of our production costs. *Fatal Attraction* did more business in a single weekend. When year-end figures were released, *The Sicilian*'s totals were beaten by such memorable movies as *Adventures in Babysitting* and *Harry and the Hendersons*.

Fortunately, Gladden's losses on *The Sicilian* were balanced by the surprising success of our other 1987 release, *Mannequin*. A comedy that depended on magic—Kim Cattrall plays a mannequin that comes to life—*Mannequin* was the opposite of *The Sicilian*, in every way. It was relatively easy to produce, and our domestic gross of $40 million was four times what it cost to make it. It wasn't a great piece of art, but enough people liked it. More important to us was the effect *Mannequin* had on Gladden's finances. It produced enough profit to cover what we had lost with Cimino, and kept the company going.

We had to keep going. Gladden, indeed, my entire business empire, was always in need of cash. The horse business was in decline as Japanese investors pulled out of the global market and prices tumbled. And Numismatic Fine Arts had yet to recover from the Hunt crisis. Though NFA reported inventory worth tens of millions of dollars, and banks had lent money based on those assets, in truth our holdings were a fraction of what we claimed and business was bad. Ancient coin prices were no longer climbing, and I hadn't found enough new wealthy clients to replace the Hunts.

It wasn't for lack of trying. Throughout the 1980s, I remained one of the most active coin dealers in the business. In 1986, I purchased my first airplane, a four-engine JetStar, which made moving around the world in pursuit of big sales much easier. (When time and other expenses were factored in, it was barely more expensive than flying commercially. The jet was also a key public relations item, burnishing my image as a rich and powerful operator.)

Like the jet, my horses also enhanced my public persona, and as luck would have it, they won at regular intervals. The peak came in October 1987 at a French racetrack called Longchamp, where the venerable Prix de l'Arc de Triomphe is run. I had flown to Rotterdam to see the Credit Lyonnais gang and took some of them on my plane to Paris, where they accompanied me to the race. My entry, a three-year-old colt named Trempolino, was one of Emmanuel de Seroux's great finds.

For years Emmanuel had scouted the world to find horses on the verge of greatness, horses that had run well, but had not yet reached full physical maturity. He rightly figured that those animals could grow even stronger and run even faster. Beyond a horse's conformation he also checked its bloodlines and temperament. That last element was a matter of intuition, or art, as much as science. Emmanuel, who had grown up around horses in Normandy, understood them better than anyone I ever met.

Trempolino had the look and feel of a horse about to break out. His owner, Paul de Moussac, had run out of operating cash and was considering getting out of racing altogether. We kept him racing for awhile when we bought half interest and began to train Trempolino for the Prix de l'Arc d'Triomphe.

The Arc is Europe's equivalent to the Kentucky Derby. The entire racing community focuses on this one race to determine the best horse of the year. In 1987, the favorite was Reference Point, a colt that was so dominant he frightened away many would-be challengers. A sinus infection had kept Reference

Point from competing for the Triple Crown in America. That made a victory in Paris essential to establishing him as a great horse.

Reference Point, who was a wire-to-wire, front-running horse, was a better-than-even bet to win. But two other horses were believed to have a chance. One contender was Triptych, a mare that was an extraordinarily fast-finishing racer. The other possible winner was Tony Bin, a four-year-old owned by an Italian stable. Tony Bin had racked up impressive victories, but it was not clear he could run with the likes of Reference Point.

For us, the race was a long shot for a victory, but a sure thing when it came to social opportunities, because each year at race time, Longchamp is crowded with the rich and famous and powerful. After a catered lunch in a private enclosed box I took my guests to the paddock where we all got our first look at the colt. He was a tall, strong chestnut with a white blaze on his forehead. Before returning to the stands to see the race I stopped and put $1,000 on him to win. Since the field was the toughest of the year in Europe, and Trempolino was relatively unknown, I got twenty-to-one odds.

As the race began the horses fell into the order predicted by the oddsmakers, with Trempolino lagging. However, Reference Point was unable to break away. With many other horses pressing her, she was forced to use up energy. About halfway into the race of roughly one and a half miles, Trempolino began to move. With his mane flying, he swung outside and began to pass the field. By the time the horses pounded down the last quarter mile of grass it was apparent to everyone that Trempolino was going to win. Tony Bin chased hard, but couldn't close the gap. Triptych finished a surprising third, and Reference Point fell to eighth. Trempolino broke the record for the race by 1.4 seconds.

Though I tried to act as if the finish was something I had expected, in truth I was shocked. My share of the winner's purse was $500,000. President François Mitterand presented the trophy, and my bankers were thrilled to be introduced to him just outside the winner's circle. Later, I would also introduce them to other owners who had entered the race, including a few Arab sheiks and the Aga Khan, the legendary billionaire leader of the world's Shia muslims.

Trempolino's value rose several times over the moment he crossed the finish line, but we resisted selling, and instead flew him to the United States for the Breeders' Cup. There the favorite was Allen Paulson's horse, Theatrical. Trempolino almost pulled off the upset, but finished second. Nevertheless we won $400,000, and that showing further enhanced his value. Emmanuel negotiated on the spot for his sale to Gainesway Farm in Kentucky as a stallion, for $8 million. In six weeks my $400,000 purchase of half a horse had netted me $700,000 in winnings, and $4 million for his sale. Oh yes, there was also the $19,000 profit I made betting $1,000 on him at the Arc de Triomphe.

The profit I made on Trempolino was widely reported in the racing press and bolstered my reputation. It gave us an infusion of cash, at just the right moment. But it didn't provide a long-term fix. And it did nothing to protect us from the kind of little surprises that can severely damage any business. For example, even as we were putting our horse operation on steady ground, Summa Gallery was struck by a development that severed our link to the Getty Museum, and all those sales we had made to donors seeking tax breaks.

The Getty connection was broken when Jiri Frel's superiors—alerted by the Internal Revenue Service—discovered that he had accepted gifts for the museum and then helped donors value them for tax purposes, at hugely inflated costs. I had made the original sales for many of those items, and helped obtain the valuations. But it had been Jiri who was the central figure in all the transactions, which totaled more than $12 million. All of this was revealed in the *London Times* by none other than Thomas Hoving, the same Thomas Hoving who, as curator of The Metropolitan Museum of Art in New York, had bought the infamous Euphronius krater. Once the publicity hit, Jiri quit the museum and fled the country, leaving his wife behind. I never saw him again.

I understood why Jiri ran. When you have worked hard and built something substantial, it hurts to see it fall apart. In my case, everywhere I looked, once-vibrant businesses were bleeding dollars and we were struggling just to meet our payroll and finance payments. Sure, I worried that some of our shady moves might be uncovered, but I was more concerned about making sure all the people who depended on me continued to have jobs and paychecks. And I was fiercely protective of my own image.

My pride extended to my friends, and even to my wife, Jane. I worked longer and harder, spent more time on the road and poured more energy into my businesses, but never told her or anyone else outside my businesses what was happening. I was especially secretive where Jane was concerned. She did see that I was distracted, but never knew why. Even on vacations, I would spend most of my time on the phone doing business. And I spent so little of my time at home that I really only knew my way around a few of the rooms— our bedroom, the kitchen, and a little office I kept there. If you had asked me to locate a hammer, or a lightbulb, I would have had no idea where to look. I was, no doubt, a mysterious figure to my daughter, Katie, and later to my son, P. J., who was born in 1985 on my birthday, April 17. I loved them very much, but was so preoccupied and frantic about business that I was an absentee parent. That is one of the great regrets of my life.

The people who were fully informed about my problems included David Begelman, Steve Nessenblatt, and Su Waks, all of whom were depending on me for their own wealth and success. We spent hours talking about new sources of cash, whether they lay in our existing businesses or in new projects. As sympathetic as he may have been, David offered little in terms of a solution. He was always optimistic about his movies—work was beginning on *The Fabulous Baker Boys* with Michelle Pfeiffer—but he never volunteered to cut expenses or his salary. In fact, he kept drawing more and more out of Gladden, until his annual pay reached $1 million.

All of us, Steve, Susan, David, and I, could justify the financial deceptions because we firmly believed that we would eventually find legitimate ways to earn enough money to make everything all right. One blockbuster movie, or one shrewd new business deal, would set everything right. I was constantly on the lookout for the right opportunity, always trying to find a way to turn a small investment into a big enterprise. Wherever I went, out to dinner, on business trips, even vacationing with family, my mind would grind on the problem. On one family ski trip I spent so much time on a pay phone outside a supermarket that I nearly got frostbite.

Although it might seem from the outside that I was unrealistic, even grandiose in my ambition, given the businesses I knew and the context of the times, my dreams were not so outlandish. A single hit movie could generate $100 million in profits and get me back on the straight and narrow. At the same time, businessmen and investors in many fields were making huge profits, not through innovation and invention, but through creative financing. This was the mid-1980s, when Ivan Boesky was publicly extolling the virtue of greed, and leveraged buyouts were making speculators ridiculously wealthy. It was not unreasonable at all for me to hope that I could do it, too. That is why I obsessed over finding the deals, and saving my empire. I believed it would happen.

One of the few places where I could relax, and lay all my worries aside, was The Los Angeles Forum, where I would lose myself in rooting for the Kings hockey team. After years of buying tickets from the same scalper on the corner of Manchester and Prairie, I had bought season tickets—section 10 row J, near center ice—and had become ever more devoted to the team.

To most people in Los Angeles the Kings were an afterthought, a team you might consider watching when the Lakers were on the road and the Dodgers were dormant for the winter. A small corps of fans, many of them transplanted Canadians, came to every game, but they could barely fill half the seats. Sellouts were as rare as hockey rinks in Hawaii.

Around the National Hockey League the Kings were regarded as a competent, if not fearsome organization. The team always had some good players.

Marcel Dionne was a genuine star in the 1970s and '80s. So was Dave Taylor. But overall the Kings were inconsistent, and their record in the playoffs, which is what really counts, was truly terrible. Between 1968 and 1985, they won just four out of sixteen playoff series. And they never once made it to hockey's version of the Super Bowl, the Stanley Cup Championship.

I wanted to see the Kings win the Stanley Cup, but I loved the team, and the game, despite the fact they never did. Ice hockey is a blend of speed, balletic grace, and raw muscle that is unique in sports. I never got tired of watching the players perform, and when I lost myself in the game, I was relieved of all the anxieties that dogged me from day to day. It was a kind of therapy, which I needed more and more.

The Kings were owned by Jerry Buss, an engineer and real-estate magnate who had received the hockey team as part of a $67.5 million deal in which he purchased the Great Western Forum arena, and the L.A. Lakers basketball team from Jack Kent Cooke in 1979. Led by Kareem Abdul-Jabbar, the basketball team was the hottest sports franchise in town, and Jerry added to its value by drafting and then signing Earvin "Magic" Johnson. In his very first season, Magic helped bring the team to a championship.

Hollywood flocked to The Forum, and the Lakers games became hugely popular social events. Though Jack Nicholson would become the team's most avid movie-star fan, on any given night a ticketholder might also bump into Dustin Hoffman, Madonna, Tom Cruise, or Michael Douglas. If the celebrities weren't enough of a distraction during timeouts, there were the Laker Girls, the hardwood-floor version of *Baywatch* babes. Taken together, the marquee players, the championships, and the glamour made the Lakers one of the greatest sports draws in the world. The press, and pretty much everyone else, began calling the games "Showtime." And Jerry Buss, the architect of that success, became the happy host of the longest-running party Los Angeles had ever seen.

Buss and I actually met first, before his Laker days, at a coin auction. He was a collector with a good eye for value. Later he had noticed me at the

Kings games, and from time to time invited me to sit with him in the owner's box, which was located behind one of the nets, very high up. Jerry was usually accompanied by one of the many young women he met at L.A. nightclubs, and he ordered that the TV cameras be trained elsewhere because his long-time girlfriend, mother of his children, might be watching. Besides serving as a hiding place, the box gave Jerry a view of the entire Forum. That was because it was located high in the cheapest seats. Aside from a glass partition, nothing distinguished the box. It had the same small chairs and the same narrow aisles, as the surrounding sections. When I asked him why he didn't take a better spot in the arena, Jerry made it clear that he needed the income from the paying customers who occupied the best seats.

The truth was, Jerry often seemed to need cash. Even though he was winning NBA championships, and paying millions upon millions to athletes like Magic Johnson, he frequently asked me for loans for what should have been small amounts—$25,000 to $50,000—to someone of his apparent wealth. The key word was apparent. Like a great many seemingly rich men and women, Jerry carried an enormous amount of debt, and he often had to borrow here to pay a loan there. I never asked him why he needed the cash. Los Angeles real estate was in a slump, so that could have had something to do with it. And then there was his habit of playing in extremely high stakes card games. In the end, it didn't matter why Jerry needed the money. I had it to lend, and a relationship built on friendly loans to someone like Jerry Buss could only be a good thing.

Over time Jerry's debt to me grew to $1 million. In that same time, his businesses did not improve. Pressed by his creditors, he came to me with an offer that would change my life—a quarter interest in the Kings for $4 million. I wouldn't have to pay the $4 million up front. Instead, I would forgive the $1 million that Jerry owed me, turn that into a downpayment, and finance the rest. I wouldn't be a silent partner. Jerry wanted me involved in managing the team. And he would also give me an option to buy a bigger share of the team, up to 49 percent, in the future.

"I know you love the Kings," said Jerry, "so I want you be to involved with the team, with the operations."

Jerry was right. I loved the Kings, and I wanted what he was offering. The team had a handful of solid veterans, and a very promising crop of rookies. Luc Robitaille, Jimmy Carson, and Steve Duchesne could be the nucleus of a powerful team.

These quality players made me think the Kings were an exciting deal. But as usual, when it came to something new, Steve Nessenblatt and Su Waks were skeptical. They thought $4 million was too much, especially given the pressures bearing down on Gladden and the sour market for NFA's coins. But I kept emphasizing the fact that the downpayment was already paid, in the form of the loans to Buss, and that the note for the remaining $3 million would be covered by my share of the Kings profits. Who knows, I argued, maybe I can improve the team's operations enough to actually generate some solid profits that would ease the pressure on all our other businesses.

Our debate over the wisdom of the deal continued as one of Jerry's key aides, Kenny Doi, put together a report on the Kings' financial condition. Like many of Jerry's executives, Ken's main qualification for his position was that he was an old and trusted friend. He was actually a pharmacist by training, and though he was a very nice guy, he was completely out of his depth. He reported the team was solvent, and that its market value was roughly $16 million. I considered his report to be less than authoritative.

Although Ken's numbers were squishy, and the doubts raised by Steve and Su were realistic, nothing could diminish the excitement I felt about owning a big chunk of a National Hockey League team. Pro teams are businesses, but they are also great big glamorous toys for their owners. They allow grown men to express little boy fantasies, to channel their competitive instincts and aggression. Pro sports also offer owners who were never on teams in high school and college a shot at the action at the very highest level. It's the ultimate redemption for the kid who was always on the bench, or worse, in the stands. For those reasons I would have taken Jerry's offer under almost any circumstance, and when they came to understand that, Steve and Su gave me their support.

Just before the start of the 1986–87 season, Su and Steve went with me to the closing of the purchase, which was done in a conference room at Security Pacific Bank. Jerry's lawyer Jim Perzik was there, and so were a bunch of bank officials, who didn't even bother introducing themselves. Finally Jerry arrived, dressed in his usual jeans and casual shirt and carrying a hockey stick signed by Marcel Dionne, which he gave to me as a gift. He greeted my group and Jim, but didn't even look at the bankers.

Very little was said as we signed all the papers. With the last signature, I held out the check for the $3 million. Jerry took it, but held it for just a split second before one of the bankers rudely snatched it out of his hand. Jerry looked at them—his face the picture of disgust—rose, and then quickly left. Not knowing Jerry's true financial condition, I was taken aback by what happened. Obviously Jerry was so shaky financially that the bank insisted on receiving the check immediately. It might have even been the difference between solvency and bankruptcy. But given the condition of my own accounts, and the fact that my seemingly solid empire was held together by little more than the force of my personality, I could hardly pass judgment on him. We were, in many ways, the same: men whose public images of wealth and power exceeded private reality.

The Jerry Buss I knew in the 1980s was a complex, even paradoxical man. He was extremely bright and very well-read. Where the Lakers were concerned, he was keenly competitive. He wanted to win, and was willing to pay players the salaries they demanded if he thought they could produce championships. But while he applied that strategy with the basketball team, to great success, he never quite did it with the Kings. Maybe he didn't understand hockey, or maybe there weren't enough hours in the day for him to build two successful franchises. Whatever the reason, under Jerry the Kings were as disappointing as the Lakers were exciting.

Once I got inside the Buss operation, I could see more clearly why his success had been limited. It was obvious, even in the way the offices for The Forum, the Lakers, and the Kings were organized. They were not really organized at all. Most of the people who worked for Jerry had overlapping duties, and they were thrown together in a chaotic warren of indistinguishable offices that lined a hallway in the basement of the arena. There was not a Kings operation or a Lakers management team—but rather, an amalgam of people who simply did what Jerry wanted done. Many of his key officers were reliable old friends, but not sports-management pros. They had been unable to make the Kings a successful, stand-alone business with its own identity.

Fortunately, I could also see that the Kings had a potential value far exceeding the $16 million estimate that had been the basis for my buy-in. Southern California was an enormous, wealthy sports market, and as the only NHL team on the entire West Coast, the Kings had no competition for fan attention. But if the team were ever to capitalize on its opportunities, it had to do two things. It had to develop a style that was flashy enough, and entertaining enough, to compete for public attention in a place where people have a wide choice of entertainment and spectacle every night of the week. Second, they had to win. If the Kings did both of those things, they would have a great story—full of characters, drama, and victory—to sell to a public always ready for a good tale.

Of course, turning a team around is difficult. Consider the Chicago Cubs. A century of trying hasn't worked there. But the challenge didn't faze me. If I have any talents at all, they lie in promoting and building value in properties that others overlook. I saw the Kings as a wonderful opportunity and as a departure from the stress and strain of my other businesses. I loved the game, and the team. I had not felt so much pure excitement since I had smuggled old coins out of North Africa in the early 1970s. In the back of my mind there grew a dream to make the Kings entirely mine.

7

THOUGH I HELD JUST ONE QUARTER of the Los Angeles Kings' stock, Jerry Buss wanted me to be the active owner, the one who was the public face of the team and its long-term strategist. I hoped that over time we might draft and trade for some great players who could lead us to the Stanley Cup. But in the short run I would use my skills as a promoter—a storyteller—to generate enough excitement about the Kings that people might actually come to The Forum and watch them play. It was a delight, really, to focus on building up the team, creating excitement about something I loved, as I had with ancient coins.

In that first season, the story was about a quirky, thirty-six-year-old entrepreneur who made his first millions in the obscure world of ancient coins and had a dream come true when he grabbed a chunk of the Kings. I was the fan-turned-owner—plainspoken, passionate, and determined—who gave his faith to a team that, based on its record, might not have deserved it.

I sold my story by being accessible to reporters, and answering their questions honestly and candidly. That was then, and remains today, a rare attitude among sports team owners. In every league, and in almost every American city, teams antagonize and alienate the press as a matter of routine. Thin-skinned owners bear grudges about the mildest criticisms. Prima donna players boycott interviewers. Most of those who deign to speak to reporters offer nothing but cliches. "We'll play 'em one at a time." "I gave it 110 percent." The result is boring coverage at best, or hostile reporting, which hurts attendance.

Instead of following that tradition of antagonism, I worked hard to give the press what they wanted. When the Kings lost I would say, "We sucked." Once, when a losing streak grew too long and a reporter asked if I might trade some players, I shocked him with my answer. "Hell no," I said, "I'm not letting them off that easy. If I have to sit and suffer through this, they are going to sit and suffer through it, too." Quotes like these made headlines, and the headlines brought people to The Forum. People began to recognize me at the games. Some even cheered when I walked by. I loved it, and I often fantasized about what life would be like if the Kings were my only responsibility; if there were no Gladden, no NFA, no EAB, no Credit Lyonnais.

Away from the Kings, one of the big unresolved issues that dogged me was the $25 million deal with Ray Dempsey, which was designed to get EAB out of Gladden and secure his big bonus. Soon after the plan was crafted, EAB had notified Credit Lyonnais that it was eager to get out of movie funding altogether. The Europeans had been looking in vain for other partners to replace EAB, so when the so-called outsider investors appeared, they seemed to be the perfect answer to a sticky problem.

The negotiations were tough because Steve Nessenblatt, once he got on board, was an energetic and aggressive advocate for the deal. Keeping in mind, of course, that I was actually the "outside investor" called Congress, Steve made demands that would benefit us immensely. Under his terms, Congress would be paid 9 percent interest on its investment and, should Gladden's films make a profit, would draw a 40 percent share. Both of those conditions were accepted by Credit Lyonnais.

The final talks on the deal took place at the bank's offices in Rotterdam, where Steve, David Begelman, and I met with Afman and his bosses. There, Steve got Credit Lyonnais to accept that I would no longer be personally responsible for Gladden's debts. This was supposedly because the investors were friends, and they were going to depend on me to make them whole in the event of disaster. I couldn't do that if the banks were first in line. Finally, he said the deal would require that Credit Lyonnais increase its lending to Gladden, so the company could continue to operate.

If Afman and his superiors had been genuinely concerned about protecting their bank, our demands would have been refused. Why would Congress get first shot at profits plus a juicy 9 percent dividend? Even more alarming was the requirement that my personal guarantee be removed from the Credit Lyonnais debt. Under normal circumstances, no serious lender would have agreed to let me off the hook, but they did. In fact, they showed hardly any concern at all. That may have been because the Cannes debacle still hung over their heads, and they were afraid of what we might do. Or it may have been because they were too heavily invested in Gladden to let it fail. This often happens when a bank's commitment to a large borrower gets out of hand. The threat of a bankruptcy, and a default on the loan, is so enormous that the bank keeps pouring in money and hoping for a turnaround. It happened with Donald Trump in the late 1980s and early 1990s, as his net worth fell by billions of dollars. He was so big his bankers couldn't let him fail, so they kept restructuring his debts until his businesses recovered. All along, The Donald continued to live the life of a billionaire.

Just days after our talks were finished in Rotterdam, the money that was the focus of the whole scheme began to move from account to account like the little metal ball in a Rube Goldberg contraption. The journey of the cash began with a $25 million check, a personal loan, EAB wired to one of my personal accounts. Leaving $5 million to cover interest payments, I then sent $20 million to an offshore, dummy company called Jura. From Jura the $20 million went to Congress, which was overseen by my Swiss lawyer. As each of those steps were taken, officials at EAB nervously monitored the money's movement, pleading for instant notification as deposits and withdrawals were made.

On the very day that Congress received the $20 million in Zurich, it was wired to Credit Lyonnais in Rotterdam. There, it was posted to an account for EAB. In a little more than a day, EAB's Dempsey had gotten out of the movie business and erased a risky $20 million loan. But the dealing wasn't finished. On that same day, Credit Lyonnais dumped another $10 million into Gladden's line of credit. That was the cash we needed to keep on making movies. I took real pleasure in knowing that Credit Lyonnais was even further committed to Gladden. The old adage—keep your friends close and your enemies closer—is hard to refute. The more tightly Credit Lyonnais was bound to me and Gladden, the more secure I felt.

There was just one problem. All of the loans and transfers had been done on the basis of less-than-formal agreements with Credit Lyonnais. It was understood by all parties that more detailed and binding documents would be hammered out and signed to cover the deal retroactively. That was an unusual, but not unheard-of, approach. We all believed the lawyers would wrap up all the details without any problems.

I may have been too busy to keep track of it, or maybe I just didn't want to know if there were any problems, but month after month passed without those final documents being completed. Eventually I pressed my staff to find out what was wrong. They identified the bottleneck as a young lawyer named Phil Grosz, an associate at the Los Angeles firm of Loeb and Loeb, who was representing Credit Lyonnais. Grosz was a nerdy guy—black hair plastered down, thick ugly glasses—but the perfect man for the task of plumbing arcane documents to discover their key points. Unlike Franz Afman and company, Grosz had zeroed in on the clause that got me out of my personal guarantee on the line of credit.

"We really don't know who is behind Congress, but we know that Mr. McNall gets tremendous benefit from this," he told my lawyers. "Therefore, if it is one day determined that it's him, that Bruce McNall is the investor, then the guarantee should come back into place."

Grosz had us in a bind. If we fought him too vigorously, it would signal that perhaps I was the secret investor behind Congress. But if I signed off on his language, it placed me at risk, should the truth come out. For a while I fumed about what I should do. I expressed some of my anger at Steve who, I thought, hadn't used all his charms to push the deal through. He had handed the job off to a less experienced attorney, Martha Ayers, and she hadn't protected us. But the truth was, Grosz was the type who couldn't be schmoozed.

Many months went by as first Ayers and then Steve himself delayed Grosz. Finally, after a year, Credit Lyonnais instructed Grosz to give us twenty-four hours to sign, with the caveat he constructed, or they would move to get all their money—by then $70 million—back. This was all presented to me suddenly one morning by Steve and David Begelman, who came into my office white-faced and sputtering.

"Wait a minute," I said. "You were there, Steve, and so were you, David. They agreed that I would be taken off the loan, period. That was the deal." We got Franz Afman on the phone and he confirmed it. "You are right, yes," he said in his clipped, accented voice. But then he added that the lawyer, Grosz, had made the people back in Rotterdam wonder if, indeed, I wasn't behind Congress. No matter what we had said, and shaken hands on, the terms had changed. We had no choice. We signed.

Throughout that period, I could see that both Steve and David were being affected by the stress. Steve seemed to require more and more cash. I had no idea where it was going. David was irritable and lived for his weekends, which began with the ritual of a high-stakes poker game, held every Friday in a private room at a trendy restaurant in Beverly Hills called Mr. Chow. The games were attended by old-school movie people, including Walter Matthau. I suspected that, while the games provided an escape for David, they weren't helping his financial situation because he, too, seemed to draw more cash out of our businesses with every passing month. I could hardly blame them. We were all under tremendous pressure, and I, too, found relief in a lifestyle others would find excessive.

If I worried at all about the $70 million burden that had been shifted back onto my shoulders, it wasn't for long. My anxiety was eased by the leverage—a possible lawsuit—I would always hold against Credit Lyonnais. Besides, we truly believed we were going to make a movie or two that would literally gush cash. David was developing an oddball script, tentatively called *Hot and Cold*, that had the potential to be a smash with the twenty-and-under audience that dominates among ticket buyers.

Along with the possibility that Gladden would produce a blockbuster were the myriad business deals that came to me simply because I was famous and, as far as anyone knew, extremely rich. Almost daily I fended off schemers and dreamers who came to me with ideas for inventions, restaurants, marketing companies—you name it. One fellow wanted me to invest in bottles of wine. Another asked for money to expand a nude bar. All of those ideas were rejected. But I also received many serious proposals. For a while I pitched ancient coins on a TV shopping channel. The results weren't worth the effort. After that I teamed with American Express to market ancient coins via advertising added to their billing statements. We sold thousands of coins, but they were mainly the inexpensive, common types that yield very little profit.

Experiences with the likes of American Express brought me into contact with a level of American capitalism that few people see. For example, lunch with top executives at their headquarters always involved, not a trip to a fine restaurant, but a short walk to a lavishly appointed private dining room where white-gloved waiters served us dishes that would earn a five-star Michelin rating.

The leaders of American Express weren't the only Wall Streeters who believed I could make money for them in a new-fashioned way. In 1986, Steven Brooks of the brokerage house Merrill Lynch approached me about creating large horse syndicates for their high-level clients. Brooks, a tall, blond, straight-backed captain of Wall Street, had heard of the success I had syndicating the Hunts' horses, and believed I could repeat it. As attractive as it all seemed, I had to tell him that the horse business was in a down cycle and it was not the time to start something new. That honest assessment made him even more interested in somehow doing business with me. He came back with the notion of an investment fund that would deal in ancient coins.

The idea involved creating a large fund of capital—$7.25 million to start— that I would use to buy ancient coins. Since we were in the middle of a bull market for coins, in which prices had more than doubled in three years, the Merrill Lynch people saw great potential for profit if we held our collection for a few years and then sold. I had seen the same price rises, which were stimulated in part by the aggressive buying of my own clients, including the Hunts. Though I had some doubt about whether the run-up could continue, I thought we could make money with the fund. I certainly would profit from the $500,000 salary I would earn, and commissions that would likely exceed $1 million.

The materials we prepared for potential investors—including a prospectus and a fancy brochure introducing readers to the world of ancient coins—came in a fabric-covered box bound by expensive black ribbon. Inside were beautiful illustrations and a sales pitch that urged readers to invest in history and, at the same time, get into an investment that regularly returned 20 to 25 percent gains. The small print indicated that such gains were not guaranteed, and since we were creating a limited partnership, not a stock or bond fund, our fees could top 15 percent. But, of course, that wasn't emphasized as I flew around the country to Merrill Lynch offices and met with their biggest clients. In a few short months we had enough commitments, at $50,000 minimum, to start operating. We hired a staff that included two people who came from EAB, and a numismatist who had been the head of ancient coins at an old London firm called Baldwin and Sons.

The goal of the partnerships—named Athena I and Athena II—was clear. Buy low and sell high, as high as 50 percent over our purchase prices. From the very start I used NFA to create favorable conditions. I gave the funds favorable terms as they bought coins from NFA and its clients. When it came time to sell, I tried to get high prices from my NFA clients, allowing the Athena investors to get their gains.

But there was risk in the coin market. Much of the recent increase in ancient-coin prices had actually been caused by my activities on behalf of the Hunts. With the Merrill Lynch group I hoped I would spur another run-up, which would benefit us all. But I couldn't be sure that when it came time to sell, and reap profits, anyone would pay our prices. Fortunately that problem was years in the future, and I had to hope that with our buying we would rev up worldwide interest in those investments. Certainly there was hope throughout the business that my big new fund would raise prices for everyone. Just a handful of insiders expressed any doubts. Silvia Hurter at Bank Leu was one. Silvia and I always had a testy relationship, and I recall her lecturing me on her belief that collectors were far better clients than investors. "In principle, I agree," I recall telling her. "But where the hell are all the collectors? They aren't exactly lining up to buy, are they?"

New businesses like the Athena funds held hope for the future. They also satisfied my need for excitement and speed. Someone else might enjoy slowly building wealth in traditional business. I got bored too easily. And even though I was carrying big financial burdens and responsibilities, I wanted to have fun. Give me the excitement of a horse race, a coin auction, a hockey game.

Hockey held my interest so completely that I never doubted I would exercise the option that Jerry Buss had given me to purchase more of the Kings. I was a little less certain when, in early 1988, he offered me the whole operation—the NHL franchise, a minor league team in New Haven, and a cluster of related assets—for the $16 million value we had established two years before.

As we discussed the sale, Buss made sure I understood that I was buying something more than a business. "Bruce, after you do this, your life will never be the same," he said. "When I go to a club at night, I see guys that can buy and sell me ten times. They own a tool and die factory in El Segundo or something. They have all the money in the world, but they have to wait in line. They can't get a reservation. When I walk up, the doors open. When you are in pro sports, there are never any closed doors. All the doors are open."

I liked what I heard, and Jerry made it easy for me to say yes to the purchase when he structured the sale to require very little up-front cash. Most of the price would be paid by the revenues generated through TV broadcasts of the Kings games. Jerry would also retain certain funds he had taken in on tickets.

The revenue from television and those seats were important to the Kings' bottom line. Giving them up put me at a disadvantage when it came to operating the club. In essence I would always be a year behind, paying expenses first and waiting for the cash to come later. Though that was a real burden, I believed the team had been neglected over the years, and that I could make a few changes that would produce offsetting income. The team's big problem, all along, was that it never became an L.A.-style enterprise. Los Angeles is not the kind of town where a workmanlike performance gets you very far. You've got to have glitz and glamour, superstars, and sell-out crowds. Most of all, you've got to win.

Those truths are illustrated perfectly in the state of professional basketball in the city. As owner of the Lakers, Jerry Buss paid whatever was required to get the superstars who would win games and fill seats. In contract negotiations with the players, he was generous to a fault. His attitude was, "I want to win." That was a matter of ego, as well as business. He understood that people in Los Angeles had more options for their entertainment dollars than people anywhere else on Earth. He made the Lakers champions and the toast of the city.

In contrast, consider Don Sterling, owner of the other National Basketball Association franchise in town, the Clippers. Once I sat courtside with him and watched a player miss a key free throw. "Look at this guy," said Don. "I pay him $4 million a year, and he can't make a free throw." Don was trying to run the team like a business. He didn't understand entertainment. He didn't understand that he would have been better off getting a player for $8 million who could make the free throws and win games. I could never persuade him to start making trades for expensive, big-name players. Don owns a lot of real estate, and he doesn't sell. He always says that some of his highest profits come from doing nothing. Just holding on had made him rich in real estate. But in sports it had made him a loser.

I was determined to be a winner, and the financial realities of my deal with Buss and my growing debt load required that I do it fast. The one sure way to do that would be to acquire the biggest name in the sport, perhaps the greatest player to ever skate, Wayne Gretzky.

Ironically, when I was minority owner, the one big trade I managed involved letting go of a superstar, Marcel Dionne, who we traded to the New York Rangers. He was the franchise player, the greatest the Kings had ever sent onto the ice. But Jerry Buss had given me a very interesting early lesson on the value of players. He said the players are assets, like chips in a poker game. Every year that goes by, a little of that stack of chips goes away. You have to replenish that stack with new talent. If you let it go low, you are out of the game. When the trade was decided, Marcel said he understood, he was a gentleman, and that took some pressure off of me. But I was never happy about letting such talent go. I was always far more interested in acquiring assets than letting them go.

The deal for Gretzky was far more satisfying, a once-in-a-century kind of trade, right up there with the Yankees grabbing Babe Ruth from the Red Sox. Given that Boston gave up the Bambino before he hit his stride, the Gretzky deal might be considered even bigger. At the time I set my sights on him, Gretzky was more than the best hockey player who ever lived. All of Canada believed he was a national treasure, an icon of everything that was right and good about their nation. They felt that they owned him, every bit as much as they owned the expanse of the Yukon, and he, in turn, felt an extraordinary bond to them. Perhaps the only person in all of Canada who didn't consider it a matter of patriotic duty to keep Wayne Gretzky in Edmonton was the team's owner, Peter Pocklington.

I met Wayne Gretzky a few weeks after I bought my minority interest in the Kings in 1986. During warm-up before a game against Edmonton at The Forum, I went down to ice level to watch the players. I was looking to my left when all of a sudden I felt a little tap on the right side of my head. It was Gretzky's stick. The "Great One" gave me a big grin as he skated by me, turned, and then glided over.

"Welcome to the league," he said. We shook hands and chatted. Before he continued skating I said, "Hey Wayne, how would you like to be a King one day?" His response caught me by surprise. "I might not mind it," he said, and then he sliced down the ice.

At about that time, Wayne's agent Michael Barnett encouraged me to think about making Wayne a member of the Kings. Over time, he would be a central figure in my pursuit of Gretzky, and in all my dealings with him. Unlike other agents, he was always extremely fair, considering all sides in every negotiation.

A year after I met Wayne on the ice, when the Lakers were playing a big, sold-out game against the Boston Celtics, he called my office for tickets. He wanted to take a date, a woman named Janet Jones, to the game. They had met years before when she was a dancer on a TV show called *Dance Fever* and he was a guest judge. I arranged for them to sit on the aisle opposite me. It was one of Wayne's first dates with Janet, and they eventually fell in love and married. They would remember it as a key moment in their relationship. I would recall it as another opportunity to make a good impression on Gretzky, and to whisper again in his ear that he belonged in a Kings uniform. (Those uniforms, by the way, had been redesigned. Gone were the putrid yellow suits that made the players look like bananas on ice. They were replaced by neat black and gold shirts and pants. The jerseys became the hottest team item on the market.)

While I did everything I could to befriend Gretzky, I also approached Pocklington whenever we crossed paths. Pocklington was an easygoing man who wore a full beard and seemed to always have a Cuban cigar in his mouth. He had used lots of other people's money to become one of Canada's biggest meatpackers and was also heavily involved in dairies and other food companies. He had gotten into hockey by buying half ownership in the Oilers when they belonged to the now-defunct World Hockey Association. His downpayment included his wife's twelve-carat diamond ring, a Renoir painting, and a Rolls-Royce. In 1978, the Oilers acquired Gretzky and two other players from another WHA team, the Indianapolis Racers, for the grand sum of $760,000.

I always suspected that Pocklington's situation was a bit like mine, that he was heavily financed and often scrambling cash. His hockey team was not a hobby but a business that had to cover its expenses. But Edmonton was a small city where TV revenues and ticket prices would never climb very high. The NHL had begun what would be a long period of salary escalation for players, and Pocklington must have seen that he was being priced out of the market for superstars. At a 1988 league meeting, he came up to me and said, "Bruce, you remember we talked about Wayne before. Are you still interested?"

"Of course I am," I replied.

"Good, then give me a call," he said. "There might be something we can talk about."

Later, when we talked on the phone, Pocklington began by saying he was irritated with Wayne, and that he believed Gretzky wanted to be traded to a city like Los Angeles where Janet might be more comfortable. "His ego is out of control. He thinks that he's bigger than the game itself," he groused. I listened, but I doubted what he was saying. Despite his superstar status, Wayne had a reputation for being almost too decent and principled. "Gretzky is what athletes are supposed to be, but seldom are," wrote Mordecai Richler, the renowned Canadian novelist, "modest to a fault, Macintosh-apple whole-some, and an inspirational model for fans." Knowing the true Gretzky, I waited for Pocklington to reveal the real reason for his desire to sell his con-tract. He did. It was money.

"I'm going to want $15 million cash," he finally said. "That's nonnego-tiable. And we're going to want some players, too."

Given the excitement and fan dollars that a single Gretzky would pump into the L.A. Kings, he could have taken my whole roster, as far as I was con-cerned. I then formally asked for permission to speak with Gretzky, because under the NHL's rules, players under contract cannot be approached about moving teams. Here Pocklington balked. Edmonton was on its way to win-ning the Stanley Cup, again. He didn't want his star to be distracted. He told me to wait until the season was over.

I couldn't wait. I secretly called Wayne and invited him to dinner. He was in L.A. at the time, staying at actor Alan Thicke's home in Toluca Lake and seeing Janet. We met for dinner at a quiet restaurant called Matteos, where I hoped no one would notice us. Afterward, I called Wayne's father, Walter, in Branford, Ontario. Walter, whom Wayne adored, was a very down-to-earth guy who continued to work at Bell Canada long after his son was rich and famous. He appreciated that I cared for Wayne and cared about hockey. The very fact that I called him meant something, and he became an ally.

"Peter is actually talking about this in a serious way," I began the next time I called Wayne. "Before I entertain it, I want to see how you feel. There's no sense getting into a negotiation if, in the end, it's not something you want."

Wayne had heard rumors of a deal, perhaps between Edmonton and Van-couver, but he hadn't taken it very seriously. In fact, Pocklington himself had said they weren't true, and Wayne had accepted his reassurances. After all, Wayne had just led the Oilers to the Stanley Cup. It was hard for him to imag-ine that even before the tournament had finished, Pocklington had been talking trade and saying that Gretzky wanted to leave Edmonton. I also told him what Pocklington had said about his ego.

Wayne grew agitated as he heard all that, and insisted that he had always expected to play out his career in Edmonton. He and Janet were planning to marry in a couple of months, and had been house shopping there for some time. She had shipped her car north and was making friends. Recently pregnant, she had planned to give birth in Edmonton so that the child would hold Canadian citizenship.

After getting over his anger about Pocklington, Wayne told me that he would feel comfortable coming to Los Angeles. He liked the city, and Janet was already rooted there. We agreed that moving the greatest player in the history of the game to one of the two most visible media markets in the world would be very good for hockey.

In the weeks to come, Wayne and I would talk almost daily. Pocklington's price was nonnegotiable, so much of our discussion focused on the other players who would be in the deal. Wayne insisted from the start that I press hard to acquire the Oilers' Marty McSorley, a tough defenseman who could change the momentum of a game. He thought Pocklington might be willing to give him up along with Mike Krushelnyski, whom he would one day describe as "a moose on skates."

Amid all the stress of the trade talks, which were kept entirely secret, Wayne and Janet were married in a ceremony that became Canada's version of the royal pairing of Charles and Diana. The $1 million service (Janet's dress was $40,000) at Edmonton's St. Joseph's Basilica was televised across Canada and drew an audience in the millions. In that very week Pocklington gave me formal permission to deal with Wayne. Five days after the wedding, I phoned Wayne in Los Angeles. From that moment on, we worked Pocklington together, like a power play on the ice.

"Ever since he got with that broad in L.A. his ego is out of control. Sometimes he's not all that good, and that father of his can be a real pain in the ass."

Peter Pocklington's voice, and more importantly his attitude, came over the speakerphone loud and clear enough for both me and Wayne—who was secretly sitting in on our calls—to understand perfectly. The Edmonton owner was telling others that it was Gretzky who was pushing for a trade, but with me, he made it sound as if it would be a relief to shed his star player.

Wayne signaled me silently, and passed me notes with his advice as Pocklington talked about the shape of the deal. I was going to give up one of the Kings' few star players, Jimmy Carson, and our most promising rookie, Martin Gelinas. I told Pocklington that he had to give me McSorley and Krushelnyski, just as Wayne had requested. When he began to resist on McSorley. Gretzky mouthed the words, "Go on. He'll give in."

"Come on, Peter," I said. "You're not going to throw away fifteen million over some friggin' thug, are you?"

Wayne was right. Pocklington caved. He was right again about Pocklington's demand for the Kings' first-round draft picks for the next three years.

"No, no, no!" mouthed Wayne. "Tell him every other year." Following Gretzky's lead I said I would only give up the picks over six years' time. Pocklington went for it, and the terms were set.

Even as we were finalizing the negotiation, Pocklington was coming under pressure in Edmonton to stop the sale. Rumors about it had become so widespread that even members of the Canadian parliament were calling on him to keep Gretzky in Canada. Sports talk shows around the country buzzed with speculation, and fan opinion was unanimous; only a traitor would send the "Great One" south.

None of that seemed to affect Pocklington, whose final demand in the negotiation was that Wayne call him and formally request to be traded. I suspect he did that so that when the questions flew, he would be able to say it was Gretzky who wanted out of Edmonton. By that time Wayne had heard enough of Pocklington's bad-mouthing that he really did want a new team. At five o'clock on a July afternoon, he made the call from my office. Pocklington agreed to do the deal. I then turned to Wayne with one final issue.

"I know you've always dreamed of playing for the Detroit Red Wings," I said. "If you want to go there, I'll back out and you can play for Detroit." Much later, Gretzky told me that the very fact that I was willing to let him go made him certain about becoming a King.

With all the pieces fitted neatly into the puzzle, I made an urgent telephone call to Ray Dempsey, my longtime friend at European American Bank. They were the New York Islanders' bank, so they knew the hockey business. I had told Dempsey about the possible trade weeks before and, being an avid hockey fan, he had immediately recognized the value of bringing Gretzky to Los Angeles. This time when we talked I told Dempsey that the sale was ready, but I needed $15 million immediately to make it happen. Excited by the prospect of financing one of the most important sports trades ever made, Dempsey promised to approve the loan on the basis of a simple letter.

The next day contracts were signed and the cash was wired to Pocklington. Wayne and I sat down to negotiate his salary, which had been less than $1 million in Edmonton. I asked him how much he thought he should earn. "I don't know," he said. "Just pay me what you think I'm worth."

I thought about Wayne's position and the marketplace and decided he was somewhat equal to Magic Johnson. "He makes $3 million a year. How about that?"

"No, no," he said. "That's waaay too much."

We danced like that a bit longer. I offered him a small piece of the team. He turned it down. Then I asked him to write down a figure. He took a pen and scratched a number—$1,000,000—onto a piece of paper. We settled on $2 million per year, which was less than I thought he deserved, but still the highest salary of any player in the game. I also guaranteed him that if at any time another player's contract surpassed his, I would increase his pay beyond that point.

At last Wayne Gretzky was a Los Angeles King, but we weren't allowed to announce it. Pocklington wanted two weeks to continue selling season tickets to the fans in Edmonton, on the pretense that they would see Gretzky at every home game. But the silence could not be held. Talk about Gretzky's departure grew so loud that in a few days we were asked to fly to Edmonton for a press conference to break the news.

We took my plane to Edmonton. After Wayne made a few calls from his apartment, to inform some Oilers teammates, we went to the press conference. As we arrived, an Oilers public relations man handed Wayne a speech in which he would announce the trade and tell the world that it was all his idea and that Pocklington was just trying to please him. Gretzky would not have it, but he did agree to sit down for a few minutes with the Oilers coach, Glen Sather, and Pocklington himself. I was left to watch them through the glass that surrounded the office where they sat. As I waited, all kinds of thoughts went through my head, including the fear that Wayne might change his mind. But when he came out, he flashed a smile and gave me a thumbs-up sign. All that remained was for him to go before the press.

Pocklington broke the news with comments that made it sound like we had practically forced him into the sale. Then Wayne got up and began to talk. He recalled how he had come to the Oilers as a seventeen-year-old. The team had been where he forged his first adult friendships, where he had grown from boy to man. When a reporter asked him what he would remember most about Edmonton, Wayne paused, and his eyes began to tear. "There comes a time," he said, and then was overcome. He stood rubbing his eyes for a moment and then sat down. He would answer no more questions.

On the day after, fans in Edmonton burned Peter Pocklington in effigy. One prominent leader of the Canadian Parliament said the trade amounted to the loss "of a national symbol, like the beaver." The Oilers owner desperately tried to interpret events in a way that made Gretzky look like the bad guy. "He's got an ego the size of Manhattan," he complained. "And he's a great actor," he added, implying that the emotions Wayne had expressed at the press conference were not heartfelt. Others in Edmonton criticized Wayne's new wife, Janet, comparing her to Yoko Ono, whom many fans had blamed for the breakup of the Beatles. Those comments hurt both Janet and Wayne, and they couldn't have been further from the truth.

Fortunately, as much as Edmonton wailed about the loss of a favorite son, Los Angeles seemed to celebrate even more about the arrival of a new talent. Jim Murray, the dean of Los Angeles sportswriters, said that Gretzky's move to Los Angeles would do for him what Babe Ruth's jump from Boston to New York had accomplished for Ruth; it would make him far more famous, much more wealthy, and ever more satisfied with his accomplishments. After explaining all that, Murray went on to praise me as an owner of the Jack Kent Cooke mold, because I understood that sports franchises are built on the star system.

"Gretzky will fill the seats. If he can fill the nets, too, he'll be the biggest bargain since Babe Ruth. The game needs glamour more than goals. He's already pulled the hat trick. He's put hockey on Page One. In Los Angeles. In August."

Around the league, our move received nothing but support. Edmonton had been beating up on everyone for years. Without Gretzky, they would no longer be the terror on ice. Owners and general managers in Philadelphia, Chicago, and Boston said that putting Gretzky in Hollywood would be good for all of hockey because it would raise the sport's image across the United States. Calgary's Cliff Fletcher exclaimed that the Kings had, after twenty-one years, achieved due recognition. "The credit," added Fletcher, "goes to Bruce McNall."

Having my name attached to a historic trade involving the likes of Wayne Gretzky hurled me into the public eye. One local paper ran a lengthy article under the headline, "In the Business World, McNall Is The Great One." The piece estimated my net worth at $100 million and quoted an expert who said I had already increased the value of the Kings by 20 percent. *Business Week* published a profile of me that concluded with the idea that my deal for Gretzky could be the most profitable business move of my life.

The fan response made it seem like *Business Week* was right. Season ticket sales doubled immediately. The sellout crowd at our first game in the Gretzky era was more boisterous and supportive than any I had seen at The Forum. Roy Orbison sang the national anthem, and Wayne scored a goal as we beat Detroit 8–2. He then led us to three more victories, the best start of any Kings season. We knew we had really made L.A. a hockey town when we filled the house for a game against the Flyers, on the same night that the Dodgers hosted a World Series game against Oakland. The fans were so juiced up that they even cheered for me when I walked around the arena. The applause was intoxicating.

All the enthusiasm, the run on tickets and the victories, filled me with hope. Sure, the trade had saddled the Kings with a debt that was almost equal to the team's total value when I bought it. But there was no doubt in anyone's mind that hockey was going to be a big draw in Los Angeles as long as Gretzky skated for us. Gate receipts were going to soar, and revenue from TV and concessions could grow just as fast. In the back of my mind, I nursed the hope that I may have even taken the big step that would allow me to get out of all the financial problems that the public and media knew nothing about.

8

I WAS A CELEBRITY. I was the man who had brought the Great One to L.A. and now hosted a rollicking, star-studded party every time the Kings played at The Forum. On game nights, I roamed the stadium to cheers and applause. On off-nights, I sat on the sofas on the late-night talk shows with Pat Sajak and Dennis Miller. Almost every morning brought attention from the local papers. And just as Jerry Buss had predicted, every door was open to me. If I wanted a table at Spago, I could have it at any time, and Wolfgang Puck himself would stop by to visit. I partied with the likes of Lee Iacocca and Steve Wynn at Allen Paulson's farm during the Kentucky Derby. At Dodger games, Tommy Lasorda would take me and my son, P.J., into the locker room. Whenever I called for a favor, there was no such thing as a sold-out game or concert. I was always accommodated.

I also possessed the property and toys of a rich man, though I rarely had time to enjoy them. I had seven homes, including one on the beach in Hawaii and another high up in the Trump Tower in New York. Nine cars were parked at the house in Holmby Hills, including a Rolls, a Bentley, a Range Rover, and a gold Mercedes that the housekeeper used to fetch groceries. I hadn't flown in anything but a private jet for years.

Though the trappings of wealth were pleasant, I valued more the people who had become part of my life when the Kings were hot. Every day I received calls from members of the Hollywood A-list who wanted tickets, and I never disappointed them. Tom Hanks, Steven Spielberg, Tom Cruise, Sylvester Stallone, Barbra Streisand—all of them came to see the Kings. Many of L.A.'s luminaries attended a lot of games and became friends. Included in that group were Michael J. Fox, Peter Weller, Jim Belushi, James Woods, Andre Agassi, Paul Anka, Marlee Matlin, Chuck Norris, and Michael Keaton. From the music business came David Foster, Jerry Moss, and Brian Turner. Among the pro golfers who went to games were Craig Stadler, Fred Couples, Billy Andrade, and David Stockton. When super-agent Michael Ovitz requested season passes to certain choice seats, I called the family that held them and worked out a deal that gave them spots that were nearly as good, for free. Ovitz was so pleased he sent a big bouquet of flowers along with the check, for tens of thousands of dollars, to pay for the seats.

In most cases it took very little effort for me to make a celebrity happy. Tickets were easy. But I also arranged for them to have a private entrance and extra security. I even built a special staircase that led to my sixty-seat private box. Before each game I hosted celebrities and others—from my bankers to my staff—at the owner's table in The Forum Club. Those pregame meals became one of THE places to be seen, and there were never empty seats. At one time or another we hosted luminaries ranging from President Ronald and Nancy Reagan, to Michael J. Fox. Regulars included John Candy, Burt Sugarman and Mary Hart, and Kurt Russell and Goldie Hawn. Their daughter, Kate, always seemed to have a crush on some player. I'd tell her that very soon the young men would be lining up for dates. Even before she became Kate Hudson, actress, I was right.

The games and the dinners won me relationships with the entertainment elite. Some of the rich and famous who came to me for tickets wound up buying coins or antiquities. Others joined me in deals for horses. But the real pay-off came when they appeared at the games. In a very short time, the public realized that a Kings game was the best place in town to rub up against beau-tiful and powerful people. With Gretzky on the ice and Hollywood in the stands, the games became happenings. Young women who knew nothing about the sport dressed in their sexiest outfits and paraded the aisles. Young men flocked to be with them. Sellouts became routine. And everyone imagined I was getting richer and richer. I was, but the picture was far more compli-cated than anyone outside my circle could know.

Where the Kings were concerned, we did benefit from huge gains in atten-dance. But as hard as we tried to find new sources of revenue for the team, we seemed to get blocked at every turn. We raised ticket prices as much as possi-ble, but I wouldn't increase the price of the cheapest seats because I wanted everyone in town to have a chance to see the games. We wouldn't benefit from any increase in the sales of hot dogs or hats, either. Under terms that we inher-ited from Jerry Buss, we started out making nothing—zero dollars—on con-cession sales of food and drink and souvenirs at the arena. At an average of $6 per person, that could be a much as $70,000 per game. And forget the rev-enues from parking. Our lease with The Forum gave the arena all those earn-ings, which could be $30,000 a date.

Fortunately we did one thing that did improve cash flow: we won hockey games, twelve more than the previous year. We had the fourth-best record in the entire league, compared with eighteenth the previous year, and we finished second in our division. We did it with a great offense that lit up the goal light more than any other in the league. In his very first season with us, Gretzky broke the team record for points scored, and the team as a whole set a Kings record for goals scored in a single season. Four of our players, a high for the franchise, were named all-stars.

All the above was accomplished with a roster that was constantly shifted in an effort to find the perfect mix. I often turned to Wayne for input—though he did not run the team as some suspected—and I acquired some players at his urging. He was always looking for better goaltending and one or two tough guys to watch his back. In response, I traded for an exceptional goalie, Kelly Hrudey of the New York Islanders, and I also grabbed Jay Miller, a beefy fighter from the Boston Bruins. The team hit a little harder, skated a little faster, and developed an exciting and high-powered offense that rang the red light for goals 376 times.

All the scoring and winning boosted attendance to an average of nearly fifteen thousand, which was also the all-time record for hockey in Los Angeles. With more than three thousand extra ticket sales per game than the previous year, gate receipts improved by more than $50,000 per home game. During the playoffs we scooped up another $1 million per home game. We also brought our fans to a state of frenzy with a level of play that surprised even me.

The fans at one game got an exceptional treat when producer Joel Silver brought his crew to The Forum to shoot a scene for *Lethal Weapon 3*. After spending three days filming in the arena, they asked to do one small bit during a time-out in an actual game. Between periods we announced to the crowd that that was going to happen. Everyone stayed seated and then suddenly Mel Gibson came running down the aisles. It was a terrific experience for the fans, and I even got to play myself. (I must not have done too well, though. My lines wound up on the cutting-room floor.)

In our division semifinals we played Peter Pocklington's Oilers in a series that went the full seven games. Gretzky faced the teammates he had skated with for nine years, only now they wouldn't speak to him. When the Oilers took the lead three games to one, Pocklington crowed that his sale of Gretzky was obviously the right move. But the Kings fought back to tie the series at three each, with the deciding game to be played at The Forum.

On an April night, with more than sixteen thousand screaming fans packed into the arena, the mood for the Kings/Oilers showdown was as electrified as it ever was for the Lakers/Celtics championship duels. Gretzky scored the first goal, and the last, and we beat them 6–3. The Forum, from the stands to the ice to the locker room, was a madhouse of celebration. With sportswriters beginning to call Los Angeles "Hockeywood," it was finally clear that the Kings had made their mark on the city. The $15 million gamble had paid off. It was my thirty-ninth birthday.

In the next round of playoff games, my Kings played like they had left their hearts on the ice in the Oilers series. The Calgary Flames swept us in four straight. But the defeat didn't take any of the pleasure we all felt over the team's performance against the Oilers, who had dominated the league, and the Kings, for many years. At season's end Wayne was named the NHL's most valuable player, and I won the NHL's Executive of the Year. During his acceptance speech, Wayne began to cry as he thanked me for supporting him during the year. I shouldn't have been surprised by the emotion. As he would show time and again, Wayne is a remarkably normal person for a sports superstar. The expectations fans had placed on him were enormous, and he was sincerely grateful that I had always been available to hear him out, and act on his behalf, by bringing in players who could share the load.

Nothing I did to help Wayne was more important than my purchase, that season, of a Boeing 727, which became the team plane with the nickname *Air McNall*. The jet, which cost $5 million, was painted silver and black and outfitted with first-class seats and television screens. It had a huge galley where gourmet meals were prepared to be served on silver trays by our own flight attendants. The plane saved us a great deal of time and stress as we worked our way through the most demanding travel schedule of any team in pro sports. But Wayne, who was a terribly nervous flyer, most appreciated the fact that, as I told him, it was an especially safe aircraft, formerly owned by the U.S. government, which had it equipped with redundant safety systems. (That last bit wasn't exactly true, but Wayne believed it and actually started to relax in the air.)

That first season was not unblemished. After the all-star break, Wayne had some trouble in Detroit with our coach, Robbie Ftorek. During the game in question, Gretzky had scored five points before the end of the second period and had begun to think about breaking his personal record, which was eight. Suddenly, during a lapse in concentration, a Detroit player stole the puck from him and scored. Wayne got so angry at himself that he smashed his stick to splinters on the post that anchors the goal. Robbie, who had a rather old-school attitude toward displays of emotion, screamed, "I can't stand for that!" and benched Wayne for two full shifts of his line.

After that incident, rumors began to fly. Supposedly Wayne was demanding that Ftorek be fired, and I was letting myself be manipulated by a prima donna star. It didn't help Robbie that he hated dealing with the press and thus, they were rarely on his side. But the truth was, I ran the team, and Wayne did not pressure me to change coaches at mid-season.

Still, by the end of the playoffs it had become clear to me that Robbie did not quite fit the team we had assembled. He was perfect at dealing with young players, and squeezing the best performances out of the mid-level skaters. But he was a very forceful personality, and resisted giving extra playing time to the stars who might produce more goals. That style rubbed our veterans, and our all-stars, the wrong way. That, combined with the team's poor performance in the second round of the playoffs, led me to dismiss him.

In the search to replace Ftorek, half the people I contacted mentioned the same man, Tom Webster. He had been a high-scoring pro player and a successful coach in the minors. When we met I was impressed by his intelligence and sincerity. He seemed very human, very decent, and, most importantly, he understood our team and what we were trying to accomplish. He would give a lot more playing time to the top players, and try to get us to score even more goals. In a town like L.A., you need to make the goal lights shine as much as possible if you're going to put people in the seats.

Although fans and press like to believe that wrenching dramas accompany every coaching change or trade and player reassignment, the fact is, compared with my other businesses, managing the Kings was a low-stress affair. On a typical day, I would get to my main business offices at eight A.M. and literally surrender myself to a series of meetings and challenging phone calls. Two-thirds of my time was spent with banking issues—all extremely unpleasant—and the rest seemed to be chewed up by associates who should have been solving problems themselves. If it wasn't David Begelman handing me some disaster on the film front, it was Steve Nessenblatt and Su Waks embroiled in a power struggle.

Contrast that with what I encountered in the late afternoon after I drove over to The Forum and opened the door to the Kings offices. There, my management team included a hall of fame goaltender in Rogie Vachon, and two sports management veterans in Roy Mlakar and Nick Beverley. Roy was so enthusiastic about his work that once, when ticket sales plummeted at the minor league team he ran in New Haven, he camped on the roof until more fans bought season passes.

It was a great group, and it was no wonder, then, that I found myself devoting ever more time and energy to hockey and to the people in the Kings organization. Gretzky and I became good friends. Wayne and Janet attended the Cannes Film Festival with me in 1989. Unable to speak a word of French, and hardly a film industry insider, Wayne was a bit out of his element until we ran into actors Rob and Chad Lowe. They were big hockey fans, and we wound up spending a lot of time with them. One morning, before dawn, I got a call from Wayne. "Bruce," he said, "you gotta call Rob. He's got some kind of problem with his girlfriend, and he needs your help." I called Rob at his hotel.

"Can you do me a big favor and take Anya back to New York with you on your way to L.A.?" he asked.

I told him I was going to stop in Paris, but if Anya didn't mind the delay, I would get her back to New York eventually.

"That's okay," said Rob. "Something's happening. It's complicated. But I have to rush back to the States right away, and I don't want her involved in it."

I agreed to do the favor. The next day newspapers all over the world reported upon the existence of explicit videotapes Rob had made while having sex with an underaged girl. Police were investigating, and Rob was immediately the subject of both outrage and satire. (He eventually performed community service in exchange for having the criminal charges against him dropped.)

Anya was very shaken up. Wayne and Janet and I tried to comfort her. We ended up in Paris at the Bristol Hotel, where there was no room for Anya. She stayed with me in my room—in complete innocence. All of us went to the track, where I saw the Aga Khan, who I knew as a fellow Thoroughbred owner.

"Wayne," I whispered. "Come on, I'm going to introduce you to the Aga Khan."

Propriety calls for a certain ritual when you meet the Aga Khan. Women curtsy. Men bow. Everyone calls him "Your royal highness."

It turned out that the Aga Khan had become a big hockey fan when he studied at Harvard, and he continued to follow the game. When he saw us, he ran over. "Wayne Gretzky," he said. "My God, you're my idol. I went to Harvard, and I tried to play hockey at Harvard."

"Hey, Aggy," said Wayne, "how's it going?"

At that time, the fun with Wayne and the Aga Khan was matched by the release of what was probably Gladden's best film, *The Fabulous Baker Boys*, which starred Michelle Pfeiffer, Beau Bridges, and his brother, Jeff. Produced with none of the ego-based nonsense that occurs with many films, *The Fabulous Baker Boys* was a movie that the critics favored, and that the distributing studio, Fox, promoted well. That was probably because it had actually started out at the studio, as a favorite project, and had been forced on David Begelman. Though we didn't win an Oscar, the movie got five nominations, and the $18 million it generated in box-office receipts gave us a small profit. Still, it was no hit. In comparison, the silly film called *Look Who's Talking*, released in the same month as our movie, did $140 million.

With John Travolta carrying my movie business and Wayne Gretzky propelling my hockey team, it would seem to the entire world that Bruce McNall could do no wrong. Certainly that was the image the press portrayed. In 1990, the glossy, upscale magazine *Connoisseur* devoted three pages to declaring me "King of Coins." In the piece, old Joel Malter provided a few I-knew-him-when quotes and the writer recounted my successes with the Kings and racehorses. But the main focus of the article was my coin business. To be more precise, the Merrill Lynch coin funds. After trumpeting all my successes and recalling my precocious youth, the writer noted that the funds represented a new and untested direction in investment. "So far the limited partners have done fairly well," the author concluded. "But this business is simply too fraught with uncertainties to forecast long-term."

If he only knew.

What *Connoisseur* had failed to note was that ancient coins had entered a terrible bear market in the late 1980s, beginning a steady decline in values. Dropping prices hurt every dealer, and eroded what was left of our own holdings within Numismatic Fine Arts. The trend also made it nearly impossible for us to make any profitable trades for our Merrill Lynch investors. Nevertheless, we did post gains, at least on the books of the Athena Fund, through some highly creative techniques.

At first we worked extremely hard to acquire coins for the funds that had the best shot of creating immediate profits. We bought groups of coins, but when we split them between NFA and the Athena funds we gave the best to Athena at discount prices. Whenever someone came to me looking for a certain coin, I sold it from the Athena funds, often at the highest possible price. Profits went to the partners. In other transactions, we allowed NFA to lose money for the benefit of the funds. But those methods cost us too much to continue for long, so we had to find other ways to show that the fund was growing.

The simplest thing we did was overstate the value of the coins held by the Merrill Lynch funds. That was relatively easy to do, given that we were dealing with items few people understood, and the values of which were highly subjective. The *Wall Street Journal* will tell you what a bushel of corn is worth today. But there is no authority reporting the value of a denarius.

The most unusual thing we did to boost the funds was to borrow cash from them, to shore up our other businesses. Then we repaid it with interest. How did we do that? We created false sales, including invoices for whole lists of coins that didn't exist, which the funds appeared to acquire from small foreign-based companies—one was named Minerva—that we had set up ourselves.

Those transactions certainly violated the rules governing the partnership, and were probably illegal. (Given the choice now, I would never do it.) For a while we justified them to ourselves because in the end, we put the money back and then some. We also reminded ourselves that our partners at Merrill Lynch had put us at a disadvantage from the start. First, their brokers were not schooled in coins, and were not effective salesmen for coins. That meant that I had had to fly all over the country, at my expense, speaking to large groups and individual investors, on their behalf. Then, if I did reach some of those people, and they made an investment, their brokers took the order and carved off a hefty 15 percent commission for themselves. That was many times the commission they were allowed to take on stocks and bonds, and, more importantly, it meant that we had to generate 15 percent profits just to make our partners whole. It was too big a handicap for us to overcome.

Few people would excuse what we did. And most would likely imagine that we sat around scheming up those transactions. In fact, it was rarely such a deliberate and overt thing. Typically one of us at the top of the organization would mention that cash was running short. Payroll might be due soon, or perhaps we needed to make a big interest payment. (EAB alone expected $400,000 per month for the $25 million involved in the so-called circular transaction with Credit Lyonnais.) With the need identified, we would look for sources of cash and ways to get it.

The trick of creating false invoices and sales was something we had begun to do almost routinely after the $20 million, Bunker Hunt audit crisis. Beginning at that time, the value of our coin holdings had been significantly over-stated to our lenders. Since we claimed to have a growing, successful business, but little cash to show for our efforts, we had to report increased holdings. We did that by generating false purchase documents. By 1990 or so, the stated value of those phantom coins was $30 to $40 million.

Our deceptions might have been noticed had we not balanced them with legitimate business activity. When Johns Hopkins University moved to sell a very large and important coin collection, the president of the school came to visit. I showed him Summa Gallery, and even took him to a movie set. In the end we shared the sale with Bank Leu and our joint commission exceeded $1 million. It felt good to work with the coins, and to make real sales. In fact, I never really ceased to be a coin salesman. I can recall one party at a farm in Kentucky when Lee Iacocca and I went outside and sat down. I talked to him about ancient coins and art, probing for a connection to his family's history in Italy. He was a pretty tough sell, and in the end didn't buy. But I loved the pursuit.

In another serious piece of real business, we pushed the Athena Fund II into antiquities other than coins. Those items, which were bought and sold by dealers and museums worldwide, promised steadier increase in value than ancient coins. Once again we hoped that the presence of a new major player—Merrill Lynch—would drive prices upward. That rise didn't happen, and Athena II's value continued to decline.

Too proud to admit defeat, and perhaps a bit frightened of being found out, I refused to stop trying to save the coin business. The modern U.S. coin market, much bigger and more stable than the ancient coin market, seemed to offer a solution. I financed the purchase of 51 percent of Superior, a Los Angeles U.S. coin company, and then started a third investment partnership with Merrill Lynch, which we called the New World Coin Fund. We attracted millions of dollars in investments, but once again could not make profits. And just as we had with Athena I and Athena II, we began to use the partners' money like it was our own.

. . .

As our handling of the coin funds illustrated, there was a certain Caesar-crossing-the-Rubicon quality to our businesses outside of hockey. Once we had entered the realm of deception, it was just too easy to stay there. Certainly the pressure to find new sources of spendable money never subsided. We suffered from an almost constant hemorrhaging of cash, which went to cover bank loans, operating expenses, and losses created by falling markets and the escalating debt at Gladden. Though we had income from legitimate activities, it rarely met our monthly needs.

Fortunately for us, at least in the short term, we had other important assets, besides coins, which we could leverage almost at will. Race horses are every bit as difficult to value, financially, as ancient coins. However, if it is working above-the-board, the marketplace can determine the value of a horse whenever it is bought and sold. The price paid is what the horse is worth. The industry also depends on professional appraisers, who are supposed to be independent in their judgments.

In reality, many buyers inflate prices artificially by paying too much for horses, and many appraisers are so chummy with owners that they will try very hard to set the highest value possible on an animal. In our case, we even set up an appraisal company—run by my former limo driver—that appeared to be independent. Of course, we got the right kind of numbers from this little operation, which allowed us to claim a higher net worth for our stable of steeds.

Those are only some of the ways that the finances around horses can be manipulated. To get the most cash possible out of our horses, we used far more aggressive techniques, beginning with pledging the same Thoroughbreds as collateral to two different banks.

Double-pledging was possible because many of the bankers we dealt with were not expert in horse financing. It worked like this: First, we found a horse we wanted to buy. Then we went to bank A, which lent us the industry maximum—50 percent of the horse's value. We then presented the same deal to bank B, and also asked for 50 percent. We almost always got our money, and bought the horse, with nothing from our own pockets. It didn't always work seamlessly. Once an officer at Schroders Bank, a private lender in New York, discovered double loans on roughly a dozen horses. We avoided serious trouble by claiming an honest bookkeeping error—easy to imagine when you own parts of hundreds of horses—and rectifying the problem quickly.

In the end, all of those deals were my responsibility. But by 1990, just about everyone at the top of my management team—as many as twenty people—was involved. Remarkably, those people all came from fields and companies that require the utmost in honesty and integrity. They were lawyers, former bankers, even certified public accountants. They had worked at Arthur Andersen, Deloitte & Touche, Coopers & Lybrand, Ernst & Young, and other venerable companies. Yet, in the culture of our firms, where banks were seen as opponents and we truly believed that we would have a home-run success that would let us repay everyone, a certain level of deceit became the norm.

It wasn't as if we grabbed some guns and robbed a string of 7-Elevens. Our crimes may have been just as bad in the eyes of the law, but they were committed in a way that lacked any of the drama or danger that signals true evil. Though the scale was obviously enormous, our acts weren't much different from the little lies told when someone overstates his income on a mortgage application, or lies about her debts on a credit card application. Those deceptions are criminal acts too—which you will discover if you read the fine print at the bottom of the applications—but they are committed routinely. And when was the last time you heard that someone was arrested for doing it?

Beyond the fact that our actions were paper crimes, and performed in a quiet, gradual way, there were unique factors that made it easier for so many seemingly honest people to go wrong. One was the effect I had on almost everyone around. Over the decades I had learned how to look and sound like an immensely successful and confident person. I dressed the part, spoke with authority, and played on everyone's need to believe in me. Belief in my power, whether real or not, made the people who worked for me feel secure enough to keep on going.

Beyond their confidence in my judgment, the McNall team saw that through me they could become wealthier than they ever imagined. It had happened for Steve and Su, and I made it clear that similar rewards were available to everyone. The staff knew that I could be approached for loans, that I was likely to say yes to requests for raises, and that I enjoyed sharing the celebrity limelight. What bookkeeper wouldn't be a little starstruck sitting at the owner's table at The Forum between Sly Stallone and Magic Johnson?

I believe all of my people were sincerely committed to fixing our problems. No one grabbed millions of dollars and took off for South America. (Not that we didn't fantasize about running away. I certainly did.) Instead, the goal was always to cover our obligations until a long-term solution was found. We always talked about making the big score that would let us pay back all the banks. And according to the groupthink that came to dominate the environment inside my companies, that goal justified the means.

Whether we felt justified or not, we all suffered under the fear of failing, or being found out. Stress showed itself in different ways. For the most part, I was able to compartmentalize things in my mind, dealing with problems at work—even screaming on occasion—but hiding them at home. Jane and our children heard nothing but good news from me. However, my weight, always a problem, betrayed the pressure I felt. I ate big meals, and nibbled constantly, until I reached 280 pounds—quite a lot for someone only five-feet-eight-inches tall—and found myself out on Rodeo Drive shopping for bigger clothes.

For her part, Su Waks indulged her taste for clothes, jewelry, and other material things. Those were her rewards for playing the bad guy in our office. With Merrill Lynch, for example, she would simply deny them information, or refuse to answer questions. They would complain to me, and I would be allowed to play the peacemaker. In reality, Su would divert attention, and give the rest of us the time we needed to craft our responses. But, as tough as she seemed, Su was affected. As time wore on, she seemed less and less interested in our businesses. Sometimes she had trouble just reporting for work. She arrived later and later, and seemed to devote ever more of her time and energy to her children. I can recall many mornings when her assistant, Nora Rothrock, would occupy Su's office and we would talk about our business problems. Tall and a bit reserved, Nora was a great contrast to Su, who was short, aggressive, and even meddlesome at times. Nora was truly gifted with numbers and detail work, and she became the person who was ultimately responsible for maintaining all the different sets of numbers we used for the banks. (We called that task "continuity," the term movie producers use to describe the job of making sure a story holds together throughout a film.) Nora didn't like doing it. And she especially hated the way that Steve Nessenblatt would blow up at her if she made even the smallest mistake.

Steve handled much of the business that had to do with the horses, and the most difficult banking situations. Other people in our office praised Steve for constructing loan documents that were so complex that even experienced bankers couldn't see how they favored us. Steve was so aggressive that I always considered him to be an offensive player for our team, in comparison with Su, who was primarily a defensive specialist. I needed them both.

Effective as he was, the strain of battling the banks affected Steve dramatically. Though he made roughly a half million dollars a year, every few months he asked for a new car, and he frequently borrowed tens of thousands of dollars. He kept track in a notebook—we called it the Steve Nessenblatt Memorial Ledger—but it was clear to all of us that he would never pay back those loans. He lived too high to ever set money aside to get out of debt. I believe he needed the distraction that toys provided, and eventually that even extended to his private life. In the office, Steve could be volatile and demanding. Almost every day he made at least one of our staffers cry. And every once in a while he would blurt out something about "going to the Feds" with what he knew about our businesses. I never considered those outbursts real threats, but they reminded me that we were all bound together by what we were doing.

Because one big mistake could unravel my whole empire, I worried when Steve's substance abuse problems got worse. By 1990, he would often disappear for days and then say nothing about where he had been. Finally he moved to Lake Tahoe, where he had long been spending weekends, and announced that he was cutting back his involvement in day-to-day business. He remained available to work with our banks, and consulted by telephone. But he would not be seen in the office on a regular basis.

Though he reduced his time at work, Steve did not reduce the salary he drew, and I did not object. That wasn't because I feared Steve, but rather because I felt that given the risks he had taken and the services he had rendered, he deserved whatever we could spare. I felt the same way about all the families who depended on my employees. That is why I paid everyone so well. It was the least I could do. But it didn't stop people from wanting more. Steve's situation made Su angry and resentful. She asked for $50,000 more in pay, to bring her even with him. I turned her down, but agreed to pay some of her household expenses. Eventually these expenses—as high as $7,000 monthly—exceeded the raise she had asked for in the first place. To further soothe her feelings I gave her gifts of jewelry at Christmas, on her birthday, and sometimes as a surprise.

Not to be outdone, David Begelman continued to host lavish parties, at company expense, and to pick up every restaurant tab, whether it was for two or twenty. At Gladden he maintained a huge staff—lawyers, public relations people, and production workers—that could not be supported by the small number of films we made. Arguing with him was useless, even though I was, technically, the boss. He would look at me with an expression that said, "Who are you to question me?" and the discussion would be over. As close as we were, David rarely shared his true feelings. On one of the few occasions when he let down his guard, however, he shocked me by saying that he thought suicide was a reasonable alternative to failure. "You know, life is the difficult part," he said. "Death is easy."

If that all seems out of the norm for corporate behavior, it was. But it was not a normal corporate environment. My businesses were created almost entirely on the basis of my reputation, and built upon my relationships with highly ambitious associates. I considered each one to be an extension of my personality. The people who worked with me, especially in key positions, were like members of a family or, to be more precise, a military unit. It was us against the world. It was corporate combat.

Winning our war against growing but largely hidden debts required bold moves. We did everything we could to raise the team's profile. One oddball thing we did was play an exhibition game against the New York Rangers, in the broiling summer heat of Las Vegas. We played outdoors, where Caesars Palace chairman Henry Gluck had ice made for just one night. The gate was $1 million.

Of course, you can only play so many hockey games in Vegas. The Kings needed to find real streams of revenue to pay the notes on the team, the loan that had brought Gretzky to town, and all the regular expenses. But that would be impossible as long as we were stuck in The Forum under the terms of our lease with Jerry Buss.

At first we tried renegotiating the terms, but Jerry had set up his own finances so that he was completely dependent on the money he got out of the Kings' lease. We then considered breaking the agreement, but that would mean instant lawsuits. We even thought about declaring bankruptcy, which would free us from the contract. But I couldn't do this to my friend, Jerry. Finally we had to conclude that the only solution was to build a new arena for ourselves, and hope to bring the Lakers with us into the new place.

Pro sport was in the midst of a building boom nationwide, with new stadiums, ballparks, and arenas under construction or being planned from Seattle to Baltimore. Though most were built to replace crumbling and outdated facilities, in some cases the projects were begun simply to take advantage of a booming new market for special boxes. All the new buildings were being constructed to include dozens of glass-walled private boxes—party rooms with a view of the games—that were rented for hundreds of thousands of dollars per season. Aside from a few immensely rich individuals, those boxes were leased by corporations, and were used to reward executives and clients.

Besides the boxes, which produced millions of dollars in receipts, the new stadiums offered vastly improved amenities for the ordinary fan. New, upscale restaurants were built, as well as shopping arcades that rivaled local malls. In some places hotels were built adjacent to the stadiums, while others were constructed in the midst of large, urban redevelopment schemes. The bottom line for team owners was a huge increase in revenues, sometimes doubling what had been available in an old place.

The cost for a new indoor basketball/hockey arena could be as low as the $40 million spent in Sacramento to open the rather modest Arco Arena in 1988. But in a place like Los Angeles, building the kind of hall we wanted would run $150 million, in 1990 dollars. Obviously we would need a deep-pocketed partner, or two, to provide the financial muscle such a project would require. When Bank of America came knocking on our door, we wondered if we had found just such a partner.

For years we had used a San Diego office of Bank of America to obtain small loans for horses and other items. The executives we dealt with, Dennis Pagola and Bob Tjessfold, were always helpful, and always interested in expanding the relationship. We listened when they made pitches, but we resisted because we had built such a complex set of arrangements with so many other banks—each one lending to us based on a different set of books—that adding one more seemed unnecessary. Then Pagola and Tjessfold brought in Mike Rossi.

As vice chairman of Bank of America, Rossi commanded all of the resources of one of the most powerful lenders in the world, a company with greater liquidity than half the countries on Earth. Tall and a little heavyset, Rossi had an ego to match his power. He also loved sports. When Pagola introduced us he said, "We want to be your bank, and we want everything. The Kings, the horses, coins, everything."

Rossi wanted our business for two reasons. First, the sports business is much more fun than everyday banking. Second, the financial statement we prepared for his bank showed that I had a huge personal net worth, something in the range of $100 million. Besides my own wealth, my companies were considered extraordinarily successful, with very good credit. The carefully obscured truth was that my debts and the phantom assets on our statements had reduced my real net worth to almost zero. And our high credit rating was only possible because we were borrowing from one bank to make the payments to another. But Rossi knew none of that. He said our companies were too big to be served properly by any but the largest banks, and he hinted that Bank of America might even get behind the right stadium project. Almost as an afterthought, he added that should I ever come into possession of a basketball team, he might like to run it. He loved basketball.

Steve and I disagreed about the bank. I really thought it was a good idea. Rossi's group was offering to pay off a slew of loans, replacing them with one big note that would include an extra $20 million. And the tantalizing prospect of a partner for a new arena was irresistible to me. Steve wanted us to be in business with as many banks as possible, so that we had optional sources of money. He might have been right, but I had my eye on the cash we would net from Bank of America and the chance of making a big deal that would right all of our wrongs. We went with Rossi.

Not long after we paid off the old loans and deposited the excess cash in our accounts, Steve told our new bankers that the value of all those coins that were supposedly the base of my net worth had dropped precipitously. He didn't tell the truth, that they didn't exist, but he said that if we were forced to liquidate quickly, we'd get just pennies on the dollar. In the conversation, which Steve recorded on tape, the bankers said they didn't care. They were looking at the value of the Kings to support their loans and they were happy. In a move that seemed designed to prove his faith in us, Rossi would soon step forward to bankroll my next big deal.

9

IF THERE HAD BEEN NO HIGHS, no victories, I might have stopped all the scrambling, declared bankruptcy, and walked away. But no matter how desperate our problems got, we always seemed to find a way to keep operating without any of our secrets being discovered. More significantly, we often had highly visible successes—the kind that make headlines and get people cheering—that brightened the aura around me.

Consider the beautiful three-year-old bay colt named Saumarez, named for a British admiral who defeated a superior French armada in 1801. In 1990, Saumarez was running in Europe, and Emmanuel de Seroux urged me to take half interest in him for $450,000. Sired by Rainbow Quest, who had won the Arc in 1985, his bloodlines were excellent. He had finished strong in some significant races, with the famous rider Steve Cauthen aboard, and had won several outright. Emmanuel liked his spirit, and believed he was not yet at his physical peak.

Wayne Gretzky and I bought a 50 percent share of Saumarez and sent him to Chantilly to work with a new young trainer named Nicolas Clement. To our dismay, Saumarez ran poorly prior to the Arc. He finished seventh at the Phoenix Champion Stakes at Phoenix Park, thirty lengths behind the winner. Cauthen believed that Saumarez had literally choked during the race, a common problem that occurs when the tongue blocks the airway. The horse was fitted with a special tongue strap, which we hoped would guarantee a better run.

At the Arc de Triomphe, Saumarez was ridden by French jockey Gerald Mosse, who was just beginning to be recognized as a star rider. He and Saumarez broke out of the gate in third place and lingered there until the backstretch, when Mosse turned him loose. By the final turn, Saumarez was ahead by seven lengths. Though several horses made closing dashes, Mosse's strategy worked, and we won by nearly a length.

In the winner's circle at Longchamp I told the press I was "the happiest man in the world," and I was. Earlier in the year, Wayne and I had won the Arlington Million, with a horse named Golden Pheasant. Saumarez had given us an even bigger victory. Soon afterward we sold shares in him as a sire. The syndication was worth $8 million, of which we received half.

Each time I achieved a gain like the one with Saumarez, I bought time for my various companies and, more significantly, my faith in a future cure-all deal was affirmed. Further affirmation was provided by our hockey team. In three years I had made the Kings one of the elite teams of the NHL. The problem was, two other dominant teams played in our division. In 1990 we beat one of them—the Calgary Flames—in the first playoff series and then ran smack into the other, the Edmonton Oilers. With Wayne hobbled by a back injury that severely limited his ice time, we were swept in four games and the hockey press began to say once again that Edmonton had gotten the better of me in the big Gretzky deal. In fact, the Oilers *had* skated an entire offensive line made up of players they acquired from me in the trade. Those same players propelled them all the way to a 4–1 Stanley Cup victory over the Boston Bruins.

For me, the highlight that would stick in my mind long after the season ended was not from the playoffs but from a game in Edmonton where Gretzky just happened to break the points record held by his childhood hero, Gordie Howe. In a moment comparable to Hank Aaron surpassing Babe Ruth, Wayne made a backhanded goal to send the game into overtime and break Howe's record of 1,850 assists and goals. They stopped the game and held a ceremony on the ice. I went out there with Janet and his father. I gave him a gift of 1,851 Canadian gold pieces. I gave Howe, who was there too, 1,850 silver dollars. And wouldn't you know it, in overtime Wayne scored another goal to win the game for the Kings.

After the season, when Wayne's excellent play was not rewarded by an excellent run in the playoffs, we talked about what had to be done to build up the team. I made no secret of the fact that I consulted Wayne. Why shouldn't I ask the best hockey player who ever lived for advice?

But many fans and some sportswriters complained that Gretzky played too big a role in my management of the Kings. We were good friends and successful partners in a host of outside interests. And the plain fact was that he did influence most of the trades and acquisitions we pursued. But I never saw a problem with that. Who in the world knew more about hockey, and more about winning Stanley Cups, than Wayne Gretzky?

Besides, I knew that I could assert myself whenever it was necessary. A case in point was Sam McMaster, who served briefly as general manager. Sam was nominated for the job by Wayne, who had played for Sam as a junior in Toronto. Wayne insisted that Sam's eye for young talent was unmatched. However, when the team didn't perform all that well, I was willing to let Sam go, especially when it seemed as if players believed Wayne might be controlling their fates through Sam. None of that was true. He was not one of Wayne's stooges. But the only thing I could do to clear the air was replace him.

With winners like my horses, and the Kings, our confidence was high enough that in that time period, Steve Nessenblatt actually informed European American Bank that we were operating from more than one set of books. That conversation came about when the bank's new management team, which followed Ray Dempsey's crew, began to review our accounts. They were apparently unaware of the circular arrangement that had been used to get EAB out of Gladden. Steve told them all about it, including the part where I was assured that I would never have to repay the principal—$20 million— used to pay off Credit Lyonnais. At one heated moment in the conversation, Steve told the bankers "if I go to jail, we can go together." That seemed to settle their worries about our loans, because they quickly stopped pressing for more payments. They knew, of course, that EAB officers had urged us to hide that loan from Credit Lyonnais.

Though it was a rare event, it was not uncommon for bankers to perform their own little manipulations. More than once we were asked to juggle some numbers so that auditors, and government overseers, wouldn't catch a poorly performing loan on a bank's books. Early in 1991, a Bank of America representative hit us up for cash to pay his credit-card bills. We were happy to do it because he would soon help us finance another big move, yet another attempt to rescue ourselves. We let the end justify the means.

It began with contacts I made while serving on the board of Hollywood Park racetrack. During a big showdown I had sided with a faction, led by Harry Ornest, that successfully installed more aggressive management led by R.D. Hubbard. I believed that Hubbard had a better vision for the future of the track. He did turn the operation around, and made it extremely profitable. Ornest had once owned the St. Louis Blues hockey team and a baseball team in Vancouver, British Columbia. Nearly seventy years old, Harry was tired of teams and athletes and eager to sell his remaining sports franchise, the Toronto Argonauts of the Canadian Football League.

The Argos, as they were called, had slid with the rest of the CFL into a state of decay. The entire league's fan base had been eroded by the National Football League, which broadcast games to almost every Canadian home. At the same time, a number of NFL teams in border states—Buffalo, Detroit, even Seattle—were drawing Canadian fans to their stadiums. You could hardly blame the fans. The caliber of play was much greater in the NFL, and the production value of each event—the stadiums, cheerleaders, music, even the food—was much higher.

Considered as simply a CFL franchise, the Argos didn't make a whole lot of business sense. In fact, the only teams in the league that seemed to have a strong future were those from minor cities, farther away from the American market, where local people had fewer options for entertainment. The Saskatchewan Rough Riders and the Edmonton Eskimos were more likely to make profits than the Argos.

On the other hand, the Argos did play in Toronto, the most populous and important city in Canada. And they occupied the country's best ballpark, the $315 million SkyDome. As I studied the team, I realized that its most valuable asset was the long-term lease giving them the exclusive right to all football played under the dome. Given that Toronto already sported a baseball team that played in the American League, and talk was circulating about an NBA franchise, it was reasonable to think that the NFL might also be lured to Toronto. The Skydome lease would give whoever owned the Argos a huge advantage in the fight for the franchise. And an NFL franchise can be worth hundreds of millions of dollars.

The idea of switching the Argonauts to the NFL was not part of my negotiations with Harry Ornest. We stuck to the basics—the team's expenses, cash flow, and assets. Harry wanted $5 million, and was willing to finance a big piece of it. The Bank of America agreed to provide a line of credit for the team's operation.

As I considered what would be needed to promote the Argos, I decided to bring in a couple of partners. I turned first to Gretzky, who had loved the team as a kid and was the most revered athlete in Canada. It didn't take him more than a minute to decide he wanted to do it. Then I went to actor/comedian John Candy, who was born and raised in the Toronto area. He leaped at the opportunity.

I could not imagine an owner better equipped to promote the team. Candy, who could make you laugh by merely raising an eyebrow, was a sports nut. In L.A., I had made him the celebrity captain of the Kings. He then took it upon himself to film, for free, an absolutely hysterical commercial in which he played a TV reporter searching for celebrities at The Forum. As an actual owner of the Argos, John would do similar commercials, make countless public appearances, and coax many of his Hollywood friends into the owner's box for Argos home games. The box, by the way, became one of John's favorite places in all the world. After we bought the team, he spent $250,000 refurbishing and decorating it with the help of a interior designer he brought to Toronto from Los Angeles.

During that time, my relationship with John became very close. Besides going to games together, we socialized. I met his wife, Rose, his children, and his mother. We shared a lot of meals together. We often talked about his film projects and the challenges of navigating Hollywood. (Like many actors, John had trouble sometimes distinguishing who his real friends were, and who he could trust.) He was fun to be around, but there was more to the relationship than that. We felt genuine affection for each other.

As valuable as Candy and Gretzky could be as promoters, to make the Argos succeed we needed to win games, and the team did not have a tradition of winning. In forty years they had taken the Grey Cup—the CFL's Super Bowl—just once. Reversing that trend would require good management—we hired Mike McCarthy and Brian Cooper to solve the problem—and a bold move, like my trade for Gretzky in 1988. Of course, we could never coax any of the NFL's best stars to Canada. But we would go after the top college player eligible to turn pro, Raghib "Rocket" Ismail.

A lightning quick offensive specialist, Rocket had set records as a receiver and kick-returner at Notre Dame. Edged out of the Heisman trophy by Ty Detmer, he was nevertheless named college player of the year by both the *Sporting News* and the Walter Camp Foundation. Every team in the NFL wanted him. But none courted him the way we did. We invited him to Los Angeles. I took him on a shopping trip along Rodeo Drive, and then to games at The Forum and Dodgers Stadium. He met Wayne, which was a big deal for him, and John Candy. For a while, Rocket was Su Waks's main priority. She spent days and weeks catering to him and his mother.

At first Rocket had qualms about the CFL, but we had him talk to Joe Theisman and a few other Americans who had played in Canada, and they made him feel better about the league. He was impressed by the financial package we put together, which included $17 million for four years and a chance to own part of the team if its value increased due to his play. The contract was unusual because it was a personal services contract, which meant that Rocket would be required to perform duties off the field as well as on. But the amount was far in excess of what he would have earned in the United States. His agent had made certain of that.

Although the numbers were persuasive, I came to believe that two other factors made Rocket take our offer. The first was the idea that he would raise the profile of the entire league and, like Gretzky, become the face of the sport. Second was a secret arrangement I made with Al Davis, owner of the Oakland Raiders. Davis and I spoke several times during my negotiations with Rocket. I told him that we would likely release Ismail after two years, making him eligible to move to the NFL. Davis then drafted him, banking on a future deal that both he and Rocket would find profitable.

When the press learned that Ismail would be an Argo, the story was front page from coast to coast. The Sunday magazine of the *Financial Post* put me on its cover, touting me as the potential savior of the entire CFL. The only troubling sign amid all the hubbub was Rocket's discomfort with the media and fans. He was a positive, fairly charming young man, but he clearly did not like doing interviews or making public appearances. Getting endorsement deals for that kind of athlete would be tough.

A number of sportswriters noted that I was handling the Argos the way I had managed the Kings, but it took the dollars-and-sense view of *Business-Week* to recognize that I was also pioneering a new kind of owner-athlete relationship. In just a few years I had gone from Wayne Gretzky's boss to his partner. I had introduced him to horse racing, where he had done quite well, and he had gotten involved in the Argos in a way that surely pleased much of Canada. The most visible deal Wayne and I ever made involved the purchase of a scrap of cardboard just a few inches square. Okay, it wasn't just any scrap of cardboard. It was the T206 Honus Wagner baseball card.

I had just started a joint venture—to sell high-end sports memorabilia—with a company called Upper Deck, when the Wagner card came up for sale. I am not an avid sports card collector. But in every field there is an item that even outsiders recognize as the most important. In ancient coins it's the Athenian decadrachm. Among those who collect pennies, the 1909 Lincoln SVDB is the ultimate. In baseball cards it's the Honus Wagner card from the T206 set, a mint-condition example of the most valued card on Earth.

What makes the 1909 Wagner card so valuable? It's another case of a good story equaling cash. A great shortstop with the Pittsburgh Pirates, Wagner was adamantly opposed to smoking. But when the Piedmont Cigarette Company planned to put his picture on a card to be inserted in packs of smokes, he faced a dilemma. Sportswriters served as rights agents for the company. Wagner liked the writer who handled Pittsburgh, and didn't want to deprive the man of his fee, so he paid him $10 to keep his picture off the card. How was it that the card was made anyway? Moved by Wagner's generosity, the writer refused to cash the check. Unfortunately the shortstop's preference wasn't heeded by the company, and the card was printed anyway. Among the fifty known to exist today, the one offered for sale in 1991 was in the best condition. It was practically perfect, showing a somber Wagner, dressed in a uniform buttoned up to his chin, and the words beneath: WAGNER, PITTSBURG.

In early 1991, old Honus's sour face stared out at me from the pages of a catalog from Sotheby's auction house. When Wayne came in the office that day, I showed it to him. He had collected baseball cards as a kid, and had heard of that one. "Hey," I said, almost kidding, "you want to go in with me on this?" For me it would be both an investment, and great publicity for my project with Upper Deck. Wayne simply thought it would be a very exciting to own a piece of history.

The catalog suggested the card's value was $100,000 to $200,000. However, I knew from experience, beginning way back in the coin business, that anything could happen at an auction. Wayne and I agreed we would spend $250,000 if required. On the day of the sale we made a conference call to New York, so that we could bid long-distance. The bidding reached $300,000 before we could say anything.

"Wayne, what do you want to do?" I asked

"Let's go," he said.

And we did. Bang, bang, bang before we could catch a breath we had paid $400,000 to capture the card. With commission, the total price would be $451,0000, a world record for a collectible card. We heard cheering in New York, and immediately the person on the phone wanted to know if Sotheby's could release the names of the buyers. For me, that was the whole idea.

The purchase of the card put me in the spotlight once again, standing next to Wayne Gretzky. Not long afterward, the magician David Copperfield invited us, and the card, to participate in a TV magic special. The show was filmed on a soundstage in Las Vegas. With us standing right there, he took the card in his hands, and appeared to tear it up. Though he had assured us the card was safe, Copperfield was convincing enough to make me sweat a bit before he appeared to magically put it back together.

We took the card on the road again when a national convention for sports memorabilia was held at the Anaheim Convention Center. The card was sealed in plastic and set on a well-guarded pedestal. Thousands of people lined up to walk past it, like the crowds at the Tower of London gazing at the crown jewels. A poster showing Wayne and me with the card was offered to the viewers. I probably signed two thousand of them in the one day I spent there.

. . .

If you think that signing thousands of autographs is a boost to the ego, try basking in the cheers of forty thousand football fans who believe you have come to save their team and maybe their league. The Argos' Rocket-powered home opener was scheduled for a midsummer night when the Toronto Blue Jays baseball team gave up the field. I took the Kings' silver-and-black 727 to Toronto, with a crowd of people that included Jim Belushi, Mariel Hemingway, Wayne, and our friend from Bank of America, Mike Rossi. Ten limousines met us at the airport. By the time we arrived at the SkyDome, it was literally vibrating with excitement.

We won the game against Hamilton 41–18. Hobbled by a slight injury, Rocket didn't exactly soar. The stars of the game were quarterback Ricky Foggie and running back Mike "Pinball" Clemons, a five-foot five-inch fan favorite. Foggie, Clemons and our halftime entertainers gave so much that few noticed that Rocket had fizzled. All through the game John Candy wandered the stadium, leading cheers and getting the crowd excited. At halftime his friends Dan Aykroyd and Jim Belushi put on a Blues Brothers concert, with John and Mariel joining them at the end.

Word of the excitement generated at the game spread quickly. That season attendance grew by more than 20 percent, as the Argos drew more fans than they had had in more than two decades. As Ismail began to perform, running back kicks and catching long passes, we even boosted the crowds at other stadiums around the league. More than fifty-three thousand people turned out in Vancouver to see the Argos and Rocket Ismail battle against the Lions, led by the league's other famous American player, Doug Flutie. Ismail caught a pass for the first touchdown of the game, but Flutie threw for three scores in what would be a rare loss for the Argos.

Over the course of the season Rocket performed well, but not in a dominating way. To be fair, it's rare that a football player can affect a game the way a Wayne Gretzky can in hockey. For one thing, the division of offense and defense means that no one plays every down. Even so, I was a little disappointed by Rocket, especially off the field. His media presence was limited by his shyness, and his endorsement value never really rose. Nevertheless, he helped bring us thirteen wins, the second highest in team history.

At the end of the regular season the Argos stood atop the Eastern Division with a 13–5 record, the best in the league. We achieved it with explosive offensive play. In one game against Edmonton our quarterback threw five touchdown passes, three to Ismail. Rocket almost broke the team record for average yards gained per catch (20.3). Overall, the 1991 team posted the second highest point total in more than one hundred years of Argo football.

The largest SkyDome crowd in eighteen years saw us win our division playoff game, and then we went to Winnipeg for the Grey Cup game with the Calgary Stampeders. The cup game was played on November 24, but it was cold enough—15 degrees—to feel like February. Martin Short, Mariel Hemingway, Jim Belushi, and Alan Thicke all came to Winnipeg and froze in the stands. I never felt so cold in my life as I wandered between the sideline and a sheltered area next to the field. The game went well for us and we led from early on. But in the final quarter Calgary scored a touchdown and pulled within one point.

After Calgary's touchdown, Wayne, John Candy, and I went down to the sidelines. We tried to encourage the players. As he ran out with the kick-receiving team, Rocket turned to me and said, "Don't worry. I got this."

The kick flew to the thirteen yard line where Rocket fielded the frozen ball and began running. Wayne, John, and I started screaming after he dodged the first few tacklers. Soon we were following him down the field as he ran eighty-seven yards for a touchdown. We won by a score of 36–21. When we got back to Toronto they gave us a parade, and we three owners rode together in the same convertible.

The Argo championship was a personal thrill and it did rejuvenate football in Toronto. But as soon as the season ended we knew that we were still losers in the ledger books, where, despite huge increases in ticket sales, we were still millions of dollars in the red. The most troubling aspect of our finances was the fact that we had won everything there was to win, and still didn't turn a profit. It might have been better, from a business standpoint, if we had lost the Grey Cup game. That would have given us something big to shoot for in the next season, and a reason for the fans to cheer us on. Now, having achieved the big goal in our first year, we faced the much more difficult challenge of repeating as titleholders.

With that in mind, I began to get a little more serious about the NFL. I even went to Cleveland for secret meetings with Art Modell, owner of the Browns. Art made it clear to me that he couldn't make a go of it in Cleveland and was going to move his team, despite the uproar it would cause in the city. Toronto was on his list of options, and since the Argos held the football rights at the SkyDome, there was an opportunity for us to do business together.

No matter what Modell and I discussed, it was all speculation until an actual deal was proposed. Even then, we had to navigate the NFL's rules and the opposition that would surely arise in Cleveland. At the same time I would have to bring along my partners and the fans in Toronto who remained attached to the CFL. Wayne would likely choose the best option from a business standpoint, but I could not make the same assumption about John Candy. In our first season he had fallen madly in love with the team. In fact, he had begun to spend far more time on football than on his career as an actor. He made friends with the players, cooked team dinners at his home outside the city, and even worked out with some of the linemen. He had become an Argo right down to his soul.

"Who can doubt this man . . . everything McNall touches turns to gold."

I didn't say it. *Sports Illustrated* did. And they weren't alone. Across the U.S. and Canada the media portrayed me as the man I wanted to be—rich, powerful, successful, charismatic. It was true, if all you considered was how well my horses ran and how many games my teams won. The only sour note in a symphony of praise came from *Forbes* magazine, which printed vague doubts about my finances. Few of the people I dealt with paid much attention.

Forbes is a cranky old Eastern publication. What could they know about the high-flying entertainment industry?

I was still determined to find a miracle that would rescue all my businesses. The most obvious thing I could do would be to win the Stanley Cup, which would generate millions in immediate income and, more importantly, raise the value of the Kings. A championship would also inflate my perceived value as a businessman, making it easier for me to find new deals and get better terms from banks and others. Everyone wants to ride with a winner. And once they get on board, they will do what it takes to keep the ride going.

I couldn't put the puck in the goal, but I could try to get the kinds of players that Gretzky needed to help him seize the championship. In 1990, I made one of the most controversial moves of my tenure as owner when I traded Bernie Nichols to New York for Tony Granato and Tomas Sandstrom, two younger players with great potential. It was a difficult decision because Nichols was a longtime King who had scored seventy goals the previous season. He was also a personal friend, and the tale of how I broke the news to him became a bit of NHL lore.

Normally a general manager or coach would tell a player he had been traded, but Bernie and I were close. I knew how much he loved the team, and Los Angeles. His wife, Heather, felt the same way. When it turned out that the trade was finalized on the day of the All-Star game, an All-Star game that Bernie had been selected to play, I went straight to see him. He was obviously upset, and we spent a little time talking about how much he had meant to the Kings. Then he had to change his jersey, from the West All-Star team to the East team. I'm not sure if an All-Star player had ever been traded out of his division on game day like that.

Granato and Sandstrom turned out to be great new additions to the Kings, but we needed even more depth. In May of 1991, my general manager Rogie Vachon pulled off a complicated deal that brought us Finland's greatest athlete, right-winger Jari Kurri. Along with being a perennial all-star, Kurri had played ten seasons with the powerful Edmonton Oilers, eight of them alongside Gretzky. We would reunite them, add left-winger Tomas Sandstrom to the line, and instantly own the best offensive unit in the NHL.

The same complicated deal brought us Jeff Chychrun, a six-foot four-inch, 215-pound defenseman. Hardly a scorer—he had just three goals in two hundred games—Chychrun was a player you throw onto the ice to intimidate opponents. As much as Wayne had spoken against the violent strain of hockey that Chychrun represented, it was a fact of life in the NHL. We needed guys like him to protect our smaller, speedier scorers.

A few fans questioned my moves. One wrote to the *L.A. Times* to say that although I had made a fortune on antique coins, I would "not win the Stanley Cup buying antique hockey players such as Jari Kurri . . ."

The response among the Kings players was different. On the day he found out about the deal, Wayne took me and Marty McSorley out to celebrate at one of his favorite restaurants, up in the Hollywood hills. Wayne had more big-league ice time logged than Kurri, but could still skate and score with the twenty-year-olds. He knew that Jari could still play, and he talked about a breakthrough in the coming season. We all hoped we would get past two rounds and into the finals. But in the months to come, Wayne's father would suffer an aneurysm, and his anguished son would have the worst hockey season of his life. Our Stanley Cup dream would be delayed for a year.

No sane businessman puts all of his hope into a sports franchise and its championship run. That's the quickest way to the nuthouse, or the poorhouse. I certainly wasn't focused solely on the Kings. I had other opportunities and problems to deal with, and somehow I managed to attend to them all.

Among the problems, Gladden still festered. Every week I met David Begelman for lunch and we reviewed the company's situation. The debt held by Credit Lyonnais was well over $100 million. On the positive side, our library of finished films, from *Mr. Mom* to *The Fabulous Baker Boys*, generated some income from video rentals and TV fees. Better still was the news from our recent release, *Weekend at Bernie's*, a creepy-strange comedy that grossed $30 million. *Bernie's* offset *Mannequin Two: On the Move* and a film called *Short Time*, which together earned just $8 million, far less than it cost to make them.

The real trouble was not the performance of completed films, but the future. *Mannequin Two* had been number ten in our ten-picture arrangement with Fox. We would need a new distributor to finance new productions and get them into theaters. David had been working the town, pouring all the charm he had polished over his seventy-plus years, into the task of finding a new deal. Though every door he knocked on opened, he met resistance when he got inside. Gladden had never made a breakout film. David was seen as someone who might be too old to understand the youth-dominated movie market. And then there was his history. Not everyone had forgiven David's sins.

Even as David gamely trouped from one executive suite to another, a team from the new management group at Credit Lyonnais came to Los Angeles to review our prospects. I had lunch with them in Century City. I began the meeting by reviewing the bank's role in the Cannon fiasco.

"You understand, I hope, that what happened is the result of the bank's actions," I said. "You are not going to get repaid." When they sputtered something about taking over the company, I told them that would be fine. "Go ahead, take Gladden," I said. "But if you come after my personal guarantee, I'll sue you."

In the short term, no one at Credit Lyonnais had any interest in forcing the issue. But it was obvious that bankruptcy loomed over the company. David put the best face on things. He continued to scout new scripts and stars. He seemed to believe that our struggles were temporary. We cut back on some expenses, and let some people go. But David's million-dollar salary and enormous expense account were sacrosanct. For him, keeping up appearances was not just a matter of maintaining the facade of a successful businessman. The appearance of success defined him. Without it, he would be nothing. Worried about his state of mind, I encouraged him to soldier on, and assured him I would try to keep the bankers away.

. . .

The best banker repellent in the world is cash, and I worked feverishly to get it. For a brief time I believed that the answer to all my troubles lay a mile and a half below the surface of the Atlantic Ocean, aboard a nineteenth-century steamship called the S.S. *Central America*.

Practically forgotten, the sinking of the *Central America* was a pivotal historical event. In late summer 1857, she had sailed from Panama carrying literally tons of California gold and more than five hundred passengers. As the ship rounded the tip of Florida, it was struck by a ferocious hurricane. For three days the crew fought against leaks that threatened to douse the coal-fired boilers. When they finally lost the fight, everyone aboard joined a bucket brigade that kept the vessel afloat another thirty hours. Nearly all the women and children were successfully transferred to a passing ship, but 425 men drowned in America's worst civilian shipping disaster. The loss of the gold, bound for banks in New York, created a national financial panic.

Eclipsed by the Civil War, Lincoln's assassination, and the Reconstruction, the tale of the S.S. *Central America* was largely forgotten until a Midwestern engineer named Tommy Thompson became enthralled with the notion of finding her and claiming the treasure. Thompson and two partners raised $12 million and developed both the technology and the research to find the ship. In 1988 they succeeded, locating her lying right side up on the ocean floor, eight thousand feet down.

With a one-of-a-kind recovery sub named *Nemo*, Thompson and his team quickly found *Central America*'s spectacular trove of gold. Solid bars, the size of bricks, were scattered by the hundreds on the seabed. Stacks of gold coins looked as if they had been gently knocked over on a table. Many were identified as freshly minted "double eagle" gold pieces, worth $100,000 apiece. Oversized gold bars, one the largest ever seen, were stacked one upon the other like cinderblocks. Piles of gold dust, left behind as carpet bags dissolving in the seawater, waited to be vacuumed up.

As raw gold, *Central America*'s treasure was immensely valuable. However, the cache would be worth much more if each of its pieces were preserved and then sold as a collectible item. Estimating how much money the hoard might bring was difficult, but the figure could have been $1 billion or more. Of course to get to that figure you had to parcel it out very slowly, to avoid flooding the market and thereby lowering prices. The trick was to maintain interest in the gold, through carefully orchestrated publicity, so that each new lot offered for sale would find eager buyers.

I explained all of this to Tommy Thompson many, many times. We got to know each other because Superior Coins, one of the companies I controlled, had signed a promotion agreement with his firm. The deal, in which we put up $3 million, allowed for us to make money on the S.S. *Central America* story, through movies, books, even a theme-park ride. We worked hard on those kinds of things, but every time I presented an idea to Thompson, he couldn't make a decision. He would keep me on the phone for hours, sometimes five or six hours, examining something as simple as the development of a movie.

In his own work, Thompson's compulsive approach had been the foundation of enormous success. Before ever going to sea, he had spent more than five years asking questions and seeking answers about the S.S. *Central America*. He had plugged thousands of bits of data into a computer model that had suggested the ship would be found in an area of the ocean that was one thousand two hundred miles square. More painstaking work had gotten him so much closer to his goal that when he finally sent his custom-made, truck-sized robot for the first time, it landed almost on the deck of the sunken ship.

Experience had taught Thompson that his modus operandi worked, and like the guy with a hammer who thinks everything is a nail, he applied it to every problem. I would spend hours and hours on the phone with Tommy discussing promotions. Su Waks, Nora Rothrock, and others would stand in my office door and wave good night. The lights would be switched off in other offices. The clock might tick past midnight, and still Tommy would ramble on about hundreds of things that might or might not happen. Eventually he got so uptight that he prohibited me from even speaking to anyone about promoting his find, without his approval.

Frustrated as I was, I never hung up on Tommy Thompson. The stakes were too high. Surely, I thought, he understood that he must sell the gold in order to pay off all the expenses fronted by his investors, and give them profits. But on that topic Tommy could also speak endlessly about possibilities and problems. Every coin, art, and collectibles dealer in the world was aware of the S.S. *Central America* project. It's likely that half of them had already approached Thompson and been rejected. But though I had his ear, or rather he had mine, he refused to make a commitment.

He did, however, pay me to testify in his successful defense against various lawsuits filed by insurance companies and others that claimed to have legal rights to the gold. I flew to Norfolk, Virginia, where I was picked up in a car that had blackened windows. We drove around for more than an hour before we got to a well-guarded industrial building. Inside I was shown a big vault, which was opened to give me a view of more gold than I had ever seen in my life. Bars were stacked high and trays were piled with coins. At court I affirmed that what I saw, properly marketed, would bring in more than $1 billion.

Thompson and his crew won every trial on claims against the treasure. But even then he wouldn't make a commitment to anything we proposed, not for marketing, not for promotion. An IMAX movie? Let's think about it. A tour of major museums? Umm, I don't know. A feature film? Let's discuss it some more. The frustration I felt was enormous, especially considering all the time I had invested in Thompson. He knew I couldn't be compensated if he refused to act, and yet he was willing to have me develop an endless number of plans and proposals that he would never endorse.

With our debts rising, and new businesses stalled, we had no choice but to liquidate more assets. Allen Paulson agreed to buy out my shares in all the horses we owned together. He paid $10 million and ended up with some of his greatest stallions, including Strawberry Road and Jade Hunter. Our other ponies didn't sell quite so well, because the overall market was depressed.

To buy more time we then put together a collection of coins, borrowed coins, that we presented to Bank of America as assets. We brought some loan officers to the office and offered the coins as collateral for a million-dollar loan. That coin trick—my last—got us $20 million at high interest.

Although $20 million might seem like a great deal of cash, it could only get us through a few months. A bigger solution, one requiring a giant business partner, had to be found. Prior to the start of the 1992–93 season, I hired an attorney named Mark Eastman for the sole purpose of finding a way to build a new arena. Our ultimate goal would be a mega deal that would involve a modern new facility where both the Kings and the Lakers would play. Whoever built the stadium would also take ownership of the Kings, and possibly the Lakers. We could cash out for more than $100 million and, aside from the Gladden debt, be free.

In all the world, few individuals or corporations would have interest in such a project, let alone possess the money and power to pull it off. R.D. Hubbard came forward with the idea of building an arena on Hollywood Park property and acquiring the team. Another option, which took off more quickly, was suggested by Gary Winnick, a coin client who would later create Global Crossing, a behemoth in telecommunications. Over lunch one day Winnick said I needed a true entertainment company, a firm with mass-marketing expertise and very deep pockets. A company like Sony.

Access to Sony would come via Peter Guber, who had been chosen to head Columbia Pictures when the Japanese conglomerate bought it in 1989. Soon he was in charge of all of the company's Hollywood operations, which were organized under an umbrella called Sony Pictures Entertainment. Winnick and I both knew Peter. I had met him in the mid-1970s when he was producing his film, *The Deep*. He had made us feel comfortable, in his hyperkinetic way. Besides being a frenetic, exhausting person to be around, Peter is a very smart businessman with a long-range vision.

Soon after we began our talks, Peter said he could see the value of the deal we were suggesting. He wanted to do it. But Sony was a big, complicated bureaucracy, so he needed time and support. We agreed to form a couple of teams to take care of the details—mine was headed by Mark Eastman—and set them to work immediately. In Guber, I hoped, I had found the angel who would finally make my problems go away.

With L.A. Kings players.

HARRY BENSON

With Wayne Gretzky and John Candy, partners in the Toronto Argonauts.

PETER READ MILLER

In the early '80s with my first love, ancient coins.

MICHAEL JACOBS

At the 1993 Stanley Cup Finals, L.A. Kings vs. Montreal Canadiens, with (left to right) Goldie Hawn, Mrs. Nancy Reagan, former president Ronald Reagan, and Michael Eisner, chairman of The Disney Company.

DAVID E. KLUTHO/*SPORTS ILLUSTRATED*

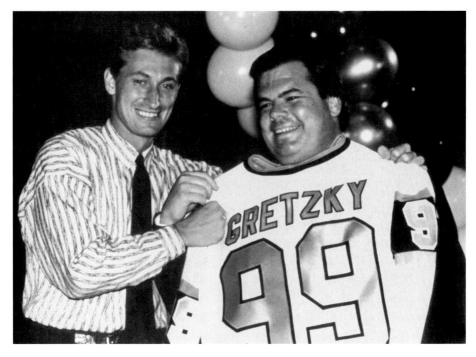

With Wayne Gretzky at the press conference announcing the "Trade of the Century," August 9, 1988.

ROBERT BECK/ICON SMI

L.A. Kings celebrating the 1991 playoff victory.

ROBERT BECK/ICON SMI

Receiving City of Hope Award as "Man of the Year" from my friend and partner, actor John Candy. Beverly Hilton Hotel, 1991.

SCOTT DOWNIE/CELEBRITY PHOTO.COM

With Alan Thicke at City of Hope Dinner in my honor, Beverly Hilton Hotel, 1991.

SCOTT DOWNIE/CELEBRITY PHOTO.COM

With Neil Diamond at party celebrating Kings opening night.

SCOTT DOWNIE/CELEBRITY PHOTO.COM

With hockey star and good friend Luc Robitaille in Kings dressing room following a victory, April 1989.

PETER C. BORSARI

With L.A. Kings coach Barry Melrose and Sony president Alan Levine.

PETER C. BORSARI

With L.A. Dodger star Orel Hershiser.

PETER C. BORSARI

With Motown founder
Berry Gordy.

PETER C. BORSARI

Celebrating the signing of
Rocket Ismail, who was
the projected No. 1 pick
of the NFL, to the
Toronto Argonauts.

AP/WIDE WORLD PHOTOS

Los Angeles, October 4,
1988—Wayne Gretzky,
Michael J. Fox, and I
pose for a photo during
a reception to celebrate
the opening of the
1988–1989 NHL season.

AP/WIDE WORLD PHOTOS

In the paddock with Saumarez before his victory in Europe's most prestigious race, "L'Arc de Triomphe." Behind the horse's head are Nicolas Clement, the trainer; Gerald Mosse, the jockey; and me.

APRH CHANTILLY

W H Hunt   N. B. Hunt

Herbert and Bunker Hunt testifying before Congress, May 2, 1980.

BETTMANN/CORBIS

Leaving the federal courthouse after entering plea for bank fraud.

AP/WIDE WORLD PHOTOS

Robert Geringer with me in prison khakis.

10

ONE MORE SEASON. WHEN HIS TIME is winding down, every athlete wants one more chance for glory. It's what owners want, too. Despite all the financial crises, and because the Kings might well be sold, I was determined to make another drive for the Stanley Cup. That is why in May of 1992, after one more no-cigar playoff series, I fired coach Tom Webster.

I felt like firing everyone. Given all the effort and money I had invested in acquiring Wayne and rebuilding the team, our first-round defeat to Edmonton was unacceptable. To be fair to Tom, he hadn't taken to the ice for us. But our problems in the 1991–92 season were as much a matter of attitude as poor play. There were important moments when too many players just didn't seem committed to winning. When that occurs, it's up to the coach to fix it. Tom didn't. There was also the matter of the twelve-game suspension he had served in mid-season for throwing sticks on the ice in a fit of pique. No coach had ever been banned for so many games.

Along with letting Webster go, I moved Rogie Vachon to a new job as my assistant and promoted Roy Mlakar to the position of president. Together we then hired our new coach, Barry Melrose. Just thirty-five years old, Melrose had been an extremely successful coach for amateur teams in the U.S. and Canada before signing on with the Detroit Red Wings organization. In the season just ended he had guided Adirondack, the Wings' top minor league franchise, to the championship of the American Hockey League. A devotee of self-help guru Tony Robbins, Barry believed that a positive attitude and intense focus could solve almost any problem in life. (He would bring Robbins in to give talks to the players, most of whom smirked and tried to leave as soon as possible.) Melrose was also more offense-minded than Tom Webster. He also favored more aggressive play. I thought the team needed his toughness.

Melrose would prove his value when Wayne was sidelined by back problems before the season even started. Gretzky had played in pain the previous season, believing he had a rib injury. A thorough exam uncovered a herniated disk, caused by years of poundings from defensemen. With the diagnosis, he was ordered off the ice to avoid permanent spinal cord damage. Doctors said it would be months before they could tell when, or even if, he could play again.

Wayne was more optimistic, declaring that he would come back in a matter of months. But we had to prepare for life without him. Melrose began preaching that his team would win, even without its superstar. The team believed him, and in the first game of the season went to Calgary and beat the Flames 5–4. They flew home happy the next day, but on a commercial jet, not *Air McNall*. To save expenses, I had leased my plane to the election campaign of the Democrat running for president: Bill Clinton.

The hockey team, which played to sellout crowds almost every game, was my refuge from all the stress of bad loans, bad art and coin markets, and bad choices I had made in the past. At The Forum I dealt with executives, rank-and-file employees, and professional athletes who knew their jobs and did them well. We solved problems together. We won and lost together. I wanted to be around them all the time.

Instead, I constantly acquired new responsibilities that made it more difficult for me to enjoy the Kings. The biggest, the job of chairman of the National Hockey League, was practically forced upon me in the summer of 1992 by a group of owners who banded together at the NHL's annual meeting. (Among them were Howard Baldwin of the Penguins; Stan Jaffee of the Rangers, who also ran Paramount Studios; George and Gordon Gund of the San Jose Sharks; Ed Snider of the Philadelphia Flyers; Mike Illitch of the Detroit Red Wings; Abe Poulin and Dick Patrick of the Washington Capitals; and Jerry Jacobs of the Boston Bruins.) The league was in a bit of a slump, and they hoped a new style of leadership would improve things.

I think they picked me because my image in sports—with the Kings, the Argos, and horses—had been inflated to the size of one of those balloons at the Macy's Thanksgiving Day Parade. I had worked miracles with the Kings and the Argos. My horses, or at least the ones people heard about, were the class of the track. If I could succeed in all those venues, they hoped, I could do the same for the NHL.

If only they knew. As I looked around the league conference table, I could see that I was probably the only one whose personal and corporate debt outweighed his assets. These were truly powerful people who controlled great individual fortunes or represented massive corporations. Yet they wanted me to replace Chicago owner Bill Wirtz, the longtime chairman, and move us in a new direction. I felt a bit like an impostor, but when they said they needed me, I couldn't say no. It was never my style to say no, especially to powerful people. My impulse was to do whatever it took to please them.

Once I was nominated to be chairman, the vote was unanimous. As soon as it was recorded, I was handed a gavel. The next item on our agenda was the matter of appointing an interim executive to handle the day-to-day business of the league. Previous president John Ziegler had, in the opinion of some owners, mishandled labor negotiations. His former ally, Wirtz, had gotten a group of veteran owners together and gotten rid of him. Wirtz's choice to succeed him was league lawyer Gil Stein.

I liked Gil Stein. He knew hockey. He knew the NHL, and he was a smart, funny man. At every league meeting he rose before the final gavel and recited an epic-length poem that recounted every thing we had accomplished with plenty of humor. The trouble was his connection to the old guard represented by Wirtz and its way of doing things. My election as chairman was proof that their day was over. I voted with the rest of the owners to name him interim president, but I was confident that the search committee we created to find a permanent leader would pick someone else.

I believed that the NHL needed the kind of management that had energized the National Basketball Association, our main rival for fan dollars. In the decade that had just passed, NBA attendance and revenues had risen spectacularly. The boom was due in part to superstars such as Michael Jordan, but it was also aided by skillful promotion by the NBA's head office. At the center of their efforts was a solid TV contract that put the game into America's living rooms every weekend all winter long.

The obvious and audacious move would have been to bring NBA commissioner David Stern over to our league. I knew Stern. We had even discussed the idea of me buying into an NBA franchise. Soon after the NHL league meetings I called him and said straight out, "The guy I want is you."

It was impossible, he said. His contract and personal loyalties would keep him where he was, no matter what kind of offer we made.

"If I can't have you," I then said, "I want either Russ Grannick or Gary Bettman." (These were the NBA's other key management people.)

"Goddamn you," said Stern, with mock outrage in his voice. "I knew you were going to do this, but I don't blame you. Don't talk to Russ Grannick. But you have permission to talk to Bettman."

A lawyer, Bettman was very aggressive, very smart, very good at dealing with the huge personalities that populate the sports business. He had handled a lot of legal affairs for the NBA, and collective bargaining. Can you imagine how much diplomacy you must exercise when dealing with employees who are immensely wealthy, and whose talents are your only product?

When we spoke, I told Bettman it didn't matter that he came from basketball. He could learn the ins and outs of hockey. What mattered was that he had worked at the top of a very successful league. Now he would have the chance to apply what he had learned as president of his own organization. He loved the idea.

Other candidates were considered by the search committee. Gil Stein remained a viable option, and other owners recommended people. At a day-long meeting we interviewed each finalist. I saved Bettman for last. He made it clear, in a matter of minutes, that he was the best choice. He knew everything there was to know about the league. He understood collective bargaining and television contracts. And his personality—tough, direct, levelheaded—was just what the job required.

The one thing going against Bettman was the fact that he was not a hockey insider. For years the NHL had suffered from an inferiority complex where the NBA was concerned. Hockey people were jealous of the money that basketball teams made, the high visibility of that game's stars, and the NBA's big TV contract. It was left for Abe Poulin, who owned franchises in both leagues—The Bullets of the NBA and The Capitals of the NHL—to give Bettman the hockey blessing.

"Why'd you waste our time?" he said, teasing. "You knew this was the guy."

All that was left was for the full board of governors, representing all the teams, to make a choice between Gil and Gary. (As acting president, Gil was entitled to make his case before the whole group.) At the meeting where we settled the issue we all counted votes ahead of time. It seemed like Gary had the edge. I went to Gil, reminded him that I thought the world of him, and gave him the bad news. "It would be better for the league for you to withdraw and make this unanimous," I said. "I will tell Gary to make sure you are retained with a good contract that protects your pension." To his credit, Gil put the league ahead of himself. He got up, made a plea for unity, and withdrew his name from consideration. Then we unanimously elected Bettman.

At the time that we selected our new league president we also moved to make a TV deal with ESPN. After a decade-long absence, we would finally get some games on an American network. The NHL would pocket just $60 million for the rights fee, a small amount compared with what other major sports leagues received for TV rights, but the cash was secondary. We were looking for exposure, and we got it.

With the president's office filled and the TV contract signed, just two major issues remained: expansion and owner-player relations. Fortunately the players association, their union really, had a new director, Bob Goodenow. Bob was a very smart Toronto lawyer but, more importantly, a great fan of hockey. We both wanted a better relationship between players and owners after a long period of tension. One big thing he did, among many, was help get players to participate, unpaid, in exhibition games that built interest in hockey across North America. That helped us a great deal when it came to expansion.

Our first immediate expansion issue involved Norm Green, owner of the Minnesota North Stars, who wanted to move his team. He was considering Dallas, but he was also interested in the Los Angeles suburb of Anaheim, where a new arena had been built. For my purposes, and the league's, it would be best if Green went to Dallas and someone new, big, rich, and powerful— someone like the Disney company—started a new franchise in Anaheim.

It would be good for the league because we would have a presence in Texas, where none existed, and because Disney would bring a certain cachet to the game. It would be especially good for me because a brand-new team, not a franchise moving from somewhere else, would have to pay a substantial sum to the Kings as compensation for invading our marketplace.

Fortunately for me, Norm Green was content to take the Stars to Dallas, especially when the league waived the transfer fee that owners are usually charged for such a move. That saved him millions of dollars. With that issue settled, I set my sights on Disney, or, to be precise, on its top executive, Michael Eisner. Since Disneyland was already the biggest thing in Anaheim, it made sense to me that they would want to own the hockey team that would play in their neighborhood.

Eisner had attended Kings games. His sons played hockey, and we knew each other well enough that I had once taken the boys on a road trip with the team. The trip had been a little too eventful. After the game some of the players had invited Michael's sons to go out for a meal. They wound up at a casino where the older boy was permitted inside but the younger one was not. He fell asleep outside on a bench. When I heard about that I had a fit, even though nothing awful happened. I had to tell Michael, who didn't like what happened but was mostly relieved that it all turned out okay. Soon we were both laughing about it.

Early in our discussions about a Disney-owned NHL team, I discovered that Michael's reputation for driving tough bargains was well earned. He began by asking me how much the league was going to pay Disney for starting up a team. That was his first thought. How much we were going to pay him. I said no, it doesn't work like that. In pro sports you pay the league to get into the game. It doesn't work the other way around, even if you are Disney.

The price was $50 million, I said. The owners of the new team in San Jose had paid that much. On top of that, if Disney played in Anaheim, the company would have to indemnify me for invading the L.A. Kings' territory. That would be another $25 million.

Eisner's answer? "No."

For months after his first rejection I held talks with Michael's business-planning people. At first, I didn't have much room to maneuver. Michael didn't want to pay more than $50 million, including any compensation for territory. But the other owners of the league counted on the $50 million entry fee, which they would divide into $2 million shares. That would leave me with no compensation at all. And as all my banks, not to mention my staff accountants, would have said, I needed that money.

The solution came from my best friend among the other NHL owners,

Howard Baldwin. Eager to have Disney associated with the NHL, Baldwin suggested that he and every other owner take $1 million apiece, rather than $2 million. Disney would still be charged the full $50 million, but I would get half of it as my compensation. The other owners soon approved, and all that stood between the league and Disney was Michael's approval.

What Michael did next shows why he has stayed at the top of one of the world's largest companies for so many years. First, he got the Ogden Corporation, which would have concessions at the stadium, to put up a big part of the $25 million for the league. He then divided my $25 million in half. I got $12.5 million in cash and a note, at a very low interest rate. Under the terms I would receive the rest over twenty years. Disney was in the hockey business, but for a whole lot less cash than anyone else. The team would be called the Mighty Ducks, and in a very short time Disney made that new brand known around the world with a delightful kids' movie by the same name.

After the sale, we talked about who might be the best person to run the team for Disney. I suggested Tony Tavaras, who I had hired as a consultant. He had run SpectraCorp, an arena management firm. They chose him, and he eventually rose to head all of Disney's sports, including the Angels baseball team, the Ducks, and affiliated operations.

When the Disney deal was done, I wasn't through. I contacted Wayne Huizenga, founder of Blockbuster video and owner of the Florida Marlins baseball team. I met him in a conference room at the offices of Clay Lacy Aviation, a corporate jet company at the Van Nuys Airport. I said, "Wayne, this league is going places. Disney's getting involved. If you put a team in South Florida, you'll never regret it." He didn't commit, but it was clear to me that I had touched a competitive nerve.

Huizenga sat on the fence through the fall of 1992. The league met in the second week of December at the Breakers Hotel, in Miami Beach. I convinced Michael Eisner to come and personally submit his application to the league owners. When he agreed, I then told Huizenga that Michael would be there and it was a perfect moment for him to come aboard, too. Both men showed up. Both applications were approved, and I received my share of the Huizenga franchise fee, along with the compensation from Disney.

In one intense flurry of negotiations I had netted $27 million. How, any reasonable person might ask, could I also be on the brink of bankruptcy? Hard as it is to fathom, hard as it was for *me* to accept, at the moment that the deals with Eisner and Huizenga were sealed, my finances had reached a new low. McNall Sports and Entertainment, the umbrella company for my sports and related businesses, was in hock to the tune of $200 million, half of which had come from Bank of America. At the same time the Gladden Entertainment film company owed Credit Lyonnais more than $100 million. We had begun to miss payments, and we estimated that the debt was rising by about $100,000 per day.

Much of the increased debt was caused by interest payments we could not handle and shortfalls in revenues. The Argos, for example, drew fewer fans than they had the year before, and failed to make it back to the Grey Cup finals. Rocket Ismail was surely no Wayne Gretzky. He couldn't match the Great One as an athlete, or as a personality. He missed many of his scheduled promotional appearances, and we fell into a dispute over payment because his contract required him to show up for those things. When the season ended in November, Rocket left the Argos for the Oakland Raiders of the NFL. He also threatened to sue us for millions of dollars in back pay.

As revenues from football and other sources slowed, I sold every personal asset I could. A very nice set of French and French colonial stamps went for well over $1 million. I got nearly as much for a U.S. coin collection. Every piece of art I had squirreled away was put on the block. I also offered for sale my homes in Malibu, Hawaii, and Park City, Utah. There wasn't much else I could do. I had never accepted a salary from the Kings, so there was nothing to cut there. My earnings from other businesses were already cut to roughly half of what they had been in 1990, so there wasn't much left to trim there, either.

I wasn't the only one who felt some pain. Many employees, especially at Gladden, were let go. But those who remained continued to receive salaries and expenses. And there were occasional, outrageous situations, that required the outlay of extra cash. A typical incident began when we were contacted by lawyers representing a number of actors and actresses—Deidre Hall and Ernest Borgnine were two—who claimed they had been robbed by one of my accountants, a recent hire named Bob Houston.

At first it was hard to believe. Bob was likable, and competent, the last person you would suspect. But he confessed that he had taken money from those people when they were his private clients. We agreed to pay them back, in order to protect him and keep the matter quiet. Though it was an expense we could ill afford, I didn't think I had an option. Bob was deeply involved in all of our dealings, and I worried about what he might do if we didn't keep him happy.

Though people rarely said anything that could be construed as a serious threat, we all understood that a word uttered to the proper authorities could bring us all down. Steve Nessenblatt was one of the few who would say it aloud. When he was upset, he would talk about giving up, telling all to the FBI, and accepting the consequences. When the people you need talk like this, you don't cut back on their salaries. We kept paying Steve $500,000 per year, though he did less and less work.

The pressures that made Steve yelp and gave all of us sleepless nights increased when Bank of America began asking to inspect some of the coins that supposedly stood as collateral for the many millions of dollars they had lent us. It was the Hunt audit situation all over again, with authorities demanding to see the goods.

This time we informed our curious creditors that the coins had been traded for an important collection of sports memorabilia, items such as game-worn jerseys, autographed baseballs, and trading cards. We then took to the phones and found items we could obtain on consignment. We got game shirts from Lou Gehrig, Warren Spahn, and Johnny Bench. We obtained contracts and checks signed by Gehrig and Babe Ruth. Some of the people in my office got a little carried away with the ruse. On their own initiative they bought modern jerseys, stained them and tore them up to make them look old. We also bought two million brand-new hockey cards, at pennies apiece, to make the collection appear to be enormous.

When the day came to present the stuff to the bankers, we had it all carefully displayed on well-lighted, gallery-style pedestals draped with velvet. The centerpiece was the Honus Wagner card. It all made a big impression on our visitors, who were thrilled to hold those things in their hands. They didn't know that we actually owned very few of the items that they saw, or that the value of it all was much lower than the millions of dollars we owed Bank of America.

I was leading two, maybe even three, lives.

As head of MS&E, I was furiously defending myself from creditors and scrambling to make more money. I couldn't hope for a hot movie, because David Begelman hadn't gotten a new distribution deal and Gladden was all but shut down. Nothing was happening with Tommy Thompson and the S.S. *Central America*. My partnership with Upper Deck to create high-end memorabilia was costing me more money than it earned. The global ancient-coin market was flat, or declining, and the same was true for racehorses.

In contrast with my struggles as a private businessman, my tenure as chairman of the National Hockey League was remarkably successful. The big TV contract and new franchises had made all of my owner friends a little richer and put some excitement into the league. At the same time Gary Bettman was winning friends and proving his competence. The pressures on me, as chairman, receded as he began to run the league.

Finally, as owner of the Kings, I guided the team through the most exciting season in its history. The year had started off well, even though Gretzky was missing, but then we hit a serious slump. Despite Coach Melrose's positive thinking, we suffered a winless streak that lasted nearly a month, from early December to early January 1993. Wayne returned on January 8, but even after he came back, the team struggled. Melrose began to talk openly about making some trades to shake things up. Then he started accusing players of simply quitting under pressure.

When it got to the point where we hadn't won in our own arena in eight straight games, we all felt embarrassed. I was both angry and disappointed. "There are times," I told the L.A. sportswriters, "when I want to put a paper sack on my head and be the anonymous owner." I had a great deal of sympathy for fans who paid $50 a ticket to see the Kings lose. "But how do you think I feel?" I asked. "I've got a $50 million investment here."

If the season was going to be salvaged, we needed to act quickly. Months earlier, when we worried about whether Gretzky would ever play again, we had talked to the Detroit Red Wings about Jimmy Carson, a center who was playing on their third line. We knew Carson had big talent. We had drafted him and he had played for the Kings in the mid-1980s. I had reluctantly traded him for Gretzky, and I always wanted him back because he was an excellent player and a friend.

We initially backed away from a deal when Detroit demanded our star defenseman, Paul Coffey, whom Gretzky considered among the two or three best in the league. The two men had played together, off and on, since they were each fourteen years old. They were teammates for almost a decade in the 1980s, winning championships in Edmonton, and they were very close friends.

But as important as Coffey was, Melrose had begun to complain to me about his influence over the younger defenseman. Coffey was the kind of defender who liked to score goals, too. Melrose feared that Coffey was teaching the younger players to adopt his same style. The coach didn't want that. He wanted defensemen who focused on stopping the other team and left the goal scoring to our centers and wings.

With our losing streak, we also needed a big enough trade to shake up the team. And we knew we would have to give up someone good to get someone good. That is why we listened when Detroit called again, mentioning Coffey and Carson. The Wings had a couple of other players—Marc Potvin and Gary Shuchuk—whom Melrose liked. He had coached them in the minors and believed he could maximize their talents. When Detroit agreed to give us Potvin and Shuchuk along with Carson, we willingly gave them Coffey, Jim Hiller, and a minor leaguer named Sylvain Couturier.

Coffey was surprised, but not shocked. He said he could handle going to a new team, but that having to leave Gretzky was "devastating." The reaction in our locker room was what you'd expect. Coffey had been immensely popular, especially with our younger defensemen, who saw him as a big brother. But no one took his departure harder than Gretzky and his wife, Janet. She cried when she picked up the phone and heard Coffey's news. Wayne was upset, and for the first time a rift developed in our relationship. It got worse when, perhaps to improve his own dealings with Wayne, Barry Melrose said the trade was all my idea. At that point Gretzky turned cold toward me.

Many fans and hockey writers criticized the move. However they did see in the trade some evidence that their long-held assumption about Wayne controlling the team was wrong. Instead, the rumors suddenly swung the other way. According to "unnamed sources," Wayne was furious and demanding a trade. I eventually had to call a press conference to put that notion to rest. The truth was that Wayne was furious with me, but he never asked to be traded.

Though we played a little better after the All-Star break, we sort of backed into the playoffs by finishing in third place, courtesy of Winnipeg, which had an even more dismal season than the Kings. We faced Calgary in the playoffs. I began to hope for a little surprise in the postseason, something to tell me all the money and emotional capital I had spent on the team was worth it. I got much more.

Los Angeles was hockey-mad in the spring of 1993 as we came back from a two-games-to-one deficit to beat the Calgary Flames in the first round of the playoffs. We then beat Vancouver in just six games to win our division for the first time in history. If we could survive another seven-game series, against Toronto, the Kings would play in the Stanley Cup finals.

The idea that the L.A. Kings might beat the storied Toronto Maple Leafs was flatly unacceptable to hockey purists in Canada. Hockey was their sport. It was played by rough, pale-skinned men who inhabited cold-weather cities. No team that dwelled amid the palm trees of Southern California could possibly beat the Leafs. It would be the equivalent of Japan beating the United States in Olympic basketball.

That was how they felt in Toronto, and I worried that our players felt the same way as they skated onto the ice at Maple Leaf Gardens for the first game. We played tentatively as the Leafs took a 4–1 lead into the final period, mainly on the performance of their star forward Doug Gilmour, who had two goals and an assist. Gilmour, perhaps that year's dominant player, had a history with the Kings. Early in the season he had slashed our Tomas Sandstrom with his stick, breaking Sandstrom's arm. Our players had said the slashing incident had been forgotten, but as the first playoff game wound down, our tough guy, Marty McSorley, did something that suggested it was not.

With two and a half minutes left in the game, the 170-pound Gilmour flicked a pass down the ice. A split second later, McSorley put all of his 225 pounds into an elbow-to-the-jaw hit that sent Gilmour to the ice. As Gilmour lay there, dazed and in pain, a melee broke out. Toronto fans, many of whom already hated Marty, threw everything they could put their hands on, including a crutch. When the ice was eventually cleaned up, the game was finished. The score didn't change, but Marty had changed something in the hearts and minds of his teammates.

The hit that Marty put on Gilmour, and the near-riot that followed, would be misunderstood by the hockey novice. Many people see the violent parts of the game, especially the fights, in a negative light. Some even think they are staged, like pro-wrestling matches. I can tell you this is definitely not true. Hockey is played in such close quarters, and at such high speeds, that physical contact is inevitable. Tempers rise along with frustrations, and sometimes players can no longer contain themselves. From a young age, hockey players are taught that it's okay to drop your stick and fight because the alternative—swinging sticks at each other—is much worse.

Think about it. Have you ever seen guys on skates throwing punches? They hardly ever land a serious blow because their footing is so unstable. They can't get leverage. I'd rather see players blow off steam, and vent their frustrations with that kind of fighting than by using their sticks as weapons.

The hard checking done by Marty and other so-called "enforcers" in the league is also a legitimate part of the game. These players are paid to make sure one team cannot bully another. They also protect players like Wayne Gretzky, whose skills and smaller size make them targets. All teams do this. It's a smart way to play the game. And the enforcer's role is a legitimate, athlete's job.

That's how Marty saw it. I can tell you from my conversations with him that he was proud to use his size and muscle to protect Wayne. He also understood that there were times when he could use his toughness to intimidate other teams and change the dynamic of a game or a playoff series. A few hard hits on the other team's star could disrupt their rhythm. A fistfight, which stops play and diverts everyone's energies, could change the tempo of a game. And certainly a big display of courage and aggression can rally a team at a moment when it was experiencing self-doubt and confusion.

This is exactly what happened after Marty's hit on Gilmour. In game two of the Toronto series the Kings skated with more purpose and confidence and won 3–2. The winning goal was scored by Sandstrom—a pleasant little irony—and our defense played very well.

We went home to Los Angeles where, before game three, we unfurled a huge banner marking the Smythe Division championship. It was the first banner the Kings ever hung, and the crowd went wild. We won the game quite easily and took the lead in the series. But with the teams evenly matched, the series eventually went to 3–3 and we prepared to play the deciding game in Toronto. The winner would square off against Montreal for the Cup.

Before the first face-off I was as nervous as a six-year-old on the first day of school. My stomach churned and I paced around the locker room. I looked so bad that Wayne had to come over and tell me to relax. "We're going to do it," he said. "You'll see."

I do believe that certain athletes have a reserve of energy, talent, and tricks that can be tapped when needed. Wayne Gretzky demonstrated that in the first period when we were down by one and he scored on a pass from Marty. In the same period he fed Sandstrom for a second score. Maple Leaf Gardens, with 15,720 souls packed inside, fell silent.

The game seesawed as we got a go-ahead goal from Alexei Zhitnik with four minutes left to play. Less than a minute later Wayne got his third goal, with a shot that bounced off a Maple Leaf defenseman and then jumped over the goaltender for a score. Toronto made one more goal, and then their coach pulled his goalie to put six skaters against our five. It was the longest forty-five seconds of my life as the Leafs swarmed all over our end. Kings defenders threw themselves onto the ice to block shots and race from corner to corner. With five seconds left we managed to clear the puck to center ice and the game was over.

I had watched the game from a box provided by the Leafs' management. John Candy, Peter Guber, Goldie Hawn, and Kurt Russell had all flown in with me to attend. When we won, we cheered and celebrated, while all around us disgruntled Toronto fans booed and growled and threw paper cups and hot-dog wrappers on the ice. When we got to the locker room, it was so crowded with players, family, and friends that you could barely move. With all the bodies jammed in there and beer spraying around, it felt like a steam bath in a brewery. But I didn't mind. I hugged every player I could get my arms around, and took my turn posing for pictures with the Campbell Cup trophy, which went to us as division winners.

Twenty-six years of frustration, from those days when I bought scalped tickets outside The Forum to my years as the owner of a team that couldn't get past the second round of playoffs, were erased that night. Though I hadn't held a stick in my hand or taken to the ice, I did feel the victory was partly mine. I had taken the gamble, with $15 million, to bring Wayne to L.A. I had put together the management team, supported the Kings whenever and however I could. And now they had accomplished what they had never accomplished under any other owner. It felt good.

The good feeling endured even as Toronto fans—shocked, drunk, angry—pelted us with eggs and rocked the team bus as we left the Gardens. It was still there when we got to the restaurant Wayne owned in Toronto for a celebration at my expense. But there, in between cheers and toasts, I began to come back to Earth. It was actually Wayne who introduced a little reality to the evening.

"We haven't really done anything yet," he said in a quieter moment. "The job is not finished."

He was right, of course, about the job being unfinished. He had been the captain in four Stanley Cup victories for Edmonton. A division championship was good, but it wasn't the ultimate goal.

Winning is good for business. Each home playoff game after the regular season brought us $1 million or more in extra revenues. But more important than the immediate income was the huge surge in the Kings' popularity that came with the Campbell Cup. Calls poured in from every corner of the city as tickets to the Stanley Cup finals became the object of universal desire. Los Angeles was suddenly a hockey town.

We would have to wage war with the Canadiens on their home ice before we got a chance to bask in our new popularity in Southern California. Facing the red-white-and-blue at the Montreal Forum was something like playing the Yankees in the House that Ruth Built. During a century of play the Canadiens had won the Stanley Cup twenty-three times. The team had a mystique that was like a seventh man on the ice for their side. They expected a win every time they skated, and so did their fans. This time around they also had the advantage of being fully rested while our guys were completely exhausted from their scrap with the Maple Leafs.

Fortunately we had important factors in our favor. For one thing, Wayne Gretzky was healthy, strong, and in good spirits. He was ready to perform at his highest level, and proved it in the first game. With a standing-room-only crowd packing the arena, Wayne dominated the game. He made three perfect passes for our team's first three goals, and then shot one into the net himself. Ironically, he even had a role in the Canadiens' single score when he accidentally tipped an opposing player's pass into our goal. With the outcome of the game, a 4–1 Kings win, his embarrassment over his mistake faded quickly.

No one was happier about the win than our left winger Luc Robitaille. Luc had grown up a few minutes from the Montreal Forum and was awed by the prospect of playing a Stanley Cup game there. He had seen hockey legend Henri Richard in the stands during a pregame skate, and felt inspired. When the game started he played with special intensity, taking nine shots and scoring a goal before the end of the second period.

Our victory in the first game shocked the Montreal hockey crowd so much that they couldn't believe we did it fairly. On the morning after, the *Journal de Montreal* claimed that I had offered my players $1 million cash, to split among themselves, for a Cup win. NHL rules prohibit that kind of incentive, and I never made such an offer. But I have a hunch about where the story came from.

Over the years I had offered players a night out on the town after an important win. I had also gotten involved in little cash-award games the players conducted among themselves. Sometimes they each put $50 or $100 in a kitty and would give it to the guy who scored the most goals, or the winning goal, in a particular game. There have been times when I have offered to double any amount they put together. But the newspaper's charge—that I threw a $1 million offer on the table before the series began—was a lie.

In game two the Canadiens played as if they were the ones fighting for $1 million in cash. They fired shot after shot at our goaltender Kelly Hrudey, out-hustled us in the scramble for the puck, and out-hit us along the boards.

Despite all of that, we managed to get the lead, 2–1, as the game went into the third and final period. Our guys started to play better, to even believe we would take two games in a row at the Montreal Forum, when Kerry Fraser, the referee, blew his whistle to stop play with less than two minutes to go.

As the players lined up for a face-off, the Canadiens' coach, Jacque Demers, called over his captain, Guy Carbonneau. They talked for a moment, and then Carbonneau raced over to Fraser the referee. From where I sat, I had no idea what Demers had told Carbonneau, or what was holding up play. I soon found out, as Fraser turned to Marty McSorley and asked to inspect the blade of his stick.

In the old, old days, all hockey sticks sported straight blades. In the mid-1960s players began to heat stick blades with blow torches and bend them a bit. By 1980, almost everyone used blades with a bit of a curve. The curve helps them cradle the puck and put more energy behind a shot. NHL rules were developed to limit this little bit of engineering. They prohibited curves of greater than one half of an inch. The rules also allow teams to challenge the legality of an opponent's stick. If a challenge is upheld, the offender must sit down for a two-minute penalty. If the challenge is denied, the team that raises the issue must sit a player for two minutes. Because of the risk, challenges are rare. Most players stay within the rule. And those who do not are tolerated under most circumstances.

It was no secret that Marty McSorley liked a big curve, maybe a curve that was too big. Opposing teams never made an issue of it. But here, with less than two minutes to play and the Canadiens about to fall two games behind the underdog Kings, Jacque Demers wanted McSorley's stick checked. Almost everyone in the building had a pretty good idea how it would turn out. McSorley's stick was declared illegal. He was sent to the penalty box for two minutes, and the Canadiens had a one-man advantage for the remaining minutes of the game.

The Montreal fans cheered the ref's decision but then fell silent to watch what would happen next. Demers took his goaltender out, which meant he would have six skaters to attack our four. Our defenders raced around our end of the ice like madmen, chasing the six Canadiens. But a two-player advantage was too much for them. It took just thirty seconds for defenseman Eric Desjardins to get into position for a slapshot that our Hrudey didn't see until it was in the net.

The Forum exploded with cheers and shouts when Desjardins scored, but he wasn't through. The game went into overtime and in the first minute of play the Canadien defenseman took a pass as he flew down the right side and fired a low shot between Hrudey's skates. For the first time in Stanley Cup history, a defenseman had scored a hat trick. Combined with Coach Demers's curved-stick-challenge, his three-goal performance had saved the Canadiens from certain defeat.

Afterward, we all felt a bit confused about what Demers had done. Some players thought it was a lame way to win a game that's supposed to be played on the ice. But others had to allow that the rule is in the books for a reason. Demers had risked being tagged for a penalty on his own team if the challenge hadn't worked out. It was a fair move, they said. I tended to agree with the sentiment voiced by Rob Blake, who said that the curved stick wouldn't have mattered if the Kings had kept the Canadiens from scoring in the last two minutes of the third period. No one on our side criticized Marty for the stick incident. All you had to do was look at his face to see how he felt about it. The only choice we had was to focus on the three home games coming up in Los Angeles.

The limos began lining up outside The Forum two hours before the start of the first Stanley Cup game ever played in Los Angeles. On street corners scalpers offered tickets for $500 apiece. We rented searchlights to give the event some added glitz. Inside, as 16,005 seats were filled, a red carpet was unfurled on the ice and the Stanley Cup, a huge sparkling silver trophy, was carried out for display. In one corner of The Forum some season-ticket hold-ers popped the cork on a bottle of champagne and toasted the team.

Everyone stood and cheered when we raised the Campbell Conference banner next to the one we had hung after winning the Smythe Division. The roaring crowd included our regular crew of celebrities, and a few newcomers including Mick Jagger, Michelle Pfeiffer, and Dyan Cannon. I had never felt more joy and excitement in The Forum. Then the game started and we fell behind 3–0.

It happened so fast that our fans were stunned into silence. Then Mark Hardy put a crunching hit on Canadien Mike Keane to wake them up again. Two minutes later Gretzky fed Robitaille for a goal and The Forum began rocking. We scored again four minutes later when Tony Granato hustled for a quick score. With their adrenaline pumping, our players swarmed around the Canadiens' goal. Taking a pass from left-wing Mike Donnelley, Wayne hit one of the most powerful slapshots I had ever seen past the Montreal goalie. The score was tied. The Forum erupted. Finally, everyone in Los Angeles under-stood why hockey, as the Kings played it, was as exciting as sport can be.

The Kings kept up the pressure, firing at the Montreal goaltender. Shots flew inches past the net, hit the post, and hit defensemen. Montreal goaltender Patrick Roy played spectacularly, bailing out his teammates time and again. A huge brouhaha broke out when Carbonneau appeared to stop the puck in front of the net with his hand—only goaltenders are permitted to do this—and got away with it. We lost that argument, the game went into overtime, and we lost the game when John LeClair scored for Montreal. It was a chilling, thrilling, fantastic game. It could have been better only if we had won.

Down two games to one, the Kings had to win or face returning to Mon-treal for the final games with the Canadiens in the lead. Wayne told our guys to get more aggressive. It was the right idea, but no one was prepared to exe-cute it. The team started game four slowly, and seemed unable to get out of first gear. The Canadiens were just a little bit sharper in a game that looked more like a preseason tune-up than a championship event. We took a 2–2 tie into overtime, and once again the Canadiens delivered sudden death with the first score. They won 3–2 and seized a commanding lead in the series. One more victory for them and the Stanley Cup would be back in Montreal.

It's hard to describe the way it felt to have reached the Stanley Cup round so full of hope only to suffer so many hard-fought losses. Patrick Roy was a big part of the Canadiens' success. He played brilliantly and then shone even brighter whenever we went into overtime. No one on the Kings team was giving up, but we felt confounded by Roy, and the prospect of winning two games in Montreal was daunting.

Too daunting. Game five ended with the Canadiens ahead 4–1. The Stanley Cup was theirs. Patrick Roy was named most valuable player for the series, an honor he said belonged to his coach, Demers, for the curved-stick challenge. Roy believed that the penalty on Marty McSorley was the difference in the series. He was wrong. The Canadiens were loaded with more talent than the Kings. And as underdogs, we had probably overachieved against Toronto. The Montrealers beat us, fair and square. But those facts didn't make the defeat taste any better.

Gretzky took the loss hard. He had been moved by the extra effort, the sheer grit of his teammates. Watching them pull so close, only to lose, made him think about retiring. "It's the hardest loss I've ever had," he told the press. He barely said a word to me in the locker room. But later I went to him and asked him to tell me what was bothering him.

"We could have won the whole thing if Paul [Coffey] was here," said Wayne, his voice clouded by anger. "I believe this, Bruce, so don't try to talk me out of it. It would have been much different with Paul."

I didn't bother to disagree, or to point out that none of us could say what might have happened under different circumstances. Nothing I could have said would have helped. But just giving him a chance to get some of the resentment off his chest was good, I think. A few weeks later, Wayne decided to come back for at least one more season. Slowly we became friends again. All was forgiven, if not forgotten. But he would never come so close again to bringing the Cup to California.

As discouraging as our loss was, as owner of the Kings I couldn't stay disappointed for long. Everywhere I went in Los Angeles people congratulated me on the Kings' performance. And as I examined the year gone by, I could see that we had made the Kings and the game of hockey matter in L.A. Where once we couldn't fill half the seats at The Forum, we now sold out almost every game. In a town where just fifteen games had once been televised in a season, we now broadcast every one. We hadn't won the Cup, but we had won over L.A., and my Kings were the hottest sports franchise on the West Coast.

Among the letters I received to thank me and the team for the season was a note from Ronald Reagan that read: "What a thrill it was to be 'right on the ice' for our first professional hockey games." Others came from Mike Medavoy, Michael Ovitz, Peter O'Mally, and Berry Gordy, whose telegram said, "You're my hero, once again." Perhaps the most heartwarming was a handwritten card from Tom Hanks, who signed: "Your loyal fan (Section 13, Row R)."

11

WHILE THE KINGS WERE WAGING WAR for me on the ice, Steve Nessenblatt and Mark Eastman had been quietly fighting even tougher battles against our banks. During the playoff season, Steve, Mark, and I focused on our problems with Credit Lyonnais. I thought we might report a higher investment in the S.S. *Central America* project than we had actually made, to raise more financing. Mark Eastman wrote up the documentation, then Steve went to Europe to see the bankers. He told them we had put $12 million into the project and that we would soon get to market some of the treasure. The revenues would be reserved to repay our debts.

In truth, we hadn't made such an arrangement, and the documents he presented to Credit Lyonnais as backup documentation were fake. But the bank accepted Steve's claim, and his pledge that the project would yield big profits, which we would pass along to them.

Between loans for horses, coins, and Gladden films, we owed Credit Lyonnais well over $100 million. But they were well aware of the trump card we held against them—their bad-faith dealings with Cannon—so they had little stomach for pressing us. Besides, they had much bigger problems.

By 1993, Credit Lyonnais was the subject of the largest financial scandal in history. Every day seemed to bring new revelations of officers taking pay-offs in exchange for approving loans. At the center of the debacle was $2 billion lent to a former waiter named Giancarlo Paretti, who had seized MGM Studios and quickly run it into the ground. Many current and former bank officers, including some we had dealt with, faced criminal charges in that affair. The French government had launched a huge investigation. Compared with those more pressing issues, Bruce McNall was not so important. They left me alone.

I was very important, however, to Bank of America. Through no wrong-doing on its part—except perhaps inattention to detail and their excitement at being in business with me—Bank of America also held more than $100 million in debt that neither the Kings nor I could repay on schedule. Before summer, they moved our account into what's called the "work-out group." Work-out is the final step before a bank tries to force a borrower into bank-ruptcy. It is where they try to find ways to recover as much value as they can. In some cases, the terms of the loan are changed. In others, they develop a plan that requires you to sell your business and turn over the proceeds.

No one who knew me during that time had any idea I was under such intense financial pressure. No one outside of the bank and those in my offices knew I was so close to bankruptcy, and we all kept it very quiet. Publicity about our problems would have made the bank look bad, and it might have depressed the value of the Kings if people knew we were anxious to sell. All information was strictly controlled. The work-out team didn't even refer to me by name. I became "Prince Charles" in the bank's memos and discussions, and the nature of my businesses was always obscured.

Although we were dealing with big numbers and large risks, there was no real animus in my relationship with Bank of America's people. We all wanted the same thing—to minimize their losses. Mark Eastman, who represented me, began working on an arrangement that had the bank forgiving about $45 million in debt, and then taking roughly $60 million from the sale of the

Kings. They were willing to give me time to work on the one big deal—a new stadium and the sale of the team—that might solve everything.

Sony was our first, best hope for a giant fix-all deal involving a stadium and the Kings. The deal I began with Peter Guber was pursued in detail by Mark Eastman, along with a relatively new member of our team, Jim Bailey. Bailey had worked for the accounting firm of Ernst & Young. In a short time with us he had moved quickly into a position of responsibility. For months he and Eastman labored to make an agreement that would transfer the Kings to Sony, and put them and the Lakers into a brand-new arena in downtown Los Angeles. The talks were extremely complex, involving not only Sony but Jerry Buss and the Laker organization as well as Bank of America.

As the arrangement took shape, Sony agreed to pay $60 million for the Kings, which was about four times what I had paid to acquire the team five years before. They would also take on all the team's debt, which meant the total value of the offer to me was well over $100 million. The negotiations always assumed that I would become chairman of a new entity called Sony Sports, which would have included the teams and the arena. I would be due a salary, bonuses, and equity, which I intended to use to pay my creditors.

While the Kings purchase was settled rather easily, the matter of the Lakers and The Forum took more work. Jerry Buss needed to be compensated for the investment he had in The Forum, since a new arena would make it obsolete. Eventually Sony agreed to do that, and they agreed to pay a premium price for a minority interest in the Lakers. Buss's part of the deal would be worth well over $200 million. In addition, Sony would build a brand-new sports palace. Before they were done, they were likely to put more than half a billion dollars on the line.

To make sure we had every chance to finish a deal and perhaps avoid bankruptcy, we enlisted Ken Klee, probably the nation's best bankruptcy attorney, to review everything in the deal. Klee brought with him an associate named Michael Tuchin, a warmhearted young man who became our day-today contact. Early on, Ken and Michael were not privy to all the fraud issues that lurked in the background. However, they quickly grasped our financial problems. They were businesslike, sympathetic, and each became a steadying presence in my life.

Strangely enough, I didn't need much comforting at the time. This might be hard to accept. Most homeowners start to panic if they fall a few payments behind on a mortgage. Here I was, with millions of dollars in debt that was not being serviced. Oddly enough, I didn't stay up nights worrying. I never turned to drink or drugs, although others in my offices did.

My relative calm was, in part, a matter of denial. I deliberately pushed my worst fears—about our possible crimes being discovered—out of my mind. That didn't require much effort, because I believed we would somehow fix everything that was wrong. We might have to sell everything, in addition to making a deal on the new arena that would free up millions in cash. But I knew we could do it.

Most of the time, the people around me believed our business could be saved, too. They also believed in me. I had that effect on people. They saw the hallmarks of wealth—cars, jets, horses, etc.—and accepted the idea that I had the resources to solve almost any problem. Even those who knew the truth—that the bank accounts were empty—had faith in my abilities as a salesman and deal-maker. For ten years, ever since the Hunt audit, I had always been able to make the magic that would save us. Why couldn't I keep on doing it?

Within my circle of key executives, we also practiced a lot of mutual reinforcement. Though she was tough on our adversaries, Su Waks could often be downright motherly and reassuring if anyone ever expressed doubts. On many occasions, she would wander into my office and deliver a little pep talk. I did the same for her. Sometimes a group of us would gather informally in my office and we would talk out the strategies that were going to save us.

But there were also moments when people showed they were feeling the pressure. Some of my key employees began pulling as much cash as they could out of the companies, perhaps anticipating trouble in the future. It was easy for me to understand why they did it. They were worried about their futures. That's why I did nothing when I heard that one of my employees was actually stealing minor antiquities. Another employee, Jim Bailey, once confronted me with his fears about our business practices and demanded extra pay to compensate for any risk he might be taking. He accepted $48,000 and stayed on the job.

At other moments, a manager or accountant might come to me just to vent anxiety. During one of those conversations, Steve Nessenblatt once even threatened to go to the media—in particular, the TV tabloid show *Hard Copy*—and tell all. I was able to calm him down, and I was sure he didn't mean what he said. However, his outburst did remind all of us that bankruptcy was not the worst that could happen. No matter what our rationalizations and justifications may have been, crimes had been committed. And if every detail of what we had done came to light, prosecutions were a real possibility.

We all knew that, and yet we kept going because we believed we could solve all the problems, and pay the worthy creditors. And most of us chose to believe that the wrongdoing we had committed was mainly a civil matter. They were not serious crimes, we thought. We had simply manipulated things to improve cash flow to cover our obligations. We knew we had been wrong and deceitful. But we didn't dwell on the possibility that we might also be criminals.

In playing dominoes, one falling tile will always tip another. The cascade might stop before the whole line is toppled, but you never lose just one. The summer of 1993 found me coping with a lot of wobbly dominoes. At the time that Bank of America placed us in what was essentially prebankruptcy, I began to get urgent calls from Tom Sherak, who was head of Fox distribution. Tom was perhaps the kindest, most generous person I had met in the film industry. He was an avid hockey fan, and a friend. He was such a good friend that a year earlier he had bailed me out of a serious problem that was a direct result of David Begelman's arrogance.

The crisis had involved the very last film David made, *Mannequin Two*, starring Kristy Swanson, the former girlfriend of my pal Alan Thicke. Production had been financed by Credit Lyonnais on the premise that Fox would release and distribute the film. But it turned out that David had already completed his ten-picture run with Fox, and they were not obligated to handle *Mannequin Two*. David had hidden this fact from me, as well as the bank, assuming he could solve the problem. But months after the film was finished there was no sign that it was ever going to be shown anywhere.

When David finally told me the truth, I knew that if Credit Lyonnais found out, they would knock down our doors demanding an end to our financing and immediate repayment. So, I turned to Sherak for a favor. He agreed to distribute the film, if we paid the cost of advertising and prints. We agreed, and we averted a crisis with Credit Lyonnais. Unfortunately, we never had the cash—$4.7 million—to pay Fox. Now Sherak was calling to ask why.

I couldn't tell him we didn't have the money, so I stalled. Then I argued that Fox had spent too much on the advertising, taking advantage of the fact that we had agreed to pay for it. I tried to sound serious, and informed Tom that we could hash it out in court. But my heart wasn't in it. He was in the right. If I'd had the money I would have paid him immediately. But I didn't, so he joined the growing list of angry creditors who crowded the phone log and filled my in-box with letters.

Hundreds of NFA coin fund investors also joined the money chase in September, after we issued a report on the Merrill Lynch Athena II fund. Though we put the best spin on the numbers, there was no way to disguise the fact that investors had lost much of what they had put into the pot. In three years, the value of a single unit in the partnership had fallen from $1,000 to $293.

That news was the beginning of the end for all the NFA funds, though it would take many months for Merrill Lynch to discover all the facts and to move for liquidation. When the report was filed, Merrill Lynch said nothing. No one even called me to find out what had happened to the funds. I can only guess that Merrill Lynch had merely assumed that it was a matter of the market plummeting. Of course, they had already pocketed millions of dollars in fees and commissions, and had no capital of their own at stake. It was only their clients who were losing money.

The public report on the coin funds was like a knothole in the fence surrounding our businesses. Anyone could look through it and get an inkling of the trouble we faced. For the people at Sony working on the Kings/Lakers/stadium project, it was one more reason to feel jittery. As weeks passed, they fretted more and more about whether we would stay out of bankruptcy long enough to finish the deal.

Mark Eastman and Jim Bailey pushed hard for Sony because every day that passed only added to the debt that would have to be paid off. But they had other motivations. First, they were both angling for high-level, high-paying jobs within the new Sony subsidiary that would run the Kings and the arena. Second, they were also negotiating big bonuses for themselves—in excess of $100,000 apiece—to be paid when the transactions finally occurred.

That self-dealing probably explains why Bailey and Eastman reacted negatively when another potential savior, an alternative to Sony, appeared on the horizon. In late 1993, I was contacted by an old acquaintance, Joe Cohen, and his partner Jeff Sudikoff. Joe and I had first gotten together in the late 1980s when I was interested in buying the New Jersey Nets basketball team with Howard Baldwin, then-owner of the Pittsburgh Penguins. Howard and I both thought of Joe, whose expertise was in cable TV, as a potential partner. The deal never happened, but Joe made a very positive impression on me. In 1993, he and Jeff ran an enormous telecommunications company called IDB Systems. Though not a household name, because it mainly served business, IDB was the nation's fourth biggest player in voice and data transmission, and growing. Cohen and Sudikoff wanted to raise the company's profile, diversify a bit, and have some fun. The Kings/Lakers/stadium deal would accomplish all of that with one grand flourish. (Eventually, however, they would take the company out of the deal and attempt it as a personal purchase.)

In a long meeting with Sudikoff and Cohen, I laid out the transaction that had been built by Eastman, Bailey, and their counterparts at Sony. As part of the deal, I was going to be left with a minority stake—perhaps 12 percent—of the company that was formed. I was also supposed to be earning a substantial salary as an executive of the new entity, but much of my earnings, and all of the profits I accrued as an owner, would flow directly to the banks.

As detail after detail piled up, even I was impressed by the magnitude of it all. Sony was going to put hundreds of millions of dollars into this arrangement. It would be the biggest single investment in a sports operation ever made. I couldn't imagine that Cohen and his partner were in that league. But I was in for a big shock.

"We'll match it," said Sudikoff, with barely any emotion in his voice. "And your share will be at least 25 percent, not twelve."

That was a huge improvement over the Sony deal. But as good as it was, I couldn't simply accept the offer. First, I had to weigh the differences between Sony and IDB. In Sony I was dealing with one of the largest, richest, most reputable companies in the world. The company had such enormous credibility that my anxious bankers would be more patient while we completed the transaction. However, IDB was also a strong company. And the offer Cohen made was substantially better for me, and would play out better for my creditors in the long run.

I decided to chase both potential partners, so I assigned Su Waks to work with Cohen and Sudikoff. Su was happy to have a big role in the our potential salvation. She got along very well with Sudikoff and Cohen, and they liked her so much that they planned to keep her in a top position after the sale. She very quickly became a cheerleader for the IDB option, making a very convincing case for their numbers. Eastman and Bailey responded by criticizing Su's work and arguing for their deal with Sony. The competition among them became so fierce that at times they wouldn't speak to each other.

Rumors about a pending sale of the Kings began circulating in the NHL at the very start of the 1993–94 season, and those rumors might have contributed to the team's dismal performance. At one point we lost ten games in a row. No one seemed to be playing up to his potential—not even Gretzky, who before the season started had agreed to a new contract paying him $25.5 million over three years.

At the December league meeting, I made it clear to my fellow owners that I intended to remain president of the Kings, and that I was really looking for a partner with deep pockets, not someone to buy me out entirely. They all knew that the Kings had to have a new arena. Most of the owners who weren't already settled into a modern stadium, with all the revenue that that implied, were scrambling to make similar arrangements.

However, none of the other owners were trying to satisfy creditors with hundreds of millions of dollars in claims. Almost every day I dealt with demands for payment. Smaller creditors—such as the landlord for our Century City offices—I simply delayed. But with the bankers, who could band together and force us into bankruptcy, I tried to demonstrate how they would benefit if they just gave me more time.

The problem was, I often found myself trying to explain a very complex problem to brand-new bank officers. The people I had dealt with over time, the ones who had made the loans to my companies, were nowhere to be found. I'd call Credit Lyonnais in Rotterdam and discover that the man I was hoping to speak with had been transferred to Vietnam. My contacts at Bank of America were scattered all over California. At European American Bank, vice presidents seemed to change with the seasons.

The confusion produced by all the personnel shifts was mutual. Around the time of the league meeting, Roger Doufours of Credit Lyonnais showed up in Los Angeles hoping that a face-to-face meeting would clear things up. I took him to lunch and gave him a little more clarity than he expected. First, I detailed again all of Credit Lyonnais's past sins, then I told him exactly where the bank stood in relation to other creditors.

"I know you want to be repaid," I said, "and I'm trying to find a way to do it. But right now all you can count on is the value of Gladden's films." I had no personal wealth to be seized, I added, and if Credit Lyonnais sued and caused our bankruptcy, even the value of Gladden might be lost. Doufours admitted that his bank had significant liability. He even said that the people who preceded him at the bank were "corrupt" and "self-serving." By the time the meeting was over, I had bought a brief reprieve. But no amount of talking and storytelling was going to delay Credit Lyonnais for longer than a month or two more. It was time to close a deal with either IDB or Sony.

I had never made a single business decision that was more important than choosing either IDB or Sony. I wrestled with it for days, listening to Su, Bailey, and Eastman argue for one side or the other. On both sides were thick files jammed with numbers and facts. And from both sides I heard highly emotional pleas. Eastman and Bailey understood that their personal fortunes, and futures, depended on me picking Sony. The same was true for Su—one of my most loyal employees—and IDB.

In the end, the scales were not tipped by my affection for Su or by the power of what Eastman and Bailey presented. Instead, it was the advice of Ken Klee, the bankruptcy expert, that settled everything. IDB was offering more for me, and hence, more for my creditors. As much as I might have loved the idea of joining Sony, they came in second.

As soon as the decision was final, I called Peter Guber and arranged to meet with him and Gary Winnick over breakfast. (The Sony sale had been Winnick's idea.) Peter had traveled with me to hockey games. He had been there rooting for the Kings in the Stanley Cup series, and he had worked very hard on our potential partnership. Losing out to IDB was a huge disappointment, and he said so. I consoled him with a bit of information that turned out to be prophetic.

"If we went ahead," I said, "Sony might one day decide I'm not the kind of person they would want heading one of their companies." The implication was clear. Though I was closing the door on a deal today, I might also be saving Peter real embarrassment in the future.

When the sale to IDB was announced, Ken Klee then pushed me to settle one more big issue. He wanted me to come clean with Credit Lyonnais on the circular transaction. We did that at a meeting with Phil Grosz, the attorney with the firm of Loeb and Loeb, who had represented the bank in Los Angeles. Grosz was the guy who had held up the circular transaction, years earlier, because he had always suspected that I was the so-called independent investor who bought out EAB. As we prepared to meet, I imagined him gloating as the truth came out, and he was proven correct.

Grosz's office was in the same building as mine. When the time came, we just went upstairs to the Loeb and Loeb conference room. I didn't tell Grosz that he had been right all along. I just described all that had occurred, in detail, so that he could understand not only the mechanics of the transaction but also my stormy history with Credit Lyonnais and the underlying motives of the people at EAB. To his credit, Grosz just listened, made notes, and thanked us for the information. For my part, I didn't dodge responsibility. I just gave them the facts.

After the meeting with Grosz, Ken Klee told me to hire criminal counsel. I retained Tom Pollack of the firm of Irell & Manella. Pollack was widely regarded as one of the best attorneys around when it came to defending against charges of white-collar crime. When I laid out the situation, he agreed I had serious problems.

If the banks hadn't begun talking to each other before I met with Phil Grosz, I could be sure they had started exchanging information afterward. In no time at all the big three—Bank of America, EAB, and Credit Lyonnais—would probably notify all the other lenders that had made smaller loans to me personally or to my companies. In my mind, each one of those nonperforming loans represented another leak in my ship.

When a vessel founders, the captain puts every bit of his energy and focus into saving it. Unfortunately, a lot of crew members focus more on saving themselves. In many ways, that was how it was at my companies in early 1994. I was racing from crisis to crisis, determined to keep us all afloat. My crewmates helped, but each one of them also kept an eye on the lifeboats.

Su had already secured her place with IDB. David Begelman was not so lucky. With Gladden no longer in business, he no longer received his salary—roughly $10,000 per week—or his expense account. Because he had always lived beyond his means, I knew David was close to broke. But he continued to drive his Rolls, pick up tabs, and lay down bets in high-stakes poker games. He insisted that he would be back in business soon. And for months he worked the town, trying to get someone to back him in a new venture. He had plenty of friends, but he was low on credibility, and none of them were offering him the financing a new company required.

One afternoon, after many weeks had passed since I last saw him, David appeared at the door to my office. He was broke, he said, truly broke. And though he understood how desperate my situation was, he had nowhere else to turn. He asked if I could spare $100,000. It would be not a loan, or a gift, but an investment. Once his new company was running, I'd have a piece of it.

I didn't doubt that he was tapped out. David's spending always exceeded what he earned, even when it was more than $1 million per year. He had hit me up for $10,000 here and $10,000 there, ever since we met. Another $100,000 wouldn't get him to next month, I guessed. But I didn't have the heart to turn him down. We had set aside some emergency funds, a couple million dollars, in accounts that could be used for this sort of purpose. In one final gesture, maybe for old time's sake, I wrote him a check for the amount he requested, and told him to cash it as soon as possible. As far as I was concerned, that was his seat in the lifeboat.

Su and David and even those employees who looted Summa Gallery were not my biggest problem. Far more threatening was the prospect that Phil

Grosz or another of my creditors would come to understand that crimes had been committed by my companies, and they would take their concerns to the authorities. I don't know whether that happened. However, I did eventually find out that one key member of my team spent quite a bit of time with agents of the Federal Bureau of Investigation in early 1994, as we desperately tried to save my companies and recover as much value as possible for the banks.

Jim Bailey had looked like trouble to me from the very first time I saw him. Hired by Mark Eastman, Bailey never relaxed, never seemed comfortable in his own skin. Awkward in social situations, he never talked about having family or friends. He often seemed jealous of the pay and perks enjoyed by Steve Nessenblatt and Su Waks. And despite his lower-echelon position, Jim acted as if he always had the right answer to any question or problem, and that he could fix what everyone else had messed up.

The key moment in my relationship with Bailey came in the summer of 1993 when he appeared in my office to complain about all the irregularities in our financial statements. At first he seemed appalled and morally outraged. He moaned about the risks he was taking with his reputation. But as the conversation went on, I discovered that his concerns were more financial than ethical. A bit more money would soothe his worries. I gave it to him and his demeanor changed instantly. He was back on the team, willing to play whatever game was afoot.

When I went with Sudikoff and Cohen, rather than Sony, Bailey's horse lost the race. He realized he would not get the big bonus he had cooked up, nor would he have a job in the new organization. At the end of 1993, while he was working within the Kings organization, Bailey began complaining to Ken Klee about what he saw as irregularities in the books. It seemed like he was trying to disrupt the sale. I fired him the first week of January 1994. On March 18, 1994, he appeared at the FBI field office in Century City with his two lawyers. He sat down with Special Agents Patricia Chamberlain and Jane Brillheart and began to tell everything he knew. (I would later need the transcripts.)

. . .

My wife, Jane, and I separated in February 1994. We had been arguing for months, mostly about my total absence from the life of our family. For the better part of a year, I had been stumbling in well after dinnertime and leaving for the office very early in the morning. I tried to stay connected to P. J. and Katie, but I had truly neglected Jane. She could see I was distracted, even troubled, but I wouldn't tell her what was wrong.

My silence made it all the worse when, after the IDB sale was announced, rumors of my financial problems began to fly. No doubt Jane got an earful from people who thought they knew about my business. When I finally began to tell her the truth, and even hinted that we might have to sell our house, she felt betrayed and deceived. The last straw came when I had to tell her that her name had been forged on some documents that had been required for various sales and loans.

After Jane heard all of it, there wasn't much I could say to make her feel better. I still had confidence that the problems could be fixed. And I was sure that the salary I would draw as president of the Kings under the new owners would maintain some semblance of our lifestyle, although cutbacks were going to be necessary. But stacked up against the shock Jane must have felt, my promises must have seemed weak. One night she said she just couldn't take it anymore; that she was moving out and taking the kids with her.

I was at work on moving day. Though immersed in the crisis there, I kept an eye on the clock and imagined when the kids would come home from school and when the car pulled out of the driveway. That night I went home to a dark and silent house. It was the biggest personal defeat of my life, but I couldn't allow myself to feel all of the pain that came with it. If I had, I wouldn't have been able to get myself up in the morning and return to battle.

The struggle included selling every asset I could. For months, we tried to find someone to buy the Argos, who were losing money every day. Eventually John Labatt Ltd., known primarily as a brewery, bought the team for $4.7

million, which was far less than Wayne, John Candy, and I put into it. John, who truly loved the team, agreed to the sale because he recognized that Wayne and I were being devastated by the team's financial losses. Still, he hated to let go of it.

On the morning after the sale, I was shocked to learn that overnight John had died of a heart attack. He had been in the middle of shooting a film in Mexico, and was discovered at the house rented for him there. Some of his friends angrily blamed me for the Argos-related stress John experienced. It was something I had thought about, but obviously his problems were greater than that. To my eye John weighed 300 pounds, and heart disease ran in his family. Forty-three years old when he died, John was eight years older than his own father had been when he, too, was felled by coronary disease. Though we had all worried about John's health, his passing was unexpected. His funeral, which I attended with Wayne, was filled with friends and family who were in utter shock.

At the funeral, I talked with Jim Belushi and Dan Aykroyd, and all of us felt an incredible sense of loss. We were also confronted by the very stark reality that we walk this earth for a very short time. Everything in life, every one of us, is fragile, and in a moment all can be lost. It was sobering.

John Candy's death added to the sense of unreality that I experienced in so much of my life in early 1994. Fortunately, there were moments of relief. The Kings did not have a great season, in part because we suffered a certain post–Stanley Cup series letdown. However we still played to a mostly sold-out Forum, and Wayne's performance continued to excite the fans. Although I couldn't go as often as before, I attended many games. It was a relief to hear fans call out and cheer, and to lose myself in the sport.

In late March, after John died, Gretzky closed in on Gordie Howe's record for goals scored in a lifetime. It appeared that he would cross the threshold in a series at the end of the month. I knew that something had to be done to commemorate the event, but I didn't know what.

I was at a loss to imagine what kind of gift might mean something to a person who was adored everywhere he went and could buy himself anything his heart desired. When I called Wayne's wife, Janet, at home, she thought about the question for a minute and then said, "How about a Corniche?"

Although I thought she might suggest something sentimental, I was pleased she had come up with something of real value. And once the proposal was out there, I tried to meet it. I contacted Joe Cohen, who was buying the team, and he agreed to look into it. Eventually a deal was made on a Rolls convertible, which cost about $300,000.

Wayne broke the record at the end of March. I was watching the game with Kurt Russell, who was so excited he wanted to jump over the glass and onto the ice. The game was stopped. The crowd rose and cheered. Wayne skated over, shook my hand, and gave me his game jersey. At the next game we gave the car to him as part of the ceremony marking his achievement. Later on, Wayne showed little interest in it, but he was excited about Janet driving it.

Moments like the one when Wayne broke Howe's record helped keep my spirits up. But in fact, I wasn't experiencing the kind of dread one might assume I would. Maybe it was because I thought that everything we had done was justified. Maybe it was because I truly believed that we had set up deals to bring in enough money to fix everything. Whatever the reason, I did not expect my entire empire to fall apart. I anticipated, instead, an orderly kind of transition. Companies would be sold or closed, but in the end I would be left to rebuild.

My confidence held in the spring of 1994, even after EAB sued me in New York, and news of their action made it into the L.A. Times. When we were asked to comment, we challenged the notion that the debt in question—the $25 million related to the circular transaction—really existed at all. When Fox then sued us for the cost of the ads and prints related to Mannequin Two we made the same kind of public argument, alleging that the studio had mishandled the film.

Right up until 6 P.M. on April 20, 1994, we held out like settlers in a wagon train under attack. Then came news that the Feds were on their way—only they weren't coming to rescue us—they were joining the Indians.

"Bruce, come here right away."

It was Su Waks, calling on the office intercom. There was a tension and urgency in her voice that chilled me. I got up from my desk and quickly crossed the thirty feet of hallway to her office. She was sitting with Nora Rothrock, and they had another of our employees, Joanna Orahek, on the phone.

"Tell Bruce what you just told me, Joanna," said Su.

Joanna's voice crackled through the speaker, with a hollowness that sounded like fear.

"The FBI was just here," she said. "Two women. They gave me a subpoena, and they wanted me to talk about the company. I told them I wanted to talk to a lawyer first, and they said okay. They gave me their cards and said my lawyer should call them right away."

Joanna was upset. Su asked a few questions and tried to reassure her. Su also asked her to fax over the subpoena, so we could look at it. When Joanna hung up, Su and Nora just looked at me. I said the first thing that came to mind.

"We're screwed."

Su insisted that it was not necessarily the disaster I imagined. The FBI might be on a fishing expedition. The inquiry might just cover some small incident involving Joanna, she said. Then the phone rang again. It was David Begelman.

"I talked to them. They were very nice," said David. "We sat down and went over a few things. I think it went very well."

Only David would have both the arrogance and the ignorance to believe that he could invite a couple of FBI agents into his home and achieve anything with charm and a chat. (I was almost that over-confident, but not quite.) It is a testament to how isolated he was from the world outside Hollywood, and how deluded he was about his own power. I can't say he was unique in that. Powerful people, especially in the movie business, often believe that the world will treat them in the same fawning way that their underlings in The Business do. That belief makes them seem shockingly naive when they bump up against another kind of power—the FBI for instance—that is outside of their realm.

After David's call, Su became as freaked out as me. We realized that there was likely to be a big investigation and that agents could be fanning out across the city to talk to anyone who might be associated with me. We had to tell all the others who were still in their offices that agents were likely to call on them when they got home. Some of those people were so frightened by the prospect of being confronted that they wouldn't go home that night.

As panic swept over us, we talked about the damning documents that filled some of our files: duplicate tax returns, different sets of books, altered contracts. Some people went to their private offices and began rifling through the stuff and feeding the most incriminating papers into shredders. I let them go ahead with this, though I knew it was a useless exercise. There was nothing in our offices that couldn't be located at some bank, or other company. But for that night, anyway, a few people thought they were doing something in their own defense.

While others did their shredding, I began calling people who were not at work. At Steve Rubinger's house, his wife picked up the phone and said, "He's a little tied up right now." I could tell by the tone of her voice that the FBI was already there. Steve later called me back and said he had talked with the agents, telling them he knew very little about our dealings with banks.

After talking with Steve's wife I telephoned Jane at her home in Studio City to warn her. I also called my horse trainer, Emmanuel de Seroux, and a woman I had recently begun dating, Mara Bruckner. None of them reported any contact with the authorities, but before the investigation was finished, they would all be interviewed. I also called my lawyers and left messages for them.

By nine o'clock that night, all that was left for me was to head home to discover if the FBI was waiting for me, too. I called Mara again and arranged to meet her at a coffee shop so I could explain a bit more of what was going on and to reassure her. In that brief conversation, I told her that everything would be okay, that I had good lawyers and we would work something out. That was mostly bravado on my part. I couldn't predict what might happen, but I feared that some of what we had done was bad enough to land me and maybe a few others in prison.

Mara was in better spirits when I left her to drive through Westwood and then up into Holmby Hills. I passed the Playboy Mansion, wondering if, when I rounded the curve on Faring Drive, I would see a couple of government cars parked in front of my home. When I saw there was no one there, I went through the gate and up the driveway, parked, and went inside.

For the rest of the night I listened for the doorbell to ring, but it never did. Across the city, agents visited the homes of Rubinger, Waks, and others. But they left me alone. Of course, I was their prime target, and obviously they were working all around me, closing the circle slowly, in the hope that they would have all the answers before they started asking me any questions. I went to bed that night, but I didn't sleep.

On the morning that followed the initial FBI sweep, a dozen-or-so key people on my staff were all in my office by 10 A.M. Tom Pollack, my criminal attorney, arrived soon after we had all gathered. He had already spoken to the prosecutor assigned to the case, Peter Spivak, and had a sense of what was happening. No one was going to be arrested and carted off to jail, he said. For the moment the authorities were interested mainly in documents.

"Step One," he said, "is don't do anything that will exacerbate the problem. By that I mean, don't hide anything, don't shred anything. Step Two should be for each of you, except Bruce, to hire a lawyer."

At that moment every person in the room seemed to take a deep breath. A few said that they wanted Pollack to represent them, too. Someone else asked why he couldn't stand up for all of us, as a group. "I can give you a little advice for the next few days," he answered. "But it is in your best interest to get individual attorneys. I cannot represent everyone here."

Pollack was right. From the moment that the subpoenas began to fly, every person in the organization had to become self-protective. Each of us had responsibilities to family and friends. Each of us had played a distinct role in what had happened. I pledged to pay the $10,000 to $20,000 fees each lawyer requested as a retainer. Some of the money came from Wayne Gretzky, who volunteered to do whatever he could.

The meeting where I told Wayne about the FBI probe remained vivid in my mind years later. I had arranged it with a call to his house, suggesting that he come to a little restaurant he liked near his home. We sat at a private table and I told him what had happened. I think he was more upset than I.

"I can't believe it," he said. "Oh, my God."

Wayne had known something of my financial problems. Certainly I had consulted him about the sale of the Kings. But he was definitely shocked to hear that a criminal investigation was underway and I was the target. He immediately said, "Whatever you need, Bruce, it's yours." I asked only for a little help with the attorney fees, and he gave it.

Like every one of the friends I contacted, Wayne was very concerned about my future, and gratified to hear I had the best legal help. As Tom Pollack and I began to prepare to confront the prosecutors, I came to believe I was in good hands. From the very beginning, we were determined to tell the truth, and I was ready to take responsibility for what I had done. I was not going to say that I just signed the papers but had no idea what was really going on. I had been a hands-on boss. I set the tone. And no matter what anyone else did, I had ultimate responsibility.

At the same time, I wasn't going to just roll over and say I was a schemer who had deliberately set out to defraud various banks. If I was going to tell the truth about my actions, I was also going to make sure the truth came out where the banks were concerned. I was going to tell the truth about Credit Lyonnais's betrayal in Cannes, and about EAB's deception in the circular transaction. I was going to talk about the payoffs requested and accepted by individual bank officers, and about under-the-table favors—like that loan to the governor of Kentucky—that the bankers had asked me to perform. Before I finished, I would make sure that all the circumstances around my problems were known, and that the authorities also understood all the effort I had put into trying to right the wrongs.

The cornerstone of my struggle to pay off my debts was the sale of the Kings and construction of the new arena. By this time Cohen and Sudikoff had decided to take on the deal as individual investors, rather than through IDB. This didn't matter to me. What mattered was that they follow through despite whatever might happen to me. When I contacted them, they said they would stand firm, and they did, despite the growing signs that I was in serious trouble.

Within a week of the FBI's move against us, rumors began to circulate around Los Angeles. UNC Pacific Airmotive Corp., which had maintained my 727, sued us for failing to pay for repairs they had done. Then one of the smaller banks we had done business with—Republic of Torrance—filed suit over nonpayment. They were joined by JMB Properties, the landlord for our offices, who said we owed almost $300,000 in back rent. All of this was revealed in a small article in the *Los Angeles Times*.

Our crisis finally made it onto the front page on the last Friday in April 1994. "McNall Being Investigated by Grand Jury" screamed the headline. The piece, cowritten by a sportswriter and a business reporter, said I was being investigated for allegedly falsifying loan documents. For once I declined to be interviewed by the press. But I gave Tom Pollack permission to confirm that we were under investigation and to state my position. "Mr. McNall believes that once the government completes its inquiry," said Tom, "no action will be taken."

That wasn't mere bravado. I knew we had done some truly egregious things. But, because the banks were so intimately involved with it all, I had convinced myself that my crimes weren't as serious as they really were. In my state of denial, I was more concerned about completing the sale of the Kings than I was about going to jail. As April turned to May, I spent a great deal of my time on the phone with bankers, urging them to delay forcing us into bankruptcy. Under the law, three lenders could band together and force it upon us. That would almost certainly kill the sale of the Kings, and kill what I thought was the best chance for us to pay off a large part of our debt.

The pleading I did with bank officers was not easy. The last of those conversations, with an officer of EAB, took place on the phone near the end of business of Friday, May 13, 1994.

"We've decided to force you into bankruptcy," he said.

"You can't do that!" I countered. "Your bank is the reason this is all happening. You were the ones who said to hide the circular transactions on the financial statements. You were the ones responsible at the start."

That argument achieved nothing. It was obvious to me that they were going through with it. It was just as obvious that the result would be worse for them than for me. I was furious. "If you do this, you won't see a nickel from any settlement!" I shouted. "You're cutting your own throat." I hung up the phone, knowing that I had to immediately close the sale with Cohen and Sudikoff before the hearing on the bankruptcy petition began. It was scheduled for 3 P.M. Monday.

Accomplishing the sale would require a gargantuan legal effort involving my attorneys, the buyers, the banks financing the deal, and every other party. The work took place in two huge conference rooms at the firm of Gibson, Dunn, and Crutcher. It began Friday and continued nonstop through Sunday. More than two dozen people spent a coffee-soaked weekend grinding out the paperwork. At one point even my ex-wife, Jane, got involved when her lawyer appeared and demanded she get payment in exchange for her signature on certain documents. We gave it to her.

On Monday, May 16, 1994, I went to the office, where a twenty-foot conference room table was loaded with documents. Cohen and Sudikoff arrived and we sat down to sign. After the last signature was made, millions of dollars were transferred to the various parties via telegraph. My personal bankruptcy attorney, Rick Wynne, raced to Federal Bankruptcy Court for a 3 P.M. hearing. At 2:59, he was on his cell phone as he walked into the courtroom. We reported to him that the monies had been deposited. The deal was complete. Moments later, the lawyers representing the banks asked Judge Lisa Hill Fenning to somehow undo the transaction. She refused, noting that the bankruptcy petition had not yet been approved, and that a trustee had not yet been named to take over my businesses. As far as she and the law were concerned, I had every right to execute the sale when I did.

(It's important to note that the controversy did not end when the papers were signed. In a matter of months IDB was rocked by an accounting fraud scandal. The company was sold, and Sudikoff and Cohen were forced to sell the Kings. A group led by industrialist Phil Anshutz and Ed Roski, an L.A. developer, bought the team. After taking control, they put the team into bankruptcy, which freed them from all of their contracts—including the lease with Jerry Buss and my employment contract, which had been of benefit to my creditors, Jane, and my children. Before it was over, they did build the new arena, now called the Staples Center. But on the negative side, I lost my contract. That meant my creditors received none of the income I could have earned. The same was true for Jane and the kids. The Kings eventually lost Gretzky, too. He became a free agent and went to St. Louis. Jeff Sudikoff, by the way, pled guilty to a felony in the IDB scandal.)

Suddenly the Kings were no longer under my control. Gladden was no more. The Argos belonged to Labatt. As soon as I had learned of the criminal investigation I had resigned from the NHL chairman's post. I had shut down the coin and horse operations. Merrill Lynch was sifting through the wreckage of the NFA coins funds and preparing to make whole those investors who had lost money. (To their credit, they eventually did cover much of what people lost.) The empire I had spent twenty-five years constructing, from my first sale at Coins of the World Etc., was gone. I was now in the business of untangling my business affairs and defending myself from criminal charges. It became a full-time job.

The two tasks were intertwined, which I discovered as I worked with bankruptcy trustee Todd Nielson. Any restitution I could make on the hundreds of millions of dollars in defaulted loans would be considered in a positive light by the courts. Of course, I didn't know exactly what kind of case the federal investigators were cooking up, because they still hadn't come to me directly. Instead they were calling in my employees and associates, one by one, and demanding cooperation. Some, like Mark Eastman and Steve Nessenblatt, stood firm. Others quickly made deals, agreeing to tell all in exchange for charges being dropped or reduced. In a short time, those people were literally gushing information in hopes that prosecutors would go easy on them. Some even resorted to accusing the innocent, including several prominent business associates and L.A. lawyers, in order to save themselves.

Most of the people close to me thought I should fight the charges. Considering the various banks' actions, they thought that I could win, and avoid jail entirely. When I looked at the history of so-called white-collar crime prosecutions, it did seem like the odds were in my favor. Many investigations of business crimes fall apart because the schemes are so complex that prosecutors have trouble making a coherent case for a jury. Even when convictions are obtained, people rarely spend much time in jail for business fraud. Executives at E. F. Hutton committed two thousand felonies in a check-kiting conspiracy in the mid-1980s, but no one did time. In 1994, Prudential Securities bilked customers out of more than $1 billion, and yet no one was jailed in that case, either.

On the surface, it did seem like I might fare well in a trial. But there was one big difference in my case. I was the chief, and sometimes sole stockholder, in the companies that got in trouble. There was no board of directors that could be held accountable. There were few corporate shields that I could hide behind. There was no doubt in my mind that a prosecutor could, and should, try to pin everything on me personally. I had to conclude that it would be best to avoid a trial, as well as the worst-case scenario of being convicted on dozens of counts.

I wasn't going to lie or deny that I had done wrong. And I was also eager to protect the people who worked for me. No matter what others said and did, I felt that as the boss, I should bear the brunt of the government's wrath. I should protect them. But even though I was determined to take responsibility, I also felt justified, given the behavior of my banks, in fighting with prosecutors over what constituted a fair deal. I believed that if all the facts came out, and everything about the banks' actions was known, the courts would be more lenient with me and everyone else who was in trouble. My criminal lawyer, Tom Pollack, agreed and began a lengthy and heated negotiation with the federal prosecutors. We were not powerless in those talks. After all, no one had more information about what had happened, and where our remaining assets might be found, than I.

While Tom worked on the criminal case, for nearly three years I spent untold hours working with the bankruptcy trustee, Todd Nielson, to determine which creditors were worthy and which ones were coconspirators. I had never met someone with a firmer sense of right and wrong, and a tougher attitude about it, than Nielson. He was a former FBI agent, a devout Mormon, and deadly serious. In our first few meetings, he seemed to regard me as guilty until proven innocent. Then I began to tell him about Credit Lyonnais and EAB. He wouldn't take my word for what had happened. But as he did his own research, he discovered that everything I had told him was true. His confidence in what I told him was bolstered when Steve Nessenblatt shared documents and tapes he had made of crucial conversations with bankers. Eventually Todd and Leonard Gumport and Sue Montgomery, the lawyers appointed to represent the creditors, concluded that bank officers had committed such serious crimes that their claims against me were diminished.

However, there was no denying I was guilty of certain frauds. Tom Pollack and I tried to determine which of the charges the prosecutors were considering were the most serious, and how to limit the amount of time I might serve in jail. I was eager to tell the government everything, in hopes that my cooperation would reduce any penalties. Eventually I agreed to participate in what insiders call "Queen for a Day." This is a meeting that is held before the government tells you what you face, or what kind of plea agreement is possible. They invite you to explain everything you can, and agree, under an enforceable contract, that nothing you tell them can be used against you.

My moment of truth-telling took place in a stark government office inside the Westwood federal building. Assistant U.S. Attorney Peter Spivak asked most of the questions. He seemed fairly sure that I was a crook, but was open-minded enough to listen to me. He was assisted by FBI special agents Sharon Elkins and Pat Chamberlain, who were lead investigators on my case. Elkins and Chamberlain glared at me through all the hours we spent together, and seemed far more determined than Spivak to see me jailed for a good long time.

Fortunately, in our federal justice system, the desires of FBI agents have little to do with criminal sentencing. Instead, the process depends on the judgments of prosecutors and congressionally established guidelines, intended to make sentences uniform across the country. The guidelines allow for time to be taken off a term if the accused cooperates fully. But it is often left to the prosecutors to recommend those adjustments.

In my case, I hoped that the facts, and all my cooperation, would count for a significant reduction in my ultimate sentence. I also knew that the prosecutors intended to recommend probation, and no time served, to reward nearly all of my employees for the help they had provided. I prayed that if a judge saw this, saw that in one case after another, my associates were being treated with great leniency, then maybe, when my case came up, I might get a little of the same.

Naturally, the U.S. attorneys knew I was hoping for that kind of outcome, so they decided to force me in front of the judge first. They planned to recommend only a minor reduction in my sentence, even though I had given up more than two years of my life to uncover facts for them and the bankruptcy trustee. (The trustee himself would testify that no one cooperated more than I did.)

While the negotiations dragged on, my travails were followed intently by the press—even national papers like the *Wall Street Journal* and *USA Today* jumped into the fray. Surely hundreds of gallons of ink were spent on articles analyzing both my successes and my failures. Most of the writers got at least part of the story right. But only one, *L.A. Daily News* writer Jim Tranquada, was able to wrap it up in a single sentence. "In the end," he wrote, "Bruce McNall wanted too much to be liked."

This was the fatal flaw that I began to recognize as I sifted through the wreckage of my businesses. I failed because I refused to say no, refused to make enemies, refused to report bad news to investors and partners. From the moment when I got in trouble with Bunker Hunt, I was unable to deliver bad news. It wasn't that I was afraid of failure. It was that I was desperate to have everyone around me, like me. At this I succeeded, even after I was bankrupt and under indictment. In the months that passed before I pleaded guilty, hundreds of people came forward, a couple of whom had lost money with me, and vouched for me. I was broke. I faced prison. But I was still loved.

I don't come from crying stock. My father never cried. Neither did I. As the plea bargaining continued, and the prospect of prison grew, I held myself together, fearing that one crack, one moment of despair, would break the whole facade. Finally, on a sunny day in December, I met Pollack at his office in Century City. He drove me over to the courthouse where a dozen reporters and photographers converged on us as we entered the building. The plea was entered in front of Judge Richard Paez, a judge recently appointed by President Clinton. The prosecutors requested that bail be set at $1 million. My lawyer argued that I was cooperating and no risk to the community. I was finally asked to post $100,000, which Rogie Vachon did for me, by pledging his vacation house.

I was in a state of shock, feeling almost like I was having an out-of-body experience. As the lawyers talked, I silently berated myself. How could I have been so reckless, so foolish? What kind of insecurity had driven me to seek everyone's approval, even if it meant breaking the law? Was I criminal, delusional, immoral?

After the judge accepted the plea and ended the hearing I was led downstairs to a courthouse facility where I was fingerprinted and mug shots were made. The U.S. marshals were very deferential to me, and as I walked by the holding cells, a few of the people within called out for autographs. In less than an hour I was out, and Pollack was driving me back to his office where I picked up my car.

Having long since lost my house, and even the furniture in it, I spent that night at a condo I had rented. A few days later I saw Katie, who was eleven, and P. J., who was nine. They understood I was in trouble, but we hardly ever talked about it. I tried to prepare them for the prospect that I might be sent away to prison. They stuck with me, as did my friends. It was at that time that I was introduced to the famous architect Frank Gehry and we became very close. A Canadian, Frank loved hockey. He also loved underdogs, and we began having dinner together about once a week. I also met a young attorney and business developer, Robert Geringer, who would come to play a huge role in my future. I met Robert through his business partner Jerry Pressman. Pressman was a big hockey fan, and good friend. Robert seemed to understand how I had stumbled into so much trouble. But more importantly, he believed that I had a future in the film business, and he was interested in being partners.

Frank provided encouragement and Robert contributed hope as the judge, prosecutor, and my lawyer spent weeks, and then months haggling over my sentence. My job during that period was to do everything I could to help the government, especially the bankruptcy trustee, locate assets that would go to my creditors. I hid nothing from Todd Nielson, not even the bank accounts that were maintained offshore. More than a million dollars were recovered from those secret accounts, and while people would continue to speculate that I kept some money hidden, I did not.

Ironically, the complexity of all my businesses and the prospect of Steve and Mark going to trial contributed to long delays in my sentencing. I was hoping that the trials would unearth information that would persuade the judge to downgrade my sentence. The prosecutors agreed to delays so that I could keep working with them, and with Todd Nielson, to develop evidence to unravel our various schemes.

I focused on this work almost exclusively, falling into a routine that had me shuttling between my lawyer's offices and the bankruptcy trustee's quarters. The only big event outside that grind occurred in the middle of 1995. David Begelman had been working the town, trying to set up a new business. He had borrowed a large sum of money from an investor, who was beginning to chase him for repayment. None of the studios were willing to give him distribution. At seventy-three, it appeared that he was finished. Hardly the type to retire, David checked into a hotel in Century City, lay down on the bed, and shot himself in the head. Hollywood was shocked. I was not completely surprised, but I was devastated by the actual event. Here was another deep loss, another illustration of how wrong things could go when people, desperate for acceptance and success, fail.

The option David chose was never open to me. I am not the suicidal type. After his death, I redoubled my effort to help the bankruptcy trustee, doing everything I could to gain credits against my prison term. Finally, in December 1996, I had done all I could for the government and they stopped granting delays in my sentencing. I was called back before Judge Paez to hear his ruling on the precise amount of prison time I would serve.

When the day came, Tom and I again drove to the courthouse and walked through the media gauntlet. Judge Paez's courtroom was a high-ceilinged space with polished wood paneling. We sat down at the defense table, to the judge's right, and waited until he entered.

When we finally began the proceedings, the government and my attorney argued over how much my sentence should be reduced because of my cooperation. Tom Pollack—who by this time was working without pay—did an excellent job, calling Todd Nielson and Leonard Gumport to testify in my favor. Gradually the credits I received brought my sentence down to between seventy and seventy-eight months. Then the judge asked me if I had anything to say.

I stood and said I was sorry, and that I recognized I had let many people down. I told the judge that I felt a great deal of remorse for my victims. I included the banks in the list of those I had harmed, but stressed particularly the people who had worked with me and, most of all, my family. "The ones I feel worst about are my own children," I concluded. With those words I choked up and could speak no more.

The judge then proceeded to sentence me to the shortest term—seventy months—permitted under the guidelines that had been set for my crimes. I was also required to pay $5 million in restitution, which would come from any income I might earn in the future. We asked that I be allowed to surrender on Monday, March 10, two days after my daughter Katie's birthday. The judge allowed it.

When the judge struck his gavel and rose, so did we. After he left the room I heaved an enormous sigh. Of course I dreaded what was to come, but it was a relief in a way to have the matter settled. Peter Spivak, the prosecutor, stood up and we shook hands. I told him that he had been fair and decent throughout the case, and that I was grateful for that. As I walked out I noticed the two FBI agents on my case—Chamberlain and Elkins—sitting in the back of the courtroom. We did not acknowledge each other.

Soon after my sentence was handed down, the prosecutors moved to resolve all the other cases. Joanna Orahek was allowed to plead guilty to falsifying tax returns and financial statements. She served only probation.

Robert Houston, Nora Rothrock, Steve Rubinger, and five others all made similar pleas, and escaped without serving time. The last to make a deal was Su Waks. She was sentenced to just three years, even though she had tried to get away with hiding money overseas. Just two of the people charged, Steve Nessenblatt and Mark Eastman, dug in for a long-term fight, declaring they would go to trial before accepting guilt. Steve eventually pleaded and got a ten-month sentence. Mark Eastman had two trials and two hung juries.

In the period before I went off to prison I found great support from a number of friends, most especially from Mara Bruckner and Robert Geringer. Smart, sensitive, and truly trustworthy, Mara refused to judge me for what I had done in my past, but was mainly concerned with how I was faring in the present. We became very much attached to each other, and I began to think we had a future. We rented a place together in Pacific Palisades, which we shared for the six months before my incarceration.

It must have been terribly difficult for her. She was getting to know me under the worst of circumstances. I had lost almost everything. I was deeply worried about going to prison. But she did not abandon me. Instead, she encouraged me to look to the long-term future, the future after prison, and she urged me to try to learn something from my experiences. Those were two good places to focus my attention.

While Mara cared for me on a deeply emotional level, I received equally sincere support on a business level from Robert Geringer. We began to talk about my finances, and how I might emerge from my troubles and be able to function in business. He provided me with an office, and we explored projects we could do together in the entertainment field. I introduced him to people I knew. He paid me a salary that helped me survive and give something to my kids. He was a quick study. I trusted him. And we both understood that when I got out of prison, we would work together.

As Robert and Mara helped me with the most critical aspects of my life, there were several others who offered friendship that was constant and unwavering. Mara and I went out to dinner with Howard Baldwin and his wife, Karen, weekly. Wayne and Janet Gretzky invited us to their home regularly. Alan Thicke regularly called to boost my spirits, as did Frank and Berta Gehry, Luc and Stacia Robitaille, and Rogie Vachon. Paul Anka invited us to Vegas, while Kurt Russell and Goldie Hawn took us to dinner. Don Sterling, owner of the Clippers, invited me to almost every home game, where we sat on the floor level together. At one of those games, Charles Barkley came over right as they were about to play the National Anthem and wished me luck. Sometimes big groups of us would get together— Howard and Karen, Wayne and Janet, Alan, Rogie, Luc, Frank—and just enjoy ourselves. Once, when I was in New York, a group of us went to Wayne's All-Star Cafe for a sort of farewell dinner. The line-up included Wayne, Mara, Robert, Alan, and me.

All of these people helped, but nothing they could say or do really distracted me from what loomed in the immediate future. I was going to prison. As the date got closer I began to focus on what awaited me there. In one of the stranger twists of my story, I was contacted by Heidi Fleiss's attorney to ask if I would speak with her. She was having real trouble coping with being a felon, and being the subject of such intense publicity. Heidi, you will recall, was the famous Hollywood "Madam" who had provided prostitutes to a huge number of famous people. Her case transfixed the public and made her a figure of derision nationwide. She thought I might understand what it was like to be a famous felon.

We got together at a restaurant in L.A., a quiet place where we wouldn't be noticed, and I tried to tell her how I was coping. First of all, I told her that I had accepted that what the public thought was beyond my control. Second, I said that I was trying to understand what I had done, and learn from my mistakes. Heidi seemed to me to be in very bad shape. She looked very thin, gaunt even, and frightened. She wore dark glasses, and seemed mired in depression.

I agreed to see her again, and I did. Once I invited her to a hockey game. We went to the owner's dinner before the game. It was packed with celebrities, but no one got more attention than Heidi. To make everyone more comfortable I took her aside with Joe Cohen's wife, Rita. We conspired to play a joke on Joe. Heidi went up to him and said, "Joe, it's been so long. What's it been, three months since we saw you? The girls all miss you!" Rita turned on Joe, demanding an explanation. Joe sputtered a defense and then we all laughed, including Heidi. My guess is that it had been a long time since she had laughed.

A few months after those meetings with Heidi, Mara and I were watching *The Tonight Show* when Jay Leno said that I was dating Heidi Fleiss. "I wonder if he's getting a discount?" joked Jay.

I was wondering where that came from. Sure enough, a week later, *People* magazine ran a story quoting Heidi saying she was in love with me and wanted to have my child. I thought it must be untrue, a case of Hollywood gossip run amok. I called Heidi and she shocked me by saying, "No, it's really how I feel." I told her I was flattered and spoken for by Mara. Heidi apologized and volunteered to talk to Mara, whose friends and family had seen the piece. Mara said it was all right, she didn't need to talk to Heidi. Of course, Heidi never stopped saying, "I'm in love with Bruce McNall."

Heidi provided some wonderful distractions and commiseration from a fellow felon's point of view. But even more important information came to me, unsolicited, from a former state senator named Frank Hill who had been convicted of bribery and sentenced to federal prison at Boron, California. Frank wrote me a series of letters telling me about how the federal prison system worked, and volunteered to answer any questions I had.

Oddly enough, lawyers, even criminal lawyers, have little understanding of how prisons work. No one could tell me about visits, phone calls, prison routines, safety, any of it. To get answers, I drove out to Boron, in the desert, to spend time with Frank. It was reassuring to see he was physically well and more or less safe. I decided to ask the judge that I be assigned to Boron, where I had a friend, and the transition would be easier.

Unfortunately, though the judge agreed to recommend Boron, he had no power over my assignment. That was up to the Federal Bureau of Prisons, and they had another idea. They assigned me to the federal prison camp at Lompoc, which is about three hours north of Los Angeles, in a farm region where the nearest city is Santa Maria.

To prepare for the transition, I hired a former Lompoc counselor who ran a service for people who were about to go in. We met a few times, and he tried to tell me what to expect. He also met with my children, and told them that I was going to a place where violence was extremely rare. He also reassured them that I would be able to talk to them on the telephone, and that they could visit.

A few weeks before my surrender date, the counselor even took us on a trip to Lompoc, to give me, P.J., and Katie a more realistic sense of what I faced. It was a surreal outing. The worst moment came when we turned down the prison road and saw the massive, high-security facility that dominates the landscape. "Oh, you're not going in there," the counselor said reassuringly. And sure enough, we turned down another lane, which led to a less-secure prison camp. I thought the place didn't look nearly as bad as I feared. There were Quonset huts and a farm. Seeing it had a calming effect on me and on the kids.

Besides getting help from the counselor, I also contacted the brother of a neighbor, who had been incarcerated at Lompoc. He spoke to me by phone and filled me in on what to bring. He recommended gray sweats, plain white underwear, cheap tennis shoes, and really comfortable work shoes. He told me to bring extra eyeglasses, a cheap radio, and a cheap watch. I got all the stuff together the week before my surrender.

With two days to go, Jane and I took Katie and some of her friends to a Japanese restaurant to celebrate her birthday. I tried to act as I normally would, but I was pretty darn nervous. On the next day, Sunday, I went to see the kids in the afternoon. I told them they could come see me soon. As I turned to leave, Katie just wandered off, unable to see me go. P. J. hugged me and said, "Don't go! Don't go!" He cried, and I began to cry. "You're really upsetting the kids," said Jane. "Just go." She was right. I tore myself away, and closed the door behind me.

12

YOU MIGHT BELIEVE THAT IN your last hours of freedom, before you are to be locked away for years, you would inhale the life around you with an intense, even spiritual appreciation. Colors would be more vivid, flavors more delicious, sounds more complex. You can believe that you would feel this way, but given my experience, I doubt you would.

On my four-hour journey from Pacific Palisades to the federal prison camp in Lompoc, a drive that took me up Topanga Canyon to the 101 Freeway, through Oxnard, Ventura, and Santa Barbara, I barely noticed the landscape that flew by. I couldn't taste the breakfast—my last meal on the outside—that we stopped to eat. I remember almost nothing of the conversation in the car. I was too much in shock, too numb, already drifting in a self-protective haze, to take any of it in.

I was driven to Lompoc by Michael Franzese. His wife, Cammy, rode up front with him while Mara and I sat in the back. Famous for leaving the Mafia and living to tell about it, Michael had become a friend in recent years. He had been in prison. He approached his duty with a calm that came from his experience. He had told me, many times, that the camp would not be as bad as I feared, or as easy as I hoped. I would soon understand that he was right on both counts.

The Lompoc camp is one of the three federal lockups—the others are a maximum security penitentiary and a medium-level prison—that occupy a sprawling property on both sides of a twisting two-lane road. No matter which facility you are sentenced to, your introduction to The System is at the penitentiary, where a slogan written on a huge boulder at the entrance welcomes you to "The New Rock." (Lompoc took over for the old Rock—Alcatraz—when it was closed.)

My three companions walked me to the gate and into a little reception building. I carried a bag that I had stuffed with books, sweatpants and shirts, a radio and, most importantly, the address book I would use to make my official list of names for visits and phone calls. We went inside and I told the guard I was there to self-surrender. He said I would have to say goodbye there. I shook hands with Michael, hugged Cammy, and kissed Mara.

Before they left, the guard took my bag and sifted through the contents. "You can't bring any of this in," he said. I didn't protest, even though I had been told that these items were okay. I gave Mara the bag. "I'll see you soon," I said, already anticipating my first visiting day. After nearly three years of waiting, we were all prepared to say goodbye. We managed to do it without tears.

I was led into a windowless holding room, where three other guys were seated on a bench. The guard gave me some paperwork to fill out. After I did, I waited there for about an hour. I felt like a robot, and I think I had the kind of experience people talk about when they have a brush with death. I was there, but I was also outside myself, observing myself.

In the next hour or so I got an inmate handbook, which was filled with warnings about infractions that would get you transferred to the high-security unit nicknamed "The Hole." I underwent a strip search that was almost microscopic in its thoroughness. I was photographed and fingerprinted, and then they asked me to wait while they cleared some press photographers away from the entrance. When that was done, I was led to a prison van for the ride to the camp. Through all of it I was relieved to see that the guards—at least these guards—were calm and professional, not the sadistic sons of bitches you fear occupy every job in a prison.

Much later I would discover that while I was being processed, Michael, Mara, and Cammy had experienced their own little adventure. They had left the reception building with my bag, walked to Michael's car, and thrown it in the trunk. But as they were leaving, they were approached by an inmate who was raking in a garden by the gate. Chris Shafer, the same Chris Shafer who had advised me on Lompoc by phone, told Michael to stop at a bend in the road and quickly deposit the bag by a certain tree.

Michael was game, though Cammy and Mara were afraid. He drove slowly to the appointed spot, which was hidden from the view of the men in the watchtowers at the penitentiary. He got out, hurriedly retrieved the bag from the trunk, and raced to put it in the hiding place. As soon as he got back to the car he saw Shafer run from the underbrush to the bag. He was pushing a wheelbarrow. He grabbed the bag and put it in the wheelbarrow, covered it with leaves, and trotted off.

The adventure wasn't over yet. No sooner had Michael restarted the engine than a prison patrol car pulled up behind him with its emergency lights flashing. The officer got out and came up to the driver's window. He asked if Michael was having a problem. He made up something about taking a wrong turn—in fact they were in a restricted area—and the officer bought it. Michael turned his car around, and with heart pounding, drove away.

"You're in A. Go in and see the OIC."

The guard who drove me to the camp was directing me to see the officer in charge in one of the two large buildings, A and B, that served as dormitories for the camp. Inside A, the OIC showed me around. A couple of offices were located by the front door, but almost the entire building was taken up by a huge room jammed with rows of double-decker bunks—150 or so—separated by tall wooden lockers. Toilets and showers were near the front of the room, betrayed by their odor.

My top bunk was in the middle of the room, but against the wall. This was good luck, since there are electrical outlets along the wall that can be tapped to power lights. Besides the bed, I would have one of the lockers nearby, and a folding metal chair, which I could bring with me to the TV room.

Because every inmate had a job during the day, at 3 P.M. the room was almost empty of people. I was sent outside to a laundry shed to obtain a stained, wafer-thin mattress and threadbare bedding. I also got a couple of prison uniforms: frayed khaki shirts and pants, all wrinkled, all too big. I got some tattered underwear and socks, too.

On my way back to the bunk I was stopped by a black man in a business suit. "McNall," he said, "my name is McFadden. What kind of job you want to do here?" I said that I didn't know, but since I had worked in an office maybe I could do clerical stuff. He said, "Okay, let me think about that," and walked away. Although I didn't know it, McFadden was the top administrator at the camp, and he would oversee my job assignments.

As I was making up my bed, men began to come in from their jobs. They seemed tough enough, but not like the fierce, muscle-bound predators you see in prison movies. Most looked at me, and then looked away. Finally one, a guy who looked like a cross between Santa and a biker whose front teeth have been knocked out, walked right to me. His name, he said, was Dayton Backes.

"You ain't supposed to be here," he said. "My bunky is coming back."

He stalked off to find out what was going on. As he did, I looked down and noticed that my bag, the one that had been taken from me at the penitentiary, was under the bottom bunk. I opened it up and saw that all my stuff was in there. As I began to jam it all in my locker a blond guy, maybe forty-five years old, came over and introduced himself as Chris Shafer. We shook hands.

"You got your stuff okay, huh?"

After I thanked him, Shafer told me how he had rescued the bag, and that this kind of thing was not unusual. He had heard I was coming, and had waited out there to see if I had arrived. Inmates at the camp were not fenced in, he said. They had jobs all over the place and could walk around. Everyone knew which trees were outside the line of sight of the watchtowers. "You'll be surprised what gets in here," he said.

Chris wandered away when Dayton returned to confirm that I was, in fact, where I belonged. Though he was a gruff, terrifying-looking guy, he was more than friendly and started running around to get me what I might need— a toothbrush, toothpaste, shampoo. Those things, along with some food items and other staples, could be bought in the camp commissary, but it was not open and it was a tradition of sorts to put together a care package for a new inmate.

Along with the care package, Dayton offered to fill me in on some of the unwritten rules of the place, and on the routine. I learned that I'd already broken one rule—directly asking Dayton what his crime was—but he said I'd get some slack on those things, at least for a while. (He was a bank robber, by the way, who committed his crimes dressed as a very ugly woman.) The prison routine, he explained, was what you'd expect, a schedule for rising, eating, working, resting. The most important moment of the day was the 4 P.M. "count" which is conducted at all federal prisons nationwide. Though prisoners were counted at other times, this was the most important one, and if you weren't at your bunk for it, you could expect trouble.

Four o'clock was bearing down on us, and the room was beginning to fill with men. Quite a few of them recognized me and came over to introduce themselves. I was not the only celebrity in the camp, though. Marvin Mitchelson, the famous divorce lawyer, was there serving time on a tax charge. Less famous, but still notable, was Charlie Knapp, who had been convicted in a highly publicized bank-fraud case.

But no one there was nearly as recognizable as me, and I could see right away that this would be both a gift and a problem. A few inmates seemed to look at me with suspicion, almost envy. But on the plus side, a lot of them greeted me warmly. One, big, tall, tattooed guy named Terry Ferguson spoke for them when he said, "Whatever you need, we'll look after you, get you all situated."

The men told me they had reserved me a seat in one of the TV rooms for a special program scheduled to air in a few hours. Sportscaster Tom Murray, then of Channel 9, was doing a special report on my rise and fall, and timed to mark my incarceration on that very day. I was exhausted, and hardly in the mood to see my troubles recapitulated on TV. But I didn't want to insult anyone or invite a negative first impression, so I thanked them for thinking of me and pledged to show up for the program.

What I really wanted to do was make a phone call, to let Mara and everyone else know I was okay. I also wanted to submit my list of phone contacts (they allowed thirty) and visitors (twenty) who would have to be investigated and approved by the authorities. Before the 4 P.M. count, I managed to find one of the counselors, a man named Solis, who gave me the forms for my lists. A short, stout man with long hair and a moustache, Solis would be the one person I could approach with problems and concerns. He seemed compassionate, if overwhelmed. He had so many people to attend to that an in-depth meeting with him lasted less than thirty seconds.

The 4 P.M. count was announced by someone shouting, "Stand up for count! Count time!" Each of the men went to his bunk and stood there, in silence, as two officers walked the rows and counted. When they finished, someone yelled, "Clear count." That was when the rush to the chow hall began. Men ran out the front door and across a little yard to line up at the door of the cafeteria.

Dayton walked over with me, and we stood near the end of the line. By the time we got in, every seat was taken, but people were getting up quickly. I grabbed a plastic tray and plastic dishes. When I got to the server, he threw a scoop of rice on my plate and followed it with what looked like meat stew. At the end of the line I picked up a cup of water and a plastic fork-spoon combination they called a spork.

I sat down with Dayton. The place was a storm of men's voices and guards' shouts. It smelled like a high-school cafeteria, and was segregated much the same way, with blacks here, Hispanics there, and whites in another area. Whites were a minority, maybe 20 percent, while blacks and Hispanics were each about 40 percent. Though each group kept to its own, there was no rivalry or warfare among them. It was more a matter of comfort than conflict.

Dinner lasted less than ten minutes. Afterward, Dayton and Terry Ferguson showed me the camp, walking with me to see the softball field, library, weight pile, and even the dairy farm. (Lompoc produces milk products that are shipped to federal facilities across the West.) There were no fences, but there were boundaries, which they pointed out. They also explained that it was important to get on a routine. You work, you exercise, you eat, you sleep. Dayton told me to find a job as soon as I could, by submitting a request—called a "cop-out"—to the guard in charge of the area where I wanted to work. Otherwise I would be assigned to the kitchen, which was the worst place to work.

When we got back to the A dorm, my main agenda was to fill out my phone list and my visiting list. Terry Ferguson volunteered to help. I realized immediately that this was because he enjoyed my company and, more importantly, it was something to do, something to occupy the time. I got my address book and read the information while Terry wrote, very neatly, like my secretary. That activity took us a full two hours.

As the time for the TV special drew close, I went back to Solis to request my phone call. It turned out that my account—all inmates place money in an account for commissary and phone privileges—was not yet established. When it was, I would receive an identification code that I would punch in with the phone's keypad. Then I would be able to dial any of my approved numbers. The calls were hugely expensive, and monitored by guards. In the meantime, the OIC opened an office and stood there while I called Mara. I told her I was safe, asked her to tell my kids the same, and quickly hung up.

Speaking to Mara, however briefly, was reassuring. Afterward I was able to smile a bit when the guys dragged me into the TV room. They had jammed it with sixty or seventy chairs, all of which faced a battered old set. The program we watched was fairly accurate, and the host made a point of reminding viewers that I was in prison that very night. When it was over, we all went back to the dorm and got ready for lights out. I climbed up into my bunk and got under the blanket, but on top of the sheets. I had been told that the guards are so picky about how you make up your bunk that most inmates just use the blanket and keep the sheets tucked in, since it made for less hassle. I put my head down on a thin, unpleasantly fragrant pillow and closed my eyes. I was too exhausted to lie there and fret. But I did think to myself, before falling asleep, that I had more than two thousand nights of prison left to serve.

If you mind your own business at a federal prison camp—in fact, at federal prisons of almost all types—you will never be raped, never be beaten, never be stuck with a shiv. Though perhaps common in state prisons, those kinds of things happen very rarely in federal facilities. When they do, they usually involve only those people who cause trouble for other inmates. And at the lowest security level, places like Lompoc, you are safe even if you are a jerk.

This doesn't mean it is a nice place. At Lompoc, the chow hall food is barely edible, the clothes are stained, ripped, and ill-fitting. The bathrooms are disgusting, and privacy, in a dorm with 150 men, is impossible. Most of the men are stable, but nutcases are common, too. One guy in the B dorm would pace the room at night and scream his lungs out. Another guy, who had been a homeless street-person on the outside, continued the lifestyle at Lompoc. He spent his days going through trash cans and smoking butts he found on the ground. He mumbled constantly about being a friend of the president and the chauffeur for various movie stars.

Though the disturbed few stood out, most of the men were just regular guys trying to do their time *without* going crazy. The majority were in for drug-related convictions. Chris Shafer and his brother, Bill, for example, had been perhaps the biggest marijuana smugglers in the country at one time.

They were rumored to have turned in many coconspirators, in exchange for shorter sentences. For that reason, they had few friends. Other inmates were serving terms for white-collar crimes, robberies at federal facilities, and various conspiracies. They were not so much violent criminals as overly resourceful and inadequately principled entrepreneurs.

The resourcefulness of the men was plain to see in the vast network of scams and businesses operated by those who lacked the outside resources to fill their commissary accounts with cash. There were laundrymen, who for a couple bucks a week dragged your bag of clothes to the washers and dryers and returned it all clean and folded. There were also men who made beds, ironed visiting-day outfits, and cooked meals. All of this was done in exchange for little items obtained from the commissary. (Other inmates traded in more illicit items, including drugs and homemade hooch, but I was never part of that.)

In little time, I had someone doing my laundry and someone making my bed. But the best service of all was performed by a chow hall cook named Hooey, who called himself "Chinaman" and insisted everyone else do the same. Chinaman was a young man who was missing nearly all of his teeth. He was a hell of a cook. He could turn government rice and whatever else he could find into a perfectly edible meal. He did this for me three times a day, delivering the plates of food directly to my bunk.

Officially, Hooey's meal service was frowned upon, but as long as we didn't make a show of it, the guards didn't seem to care. Besides, from the administration's standpoint, Chinaman was a very important man. He knew how to cook for a lot of people. His skill made the kitchen supervisor's job much easier. You don't mess that up by cracking down on him for sneaking some meals into the dorm. On the rare occasion when someone interrupted delivery, and he was thrown into a cell for punishment, Hooey would be back the next day laughing and declaring, "Nobody stop Chinaman."

Hooey refused every offer I made to pay him. I don't know if he hoped I might do him a favor in the future, but every time I tried to compensate him he would say, "No, no. You good man. I like doing this. If I need something, I ask you." He never did ask.

Another very good man in the camp was Mark Carter, an athletic-looking black man who became my personal trainer. I had arrived at camp fat and flabby. With Carter's help, I learned how to lift weights. He also walked the camp's track with me, until I was strong enough to begin jogging. With his help I lost pounds, added muscle, and got more fit than I had ever been in my life.

The weight pile is a central place in prison life all over the country. The quality of the equipment varies. Before I got to Lompoc, the federal government had decided that too many prisoners were getting too strong, so they stopped supplying new equipment. Therefore, our stuff was falling apart, and we took care to preserve it. Most inmates pump some iron, in part to maintain enough strength to ward off trouble, and in part to pass the time. People tend to work in groups, and there's a big social element in it all. In our workouts, Carter and I often talked about his Muslim faith, and he peppered me with questions about ancient history.

Inside many prisons, Black Muslims promote a kind of history that, while reinforcing their beliefs, is riddled with inaccuracies. The source of much of this stuff was Minister Louis Farrakhan, who teaches the superiority of the black race and purports to uncover hidden truths of the past. One of these was the supposed fact that Cleopatra was black. The power of this idea was that if true, it meant that all of ancient Egypt was black, hence, the origins of Western culture belong to blacks.

I told Carter that in fact, Cleopatra was Greek, 100 percent Greek. She was a member of the Ptolemaic Dynasty, which was founded in 323 B.C. by Ptolemy, who was Greek. Its members only married other Greeks. Cleopatra was the last of the dynasty. She was purely Greek. When he heard this, Carter asked me to address one of his Muslim study groups. I did, and they listened. I doubt they liked what they heard, but it got them thinking. And I managed to avoid irritating them by expressing all my ideas with great restraint and respect. The last thing I wanted to do was make them think I disrespected them or their faith. Respect is the grease that keeps prison society going.

Fortunately, the unwritten rules that guard the system of respect allow for mistakes. If you bump into someone, or step on their foot, you must immediately apologize. Verbal slights, even the wrong look, can lead to problems. Everyone understands this, even the guards, and as a result, prison interactions can be among the most polite exchanges you will ever see.

Right about now, as you read about my trainer, my cook, my laundryman, and bed-maker, you're probably imagining that I had turned myself into the pasha of Lompoc, or some such thing. In fact, a large number of inmates paid for the same services. It was almost our duty to help those who needed commissary items work to get them. And no amount of bartering changed the fact that we were locked up, denied regular contact with the outside world, denied control of our own lives.

The loss of autonomy became very vivid to me when, roughly one month into my sentence, an officer was killed in the penitentiary across the road. I had seen Scott Williams just once, when he had brought mail over to the camp. He seemed pleasant enough, professional. He was knifed and killed in a melee that left several other officers injured. Afterward, the guards locked down the whole Lompoc complex, including the camp. We were confined to dorms, with no visits and no phone calls. It freaked me out because those calls and visits were all that I truly valued in my life. For weeks, maybe months afterward, the guards acted like they were mad at the world. And they regarded inmates as their enemy.

The guards at Lompoc fell into a few categories. A few were real hard-asses, the type who sought the job because they got a rush from exercising control over others. Fortunately most guards at the camp, and many at the penitentiary and medium-security prisons, were not like that. They were strictly professional. They did their jobs but invested little of themselves in the process. At the camp level, the guards were often more relaxed, because it wasn't dangerous duty. They talked freely, and a few did more than that. One guard, named Kimball, was a terrible alcoholic who hid bottles everywhere and occasionally invited inmates to share. He was otherwise a good man, though, and we protected him by not taking advantage of his lapses.

One rung above the regular guards were the counselors, like Solis. They could help you with your phone and visitor lists. They could also help you get the right job. A great many inmates wanted to work for Unicor, a federal program that ran little manufacturing plants throughout the prison system. While every inmate earned a few pennies per hour at his job, those who worked at Unicor could get $1 per hour and more, plus overtime. At Lompoc the Unicor plant was an office furniture factory. It was next to the penitentiary, and the camp inmates who worked there took a bus to work every day.

For most of my stay at Lompoc I took the bus, too, to work at the warehouse that received every item—from food to note pads—used in the entire prison complex. I would log shipments into the warehouse, make inventories, and log things out. The warehouse jobs were highly prized, because the supervisors often let you take things for your personal use. I got new clothes, even fresh chicken, when it came in, to bring back for Hooey to cook. I did my best to nab items for others. It's prison custom to do those kinds of favors, and as a warehouse man I was flooded with requests.

In general I was treated like the average inmate who possessed above-average skills. But every now and then the fact that I was somewhat famous intruded. Take the case of the three-by-five cards. Every prisoner has a set of cards bearing his picture. They are used at the various places where he spends his time, to help guards verify his identity. One day a senior security person came and asked me whether I had actually signed these cards. I said yes, I had. "Well, don't do it again," he told me. "There's a bunch of 'em for sale on eBay."

A more constant problem associated with my notoriety involved the people who came to visit. When Mara, or Robert, or Jane and the kids came for their frequent visits, I had no problems. But when Wayne Gretzky, or Luc Robitaille, or one of my Hollywood friends like Alan Thicke showed up, the families and other inmates couldn't help reacting. Gretzky and other players signed dozens of autographs for inmates' families every time they came to see me. For weeks afterward, people would ask me about their lives and their personalities. Though they couldn't request them for themselves, many prisoners asked if I could have autographed pictures sent to their children. I did as much as I could. I knew that if one of those kids got a photo, they might believe, for a moment, that their dad can't be in all that much trouble if he can have someone like Wayne Gretzky do such a favor.

It's impossible to overstate how important visits were to me, and to all the inmates. Those who expected someone would usually iron an outfit the night before, so they would look as good as possible. I did this. And like everyone else, I would go outside and watch the cars as they approached from the distance. (Even guys who weren't expecting someone would do this.) When I saw Jane's Lexus carrying the kids, or Mara's Pathfinder, or Wayne's Mercedes, my heart beat a little faster.

Mara was my most regular visitor. I was very awkward the first time, realizing that I was a federal prisoner waiting for a visit. Her state of mind varied from visit to visit. Usually we would talk about her job and school. She brought lots of change for the vending machine, and we tried to avoid crying, to be upbeat. Mara wanted to hear details, even though some of them were unpleasant, so she could have an accurate picture of my life in her mind. We talked about the future a little bit, but it was filled with so much uncertainty that it was a futile kind of thing.

When they visited, my kids were curious about me. Each time they would start off asking if I was healthy and safe. When they felt reassured, they would then begin asking a lot of questions about my fellow inmates. They were fascinated by those people and their crimes. "What did he do?" they would ask. I would tell them what I could, but then steer the conversation back to them.

Though visitors were not allowed to bring cameras, inmates could use tokens from the commissary to have an official photographer—Charlie Knapp played this role—snap a photo. You might think that no one would want a memento from inside a prison. But the opposite was true. Everyone wanted a picture taken with their family or friends, including me. And when one of my famous friends came to visit, a lot of men used their tokens to have pictures taken with them, too. Some guards also brought cameras, which they used outside the visiting room.

My visitors could cause a stir even when they failed to see me. This happened on a weekday when Kurt Russell and Goldie Hawn were flying over the area and realized that the Lompoc camp was just below them. They landed at a local airstrip and got a car to come visit. Trouble was, the camp only allowed visits on weekends. The guard who informed them of the rule was so starstruck, however, that he gave them a tour of the whole place, complete with a ride on one of the dairy farm's tractors.

In between visits, I haunted the bank of phones that were available to inmates. I was desperate to stay in touch with people, to maintain my relationships, even though many inmates say that doing so means you do "hard time" rather than "easy time." Easy time involved abandoning hope, and contact, and hiding in the system. Hard time involves staying connected and thereby reminding yourself of everything you are missing out on every day.

For me, doing hard time was acceptable because my sentence was not so long that I didn't see an end to it all, and because I loved my life on the outside too much to let it go. So, every day, during non-work hours, I would get in line to make a call or two, or three. I called Robert and Mara every day. I called the kids once or twice per week. The same was true for my mother and father. Every once in a while I'd reach out to Wayne, or Luc, to Frank Gehry, Alan Thicke, and many others. I could talk for up to fifteen minutes. Then the phone system automatically shut off. I could redial, but I had to keep in mind that each call cost as much as $30.

At first there were no limits on calls. (They say in prison that everything gets worse, and this was true with phones as eventually restrictions were imposed.) However, there were strict limits on the content of your conversations. No one is permitted to conduct business on the phones, and discussion of contraband, escape, or crimes is forbidden as well. Guards listen. Sometimes they'll even comment. "I heard you talking to Gretzky," they would say. "Is he really going to St. Louis?" Because they listen, you had to be careful all the time. No one jokes about putting hacksaws in cakes, or whiskey bottles in boxes of cookies.

Of course, the eavesdropping could lead to some funny exchanges, too. One guy came to Lompoc, but had told everyone he knew on the outside that he was going to Paris for a year. He would get on the phone, and tell people he was calling from France. Finally, when this guy was deep into a call, a guard came over the loudspeaker and boomed, "Hey, you're here in Lompoc penitentiary. What are you doing telling people you are in Paris, France?" So much for his secret.

With my phone calls and letters, I tried to stay in the lives of the people I loved. I also tried hard to reassure them about my safety. My imprisonment was a punishment for them, too, and I never forgot this fact. I even tried to amuse them, especially with the almost-monthly newsletter-type missives I sent to Mara and Robert, who copied them and distributed them widely. One of the most popular included my very own prison language glossary of terms which included, among others, the following items:

Hoo las?—This is what you say as you approach the line for the phone, food, and anything else. You holler, "Hoo las?" and fall in behind him.

Don't trip—This is a term you MUST use if you happen to say or do something in error. It's supposed to calm the other fellow down, and communicate that you mean no harm.

Loosin' it—If you happen to forget the above term "don't trip," or if you feel your indiscretion needs an explanation you can say, "I was just loosin' it." That is, "I was just daydreaming, thinking about the outside world."

Down—This does not refer to being depressed. It refers to how long you have been in the system.

Short—This means you only have a brief time left to serve. Of course, this is in the eye of the beholder. To someone serving life, I was short the day I arrived at Lompoc.

Dog—An inmate who seems to follow you everywhere. They have nothing going for them in the prison, and hope that by hanging around they'll catch a scrap of food, attention, whatever.

On your leg—This is what a dog does when he's angling for a favor, a gift, or a kind word. He's "on your leg."

Swole—"That dude's swole" or "big swole" means he's all pumped up from lifting weights. Usually the guy who's "big swole" is a little less-developed elsewhere, like between the ears, so it's a good idea to stay away from him.

Shystee—refers to lawyers or, more generally, someone you cannot trust.

Flavor—This refers to your discernment, your taste. Say you observe that a woman in the visitors' room is very attractive. If an inmate agrees he'll tell you, "You got flavor."

Feel me—No, this isn't what you say after you've been in prison a while and your bunky looks good to you. It means "you know what I like." If

someone offers you ice cream he stole from the dairy, you may
respond with "Baby, you feel me."

Shinin'—You do this after acquiring something you feel very proud of. This
only applies to contraband. Say you've convinced a friend to wear
new Nikes to visit, and while together you slip off your shoes and
slip on his. You'll then be "shinin' " about your new shoes.

Heavy—This doesn't refer to you being overweight or too serious. It does
mean that you are a burden, too difficult to deal with. You tell this
dude, "Man, you're too heavy. Go find another sucker."

At Lompoc, I was no shystee, but I often felt like I had a whole dog pound
on my leg. The heaviest dudes were not fellow inmates but guards, who saw
me as a source of inside information about sports and Hollywood, and as
someone who was willing to listen to them talk. Perhaps the most outlandish
example of how the guards responded to my status arose when the Florida
Marlins baseball team won the World Series. The Marlins were owned by
Wayne Huizenga, who had become my friend when we were both NHL owners. Wayne, not knowing that the inmates couldn't receive the stuff, sent me,
literally, a truckload of championship T-shirts, hats, and other items. They
came to the warehouse. They were held for a while, then suddenly disappeared. Later I learned that Marlins team gear was seen all over the region, on
kids at the local high schools and shoppers in the local malls.

The shipment from Huizenga, and visits from pro athletes, made it difficult for me to avoid questions and attention. In fact, I preferred reading to idle
chatter, and did everything I could to avoid the guys who liked to stand
around and talk. Soon after I arrived at Lompoc, I had looked down from my
bunk to see Dayton playing cards with a handful of inmates. They were playing a prison version of pinochle. I had played bridge with Jane and her parents, and had a good mind for card games. They taught me and pretty soon

Dayton, Terry Ferguson, Hooey, a champion player named Earl, and I were having marathon competitions. In the winter we tried to play inside the dorm, making a table out of a turned-over wastebasket. In summer we would occupy one of the picnic tables outside. The games kept us occupied, and exempt from all the bullshitting around us. They became integral to the routine that made the days bearable.

If you were resilient, you could make change work in your favor. This was especially true where jobs were concerned. At a place like Lompoc, there were extraordinary opportunities. The dairy, for example, actually put men on horses to round up the cows each day. It also employed one inmate as a long-distance trucker to deliver milk products. He would travel from prison to prison, staying overnight in cells, but as long as he stayed on schedule, what he did on the road was his business.

My friend Mark Carter worked on a crew that was bused each day to nearby Vandenberg Air Force Base, where they did maintenance and custodial work. Once they were out there, they were treated like regular people. When a spot opened up, Carter put in a word for me with McFadden. I got the job, and soon left the warehouse for the base. It was as good as Carter said. Much of the work was outside, and with regular Air Force personnel. If a party was planned, for example, we would set up tables and chairs and then eat right along with the guests. When storms blew through, we would go clear the tree blocking the roads. And when lunchtime came, we would get Burger King with everyone else.

The job at Vandenberg was the best I would ever enjoy in prison. Every workday it gave me a chance to leave the camp, and breathe. It all ended after about six months, when I looked at the bulletin board and saw that my assignment had been transferred to what was considered the worst duty in camp, washing dishes in the kitchen. This happened shortly after a change in administration. McFadden was gone. So was Solis. In his place we got a tough-minded woman named Halaka.

Halaka had already zeroed in on me. When she could, she made me her errand boy, and she seemed to get a lot of pleasure out of ordering me around. Friendly staffers at the camp told me she had made the job switch "because you're high profile and she wants to keep an eye on you" and also "because she can." I once asked Halaka and she said, "I think the kitchen will be good for you." The subtext, clear as can be, was that she wanted me under her thumb.

There is no way an inmate can fight a work assignment or, for that matter, any decision made about where and how he will do his time. Once you surrender to the Federal Bureau of Prisons you are their property. You can be moved at will. No one has to tell you why. They don't even have to tell you where you are going. They can and will pluck you up and deposit you where they choose. This can all seem arbitrary, and often it is. Your only choice is to stay calm, and do whatever you can to remain sane. As I soon learned, that can be a challenge when you become the focus of the system.

It all began on a Sunday in 1999—February 14, Valentine's Day. I had received a letter from Su Waks. She was absolutely petrified. She was about to report to the women's prison at Dublin, in Northern California. I felt very guilty about what was happening to her. I had written to her before, telling her it wasn't as bad as she feared. But prison is a terrible thing; and for a woman with children, it might be worse.

Kimball, the pleasant old drunk, was on duty that evening. Like most of the guards, you could approach him to make an emergency phone call to someone not on your list. They were allowed to listen to the request and, if it made sense, authorize a quick call. As long as you didn't abuse the favor, it was okay.

In this case, I thought I'd better call Su and give her a little pep talk. Once she was in prison, I wouldn't be allowed to speak to her or write to her. Kimball said, "Yeah, okay, make it quick." He opened up an office—Halaka's office—as he had done for others. He was required to be with me, and he stayed as I dialed. Once the connection was made and I began talking with Su, he stepped out into the hallway, to give me a little privacy, I thought.

The next thing I knew, in walked Halaka. Her face was instantly red with rage. "Su, I'm sorry I gotta go," I sputtered into the phone and quickly hung up.

"What are you doing here?" she demanded.

"Kimball gave me a call."

"He did?"

"Yeah, isn't he right there?" I nodded toward the hallway.

"No, he's not."

Halaka was very upset. She wouldn't believe I had been admitted by Kimball, and was determined to get me to tell her how I had gotten into the office. When I kept insisting that Kimball had given me the call she threw up her hands, grabbed the phone, and dialed the penitentiary to speak with the lieutenant in charge of security for the entire complex. She spoke to him briefly. When she hung up she said that the officer was headed over to the camp. "You just stand there," she told me. She then began to leave the office and ran smack into Kimball.

"Did you authorize this man to make a call?"

"Yeah, I gave McNall a call."

"You have no right to walk away then. You're supposed to stand right here."

"I went to open the barber shop," explained Kimball.

"I don't care. You know you're supposed to stay right here with the inmate."

It was obvious to me that she had it in for Kimball. As I watched this, I thought she might have been trying to push him into early retirement, or perhaps she was beginning a bigger campaign to shake up the entire staff. Either way, I thought, I was pretty sure I was caught up in something bigger than this one phone call.

When the lieutenant arrived, all three of them talked outside the office. I stood and waited. Kimball kept saying, "Hey, I authorized it. Blame it on me. I walked away. It's my fault. It's not McNall's issue." In the end, though,

Halaka wouldn't believe him. She turned to the lieutenant and said, "Take McNall over to the penitentiary. I want this investigated."

The officer looked confused as he opened the office door and called me out. He led me outside to the truck he had driven over, and told me to get in. As he drove he said we would go talk to an investigations officer. "Maybe he can straighten this out." I wasn't too troubled. Kimball was telling the truth. I had done nothing wrong. Halaka had been startled, but maybe she would calm down.

At the penitentiary, I was taken to an office to meet an investigator. He had me run through what happened. When I finished he said, "I don't see what the problem is here. Let me call Kimball." I sat there as he dialed and then got Kimball on the phone. I could tell that Kimball was still telling the truth. When the investigator hung up he called to the lieutenant, who was just outside.

"Okay," he said. "You can take McNall back."

As we were driving back, I saw Halaka in her personal car, flying up to the penitentiary. Before we even got to the camp, a call came over the radio. "Bring him back," they told the lieutenant. He stopped, made a U-turn, and we headed back to the penitentiary. By this time I was not only confused, I was worried.

As we headed back inside, Halaka stormed by me without a word. The investigating officer almost apologetically explained, "We have to keep you here while we investigate something." I was taken to another room, where I was ordered to take off my uniform. I was searched, then given an orange prison jumpsuit. I was then handcuffed and escorted down a corridor to a row of cells. One of the doors was opened. I entered and sat down on the bottom of a double bunk. The door closed.

For the first time in my prison term, I found myself completely alone in a cold, dark, windowless cell, and I had no idea what was happening to me. In the cell there was only the bunk, a combination sink-toilet unit, and single bulb shining overhead. I had a two-inch toothbrush, a little bar of soap, and a blanket. As far as I could tell, there were no inmates in any of the other cells on that hallway.

A full day went by, but no one came to speak with me. I called out, but the guard who was posted at a desk at the end of the hall ignored me. Meals were delivered through a two-inch-high slit in the door. I asked for a phone call, paper and pencil to write letters, or a book to read. I was denied all those things. I was in the Hole.

13

A WEEK PASSED BEFORE A GUARD, someone I had seen before, happened to walk past my cell in the Hole, look inside, and say hello. I begged him to tell me why I was being held there. "I don't know what's happening," he told me. But he did get me a couple of books—a Michael Crichton and a Louis L'Amour—along with paper and pencil so I could write letters to Mara and Robert. Of course, I had no stamps, and thus no way to mail them, but getting the materials for letters was a good first step.

Up to that point, I had occupied myself with one hour per day of pacing in a fenced yard, exercises in my cell, and as much sleep as I could force upon my worried brain. Worry was my biggest enemy. I had no idea why I was being held in the Hole, no idea whether my outside contacts knew of my fate, and no idea of what the guards were saying about me. When the anxiety pushed me toward paranoia, I would talk myself down, literally commanding myself to let go of the fear. I had no control over my situation, and therefore, it was futile to dwell on it. Whatever happened, I would simply have to accept.

I was immersed in what was likely my fourth read through the Crichton novel when Solis, my old counselor, came by. He had been transferred to the penitentiary months earlier, when Halaka had arrived at the camp. He brought me a few pieces of mail. I practically begged him to find out why I was being held for so long.

"I'll try, but I can't promise," he said. "The most important thing is that you stay cool, man."

The very next day, Halaka showed up with a unit manager from the camp. His name was Bacon. They wanted to see me in an office, so they sent a guard down to prep me. The officer ordered me to stand with my back to the door and my wrists next to the slot. He reached in and handcuffed me. Then the door was unlocked and he led me, still cuffed, to the office. That was standard procedure. I would never be moved without the cuffs, and sometimes they would put me in leg irons for good measure.

I'm sure that I looked pale, a bit undernourished, and unkempt when Halaka and Bacon saw me. Everyone deteriorates when denied a haircut, shampoo, even sunlight. They looked a little startled, but quickly composed themselves.

"Do you have anything to say?" began Bacon.

"You know the facts," I said. "Kimball let me make a call. I didn't know he had walked away. That's it."

"Who's been here to see you?" asked Halaka. "Don't lie to us because we know everything. There are cameras all over this unit."

I told them about the almost-friendly guard who had come by and fetched me the books, and about Solis. In that instant I realized that they might be after him, too.

"He brought my mail by."

"Ah-ha," said Halaka.

"Anybody else?" asked Bacon

"Not that I remember."

I didn't glare at them, or cop any sort of attitude that would give them an excuse to make the interrogation go on any longer than necessary. Bacon finally said, "Look, we don't have any issues with you. But we believe that you know a lot about what's going on at the camp. You know about the officers, and what they are doing that may be improper."

"I don't," I said. "I don't know what you are talking about."

They then began to talk about all kinds of outrageous things that were rumored to be happening. Inmates were supposedly being taken for rendezvous at motels with wives and girlfriends. Guards and inmates were having wild parties with drugs and alcohol. Wholesale thefts were taking place at the warehouse, with guards fencing the stuff on the outside and prisoners sharing the cash. I had heard similar rumors, but knew nothing specific, and I told them so.

"We don't believe you," said Halaka.

"You want to get out of here, don't you?" continued Bacon. "Well, you're not going to get out of here until you tell us what's going on."

"I'm not going to make something up," I answered. "You might as well just take me back to the cell because I don't have anything to tell."

That is how it went during roughly a dozen interviews over the next two weeks. Almost daily they would call for me. I would be cuffed, taken to an office, and they would ask the same questions. The pressure became more intense. They would threaten to simply leave me there and forget me. But I refused to confirm their stories about what the guards and inmates were doing. Like I said, I'm no shystee.

The time between those confrontations passed slowly. Every once in a while I heard screams of pain from a nearby medical unit, but other than that, I heard nothing. Not a human voice, not a bird chirping, not a sneeze or cough. It was a struggle to control my fears. Was there something I had done, something against the rules, that they knew about? Was someone spreading lies about me? Though I couldn't answer those questions, I kept asking them over and over.

One morning a guard came by, handcuffed me, and led me to a special shower that had a locking door. He took the cuffs off, locked me inside, and then let me out when I was finished. On another morning, I think it was a Sunday, a Catholic priest came to my cell door. He recognized me and stopped to chat. He told me that he had heard that half the officers at the camp were under investigation. I was in the Hole because they thought I knew everything that was going on, and that I could implicate all of them.

It was a merciful act, telling me a bit more about what was happening. I recognized this, and decided to press my luck. "Would you call my girlfriend, Mara, and tell her what's happened, where I am?" He thought for a moment and looked down at the guard posted in the hallway. He then agreed to do it, and even took out a little notebook and wrote down her phone number.

It was a month more before a guard came and handed me my clothes, the sweats I had been wearing when they whisked me away from camp, and told me to put them back on. I asked him what was happening. As was usually the case, he either didn't know, or preferred to torture me by denying me the information. He just said, "You'll find out," and waited while I dressed. When I was done I was cuffed and then he opened the door. He led me to the main lobby and out the front door.

At the penitentiary gate, a white prison van pulled up and I got in. The driver told me we were going across the street to the medium-security prison. I was being transferred from the Hole to its equivalent at the medium-level place. It's called the SHU, for Special Holding Unit, and it's normally where camp inmates go when they get in trouble. It was supposed to be a little less restrictive, maybe even a step up from where I had been.

Mostly it was just more crowded. Instead of two- and one-man cells, the SHU had eight slightly larger cells with up to six men assigned to each. The exception was at the end of the hall, where a single cell was reserved for truly crazy inmates who were kept away from everyone else. After changing into an orange jumpsuit, I was put in one of the gang cells, with four other men.

Obviously the architect who had designed the Hole had worked there, too. It was the same basic windowless construction. The same door with a pass-through slit and a four-by-four-inch pane of Plexiglas. The same toilet and sink contraption. The same fluorescent light overhead. We had the added blessing of a shower head and drain in the corner, and we had access to fresh air via a few dozen holes—each the diameter of a large pencil lead—that were punched in the outside wall.

During the day it was hot in the SHU, and every man in the cell was in his underwear. At night the temperature would dive and we would all put on our jumpsuits and shiver under thin blankets. There were a few books scattered around, but no other personal effects. And though I introduced myself, we didn't talk much. Most of those men were there for just a short time. None of us seemed to have much to talk about. And a few of the guys were inmates I knew I should avoid. One had the words "Fuck" and "You" tattooed over his eyebrows.

We spent twenty-three hours a day in that cell. For the twenty-fourth hour, we were taken outside to a pen, a cage really, that was about the same size as two cells put together. It was covered, so we didn't see the sun or sky, but we got a little more fresh air and were allowed to pace around. Fresh air is at a premium when you share a cell with four men and the toilet sits up against the wall.

Some things were better in the SHU. For one thing, we had a system for sending notes and small things like cigarettes from cell to cell. First we would pull threads from a blanket to make a long string. We would attach that to a packet and then crouch by the gap between the door and the floor. If you aimed properly, you could flick the packet across the polished hallway floor. It would fly, almost like a Frisbee. The line allowed you to retrieve it if you missed. This method, called "shooting a line," worked to send things up and down the unit. There were guards who tried to stop it, pouncing on the packets like cats, but they rarely succeeded, and it only made the activity more fun.

Tobacco, by the way, reached us through a most ingenious method. Inmates on the floors above us would drop lines attached to thin cigarettes down through the tiny holes in the wall. Then we would use whatever we could—string, paper clips, bits of wire—to snag the offerings and pull them through the hole. When there's nothing else to do, you don't mind spending an hour trying to complete a hand-off that way, even if, in the end, all you get is a few grams of tobacco inside a little paper.

I spent much of my time reading the thickest books I could find (a lot of Michener) and writing to Mara and Robert. I wrote every day, and they responded almost as often. Though the content of the letters was generally positive, they were not merely reassuring notes. Mara's response to my situation was, understandably, complex. She told me she suspected I still had what she called "entitlement issues" which lurked behind all my troubles. She meant that I was always seeking special treatment, which I believed I deserved. I could agree that I may have felt that way before, or acted like it. But confined as I was, confronted with every breath by how far I had fallen, I certainly didn't feel special or entitled anymore.

Just to make sure I never relaxed, Bacon, Halaka, and others continued interrogating me, but less frequently. All their questions were about officers at the camp. At one point they began saying that I was paying off guards with money from secret bank accounts, that I had given them cars, even houses. It was ridiculous.

Perhaps they truly believed that I was lying and the pressure would force the truth out of me. I wasn't going to help them. At one point, more or less for my own amusement, I tossed them a couple of tidbits. "Did you know Kimball has a drinking problem?" I asked.

"Did you ever see him drinking on duty?" they then said.

"No."

Later I told them that some supervisors may have been giving extra food to inmates. They looked at me and laughed.

The interrogations made me paranoid, and absurd "what-ifs?" kept coming into my mind. What if some of the officers they were questioning made up something bad about me? Could the incident involving the three-by-five cards be reinterpreted as some sort of a bribe for the officers who made money selling them on eBay? Over and over again I heard, in my mind, Bacon and Halaka saying, "We can do a lot to you if we want to."

In my cell, inmates came and went. New arrivals looked like deer caught in a car's headlights. Most were young guys who had been fighting. Others had simply broken a rule. The saddest case involved a guy in his forties who was just about ready to be released. The other inmates had had a party for him. When someone made a wise remark, he flashed them the finger. A guard saw the gesture, and believed it was directed at him. It wasn't, but nothing this poor soul could say helped. He was thrown in the SHU, and his release was delayed.

Another inmate, a Mexican man, was a diabetic. It's not a good thing to be in the SHU as a diabetic. He needed insulin shots a couple times per day, but the guards were rather lackadaisical about giving him the needles and serum. He went into insulin shock a couple of times, and after we shouted for help was carted off to a medical unit.

Most inmates were held in the SHU for a month or less. The rules required that you couldn't be kept there more than six months without being charged and found guilty by a prison tribunal. Neither of these things happened to me, and eventually even the guards in the unit began to recognize the absurdity of my situation. They made me one of two inmates who were allowed out to work as janitors for the unit. I would mop the SHU area floors, wipe the walls down, pass out laundry.

As I adjusted to life in the SHU and stood firm with my interrogators, the tide began to change. Suddenly I got word that I would be allowed my first visits. Days later Robert and Mara arrived. I came out to see them in my orange jumpsuit, with my hair all wild and hanging down, and my face pale from being indoors for months on end. They both hugged me, but I could see in their faces that they were shocked. Years later, Mara would tell me that she had been relieved to see me alive, incensed by what was being done to me, and a little bit angry at me for getting myself in such a jam.

I was just glad to see them, and so excited I had trouble containing myself. I spoke very quickly, afraid that the visit had been approved by mistake and that at any moment a guard would rush over and send Mara and Robert away. I told them about what had happened to me, about Kimball and the interrogations. And I asked Robert if we should try to do something.

"Should we call a congressman or a senator?" I asked. But before he could answer I would add, "No, no. They'll punish me more if I try that." Eventually I realized there was nothing I could do, nothing anyone could do. I would have to tough it out, for as long as it took.

After that first visit, Mara came every single week. Robert came every other week. Jane brought the kids once. I didn't want them there a lot. The place was just too intimidating for them. I also saw Luc Robitaille and his wife, Stacia, as well as Wayne and Janet Gretzky. I felt a little more ashamed to have them see me in a jumpsuit and behind the high fences of a real prison, not a camp. But after a while I forgot how bizarre it was for everyone else, and just felt grateful.

Long after this period of my life was over, Mara and others would tell me that the SHU affected me more deeply than I realized. Besides looking different, terrible really, I seemed to talk and act differently. I was more frightened, more defensive, and angry. In short, I was more like an inmate at a federal prison. The System hadn't beaten me completely. I was still Bruce McNall inside. But it was having an effect.

Nobody that I was aware of had stayed in the SHU as long as me. Four months in, as I was getting my visits, and being escorted across the prison yard for them, inmates in their cells began to notice me. I would hear, from inside the walls, whistles and shouts. "Hey, Bruce," they would say. "Hang in there, man. We're with you!"

When they finally came up with my "shot"—an infraction to charge me with—it was so minor that I almost couldn't believe it. According to officer Bacon, guards had discovered contraband in my locker. Unless it's heroin or crack cocaine, a contraband shot is so low that the usual punishment is taking the stuff away from you. At worst you might lose phone privileges for a week, or get a week in the SHU.

What evil substance had been found in my gear? Ten $25 gift certificates for Barnes & Noble. My sister had tucked them in a Christmas card. They were in my name, nonnegotiable, and could be used only to purchase books via mail-order.

"My sister sent these through the camp mail," I said to Bacon. "They are still in the envelope that you guys opened. I didn't go out and get them. They came through The System, which means someone thought it was okay for me to get them. They were screened."

My shock was slowly being replaced by true fury. "You searched my stuff right away. You could have dealt with this the day after I went in the Hole," I said. "You kept me here because of this? This is like giving me the death penalty for running a red light."

Bacon didn't answer me. I signed a paper pleading guilty to possessing the gift certificates. "We're going to transfer you," he said as he left.

"Great. Where?"

"I can't tell you."

"Thanks a lot."

Soon after Bacon departed, the warden for the entire prison came by. "Hey, McNall," he said. "I know this has been a little bit out of hand. I'm going to authorize you to be transferred wherever you want. But here's the deal. It has to be at least a low-security prison. It can't be a camp. My advice would be that you pick Safford, Arizona. It's pretty close by, and it's the best." I did what he said, requested Safford, but not because I had any confidence in his advice. I just didn't know any other place to pick. He could have been recommending the Prison From Hell, for all I knew.

The next day I was told to pack up my books and papers and prepare to leave. Where was I headed? No one would tell me. I stood by the slit in the door and they handcuffed me. When I stepped out of the cell I was put in leg irons. Another chain was wrapped around my waist, and my handcuffs were locked to it. I then shuffled outside to the gate where I struggled up the stairs of a bus packed with prisoners. Among them were guards armed with shotguns.

I took a seat near a window and stared out. The driver revved the engine, put the bus in gear, and pulled away from the prison entrance. We rolled past the camp where I could see some men on the grounds. As I looked for familiar faces, I found myself squinting in the light. It had been 170 days since Halaka had thrown me in the Hole.

As the warden had advised, I had requested placement at Safford. It was much farther from my home and all the people who had visited me, but given the fact that the Federal Bureau of Prisons could send me anywhere in the country, it was a fine alternative. Though I would eventually end up there, I would have to spend a number of weeks in penitentiary limbo, while paperwork and transportation were arranged.

From Lompoc my bus went to Los Angeles to pick up more prisoners, and then north to a prison facility in Dublin, California. The next day we drove to Phoenix and a prison where I was finally unshackled, provided with a medical checkup, and settled into a big room with wooden double bunks. Phoenix was a higher security place, one level below the penitentiary, and my fellow inmates included murderers and the like. The chow hall, I noted, served much better food. It is accepted throughout the system that the tougher the prison is, the better the food will be. I believe it's because the men held in higher security settings are mean and bad enough to tear the place apart if provoked by terrible food. At the camp level, we accepted what we were fed because we were doing comparatively easy time.

When I boarded a bus for Safford, which is on the New Mexico border, I sat down next to a tall, slender inmate named Benjamin Uba. Convicted of some drug-related crime, Ben had been at the medium-security prison in Lompoc when I was there. He was from one of Nigeria's better families, and was very well spoken and highly educated. He was a proselytizing Christian, and could sometimes go a little overboard with the hard-sell for Jesus. But he was otherwise so pleasant to be around that it wasn't hard to put up with that one annoying quality.

Though I would have enjoyed bunking with Ben, we agreed to drop that idea when we discovered that Safford was highly segregated. The units men lived in, called cubes, were low-walled clusters of bunks where it seemed the occupants were either all white, or black, or Hispanic. I was advised to find a white cube, which I did. I moved in with Ralph and Dan, a couple of marijuana dealers who were very bright. Across from us was one of the guys from Waco—a Branch Davidian. He had been away from the house when the Feds had raided it, so he escaped the fire that engulfed it at the end of the siege. He was pleasant enough, but his beliefs were so strong that I avoided having long talks with him.

Besides getting squared away on phones and visits, I had two priorities at Safford. I wanted a good job, and I wanted to sign up for DAP, a special Drug and Alcohol Program. Offered to every qualifying inmate in federal custody, it allowed those with less than two years left on their terms to knock off time—up to a year—by successfully completing a nine-month course. I had first applied for it at Lompoc.

The counselors gave me a good job, in the athletic department, and they also allowed me to apply for DAP. I had one small obstacle to qualifying. I had denied, on my presentencing paperwork, any history of drug and alcohol abuse. In fact, I may have had a small problem with booze. I certainly was an adrenaline junkie, truly addicted to risk-taking. I contacted my doctors back in Los Angeles and got them to write letters saying I had a drinking problem. Then I wrote my own application, emphasizing that I had come to realize, after years of denial, that I was an alcoholic. Considering that denial is a hallmark of alcoholism, it was pretty easy for the people reviewing applications to accept this, despite my earlier claim that I was sober. I was approved.

Now the only obstacle between me and my goal was a transfer. Safford did not offer the DAP curriculum. My counselors submitted my name to programs offered elsewhere in the system, and told me to get ready for a long, long wait.

The time passed a little more quickly because this camp had pay phones that were available all day, and allowed you to call anyone anywhere and talk for as long as you wanted. This was one of my favorite things about Safford. Another was my comparative anonymity. Although some of the inmates knew who I was, most did not. This was a relief. No one asked for autographs, or tried to get me to tell stories about the old days. And since the camp was very isolated, I didn't get a lot of visits from the famous people who had attracted so much attention at Lompoc.

Mara did come, and one of her brief visits brought me an extra dose of pain. She arrived with her longtime friend, Barbara, who did much of the talking. They explained that Mara was having a tough time. "I think I need a break," she said. My time in the Hole and then the SHU had shaken her. "I'd like to have no contact for three months or so," she said.

What choice did I have? Mara had been exceptionally generous and loyal. And though she was taking away my strongest lifeline, I had to say it was okay. I accepted that I would be a little more isolated. Every morning I would run five miles and then work out hard at the weight pile, with Ben Uba. I then reported for work in the recreation department. When I finished what chores I had been assigned I went to the library and read. I tried not to let my mind wander to thoughts that Mara was having an affair, maybe even planning to abandon me.

Almost every day I touched base with the psychologist, a young woman, who had put in my bid for a DAP spot. I was rejected by DAP staffers at prisons at Terminal Island, California; Sheridan, Oregon; and Phoenix. Eventually the psychologist told me the only place that would agree to take me was a medium-security prison in Milan, Michigan. It was the most difficult program in the system. A lot of people failed it. But I could try. In March of the year 2000, my transfer was approved.

You probably know Con Air by the movie of the same name. It's the government-run airline that shuttles inmates around the country in drab, old jet aircraft. I was going to fly Con Air from Phoenix to Michigan, but the planes don't follow a very convenient schedule. They only fly when there is a full load of passengers, so I would have to wait weeks at the Phoenix prison while additional men were collected from around the West.

In the weeks there, I shared a three-decker bunk with an old man serving life for running a methamphetamine lab, and a young kid doing hard time for violent crime. Like a large proportion of the young whites in the system the kid was a neo-Nazi type. I had already learned how to be around white supremacists without either joining them or arguing with them, so we were able to pass the time in peace.

It was at Phoenix that I heard, from the staff in Robert's office, that my grandmother had died. She was the sweet lady who had lent me the money, so long ago, to buy that box of coins from the man who had come into Coins of the World Etc. I called my sister, and we had a long talk about her. I loved my grandmother very much, and her death upset me enough that I called Mara. She seemed happy to hear from me, and that call renewed our regular contacts.

I believe there is a connection between the mind and the body, and I suspect that my grandmother's death weakened my immune system enough to let some sort of germ attack. A few days after hearing she had died, I came down with an ear infection. It was brutally painful. I couldn't hear, and a watery, blood-streaked fluid began to drain from my ear. But before I could see a doctor, I was called to board a bus for the airport. I could decline, wait for medical care, and hope to fly out later. But I didn't want to take the risk of missing out on Milan and DAP. So I decided to just endure the pain.

The Con Air jet, a battered, green 707, was parked at the private aviation terminal at Sky Harbor Airport. Right next to it was the team jet for the Detroit Red Wings, who were in town to play the Coyotes, an expansion team that Wayne owned. As I prepared to leave the bus, with chains around my waist, wrists, and ankles, I prayed that I wouldn't be seen by any of the players. The prayer was answered, and I was able to climb the stairs to the jet, without anyone seeing me.

On the plane, guards took away the wad of tissue I had jammed in my ear. and soon my face and neck were wet from the fluid that flowed out of it. When they handed us paper-sack lunches, I tore a piece of the bag and put that in my ear canal. It stopped the flow for a while, but did nothing for the excruciating pain I felt as we changed altitudes.

I suffered like that for a couple of hours as we flew to Con Air's hub, the airport in Oklahoma City. There, I eventually saw a nurse. She gave me pills and drops for what was then a raging infection. It would take nearly a month to clear it up. I would never fully recover my hearing in that ear.

The Con Air transfer facility was remarkably efficient. Planes pulled up to a jetway. Inmates trundled through it into a prison where they were assigned to cells. You waited there—in my case it was almost a month—until you were called for a flight. I got summoned at 2 A.M. I joined a large group of prisoners who were moved from room to room, filling out paperwork and undergoing searches. At dawn, they put us on another plane without telling us our actual destination, and we rolled down the runway.

I'm pretty sure our first stop was in Kansas, to drop some inmates off for Leavenworth. We next set down at Terre Haute, Indiana, where about thirty men got off. Finally we landed in Detroit, Michigan, where the few of us who remained were put on a bus. We drove for about an hour, passing through snow-covered countryside, to the institution that I hoped would be my last stop before my release.

A complex of three-story buildings on a piece of land fenced with barbed wire, Milan is one of the oldest federal prisons in the country. Most of the inmates live in the old redbrick buildings that form a rectangle around a courtyard. A few newer buildings, of cinder-block construction, stand to the side of the main cluster. I was assigned to one of those, Building G, which was reserved for participants in the Drug and Alcohol Program.

It was obvious from the start that the people who ran the DAP were serious about it being a transforming experience. The first counselor I met,

Michael O'Gorman, was truly interested in the inmates. He was generous with favors like phone calls, but also firm about the program. DAP was a lot like a hospital rehab. We were forced to confront our demons, and required to change. The core of the teaching was the twelve steps of Alcoholics Anonymous.

O'Gorman constantly warned us that a single slipup could put us out of the program. If that happened, there would be no time sliced off our sentences, and no second chance to get back in. What could get you bounced out? I heard a lot of horror stories. A dirty cell, an unmade bed, even a crooked pillow could be enough. Contraband was a sure way to be expelled. But you could also get dismissed for messing up an assignment, or just having a bad attitude.

My class—officially called a *cadre*—began on the first day of August. If I succeeded, and graduated, I would be released from prison in March 2001. That was seven months before my preset release date. I was determined to do whatever it took to succeed. Unfortunately, I also had to depend on my classmates. The risk of the group dynamic became clear early on when the counselors came into the classroom where we met every morning and announced they were running out of patience with us, as a whole.

"As far as we're concerned, this entire cadre, this entire group, doesn't get it," they said. "We're still deciding, but the way it looks now, we're done with all of you."

That had come out of the blue. The men were shocked. For weeks we had been doing the assignments they gave us, keeping journals, sharing stories, without any sense that something was wrong. Now it seemed like we were all going to wash out, losing our hoped-for early releases.

"We're disgusted," said the counselors. "You can just go back to your rooms if you want. We don't care." Then they left.

Stunned, the members of the class looked at each other in disbelief. A few of the tougher inmates closed their notebooks, and got up as if to leave. Then it dawned on a few others that the counselors hadn't said that a decision had been finalized. Our response to the situation could affect their choice. Some of the men said we should stay in the room, all together, and proceed as best we could with the routine of talking about drugs and alcohol and studying the materials we had received. I agreed.

"I don't know what this is all about," I said. "But I know we shouldn't leave. We should stay in this classroom for the period that we are supposed to be here."

A moment later one of the inmates suggested I should be a leader, a spokesman for the group. They waited while I went to the counselors' offices. When I got there, I told the two officers that the cadre was still in the classroom. We weren't leaving. "But we would like you to come back, if you would, to tell us what's happening."

They said no. "You guys figure it out. We're debating how to proceed on this thing."

I said, "Okay, but we're going to continue having our class among ourselves. You guys are facilitators, but we can continue ourselves."

"Do whatever you want. Go to the weight pile, the track, anything you want. We're done with you."

I went back and told them we ought to stay. We did. We took up the lesson we had started—"Step Two: Come to Believe That a Power Greater Than Ourselves Could Restore Us to Sanity"—and stuck with it through the entire period.

The next day, we showed up on time. I took my place in front of the room to facilitate, but before we could begin, the counselors intervened. "We think you've learned a lot," they said. "You had the courage to stay. You made the decision we hoped you'd make. We're not going to shut you down."

The reprieve allowed us to continue to work toward completing the program, but the test—and I do think it was a purposeful test—made all of us even more anxious. Outside of my time in the Hole, I have never been as worried for as long as I was during those nine months of DAP. The program was my obsession, and during my free time I would focus much of my energy on homework. I was also required to sponsor other cadre members, and quite a few came to me for help.

We worked in my cell, which for the first few months was on the third floor. It was my first integrated cell, and I liked it very much because I liked my roommate, a middle-aged man named Rollo. Most recently convicted on a drug-sales charge, Rollo had been in and out of prisons most of his adult life. He was tired of *the life*, and had entered DAP as part of a conscious effort to change. If you ever saw Rollo with his shirt off, you would understand why he might want to try a different approach. His chest was pockmarked with scars from bullet wounds. "One time some buddies of mine, I thought they were cool, shot up my car and did it really good," he once explained to me. "But I don't have any problem with those guys anymore." I knew that meant he had somehow taken care of them, but I didn't ask how.

Rollo and I had an easy relationship, but the third floor got terribly hot at night, and when a spot opened downstairs, on level one, I switched. I moved in with an inmate named Scott Abrahamson, who had one of the more amusing crime stories of anyone I ever met in prison. Scott had been a cop in the San Diego area. People always told him he looked like Garth Brooks. One night he was persuaded to get up and sing a few of Garth's songs at a karaoke bar. He sounded a lot like him. Pretty soon he was wearing cowboy hats and performing in one of those legends shows in Las Vegas.

From Vegas, Scott took to the road, singing at nightclubs and casinos. He had an alcohol problem and plenty of women problems, as ladies tended to throw themselves at him like groupies. When he landed in Wisconsin, one of those women finally touched his heart. He fell in love. She began pressuring him for money. She said she needed about $25,000 in cash to pay a lawyer to get her kids away from her ex-husband. After listening to her cry about it for days, Scott decided to use what he knew from law enforcement to get the cash. He placed a call to a bank branch that was open on a Sunday inside a nearby supermarket.

"I have planted a bomb in the branch. I am going to find a stranger out-side the store, pay him $50, and send him inside to see you. He's going to think you are my sister and that you are giving him a present. He'll say the code words—Green Bay Packers. You'll give him $25,000. I don't want to see any ink cartridges in there, no markings on the bills. If you mess this up, I will blow you up."

Of course, it was Scott who entered the bank, said "Green Bay Packers" to the teller, and made off with the bag of cash. The next day the local papers described someone who didn't look anything like him as the robber. A reward of $50,000 was offered, but it looked like he would get away with it. Then there came a knock on his door, and an arrest. The girlfriend had decided that $50,000 was better than $25,000, so she had turned him in.

Stories like Scott's make you believe that there is no end to the ways that people get themselves in trouble. I had to admire him though. He wasn't bitter or depressed. He actually thought that what had happened was a little bit funny. We agreed that it might make a nice plot for a movie, with Garth Brooks playing Scott Abrahamson, pretending to be Garth Brooks.

The program got tougher as the months passed. We all were pressured to confront our "character defects" so that we could understand how we had made such a mess of our lives. You couldn't fake it. If you did, and they found out, you were dismissed. People had been expelled with two days to go. That was because the counselors wanted a very high rate of success. Anyone who seemed like he might go bad and get locked up again after being released via the program was weeded out before graduation.

To satisfy the counselors, I had to inventory the character flaws that had led to my downfall. They were real, and included, at the very top, my sta-tus as a master of manipulation. Over and over again I had to acknowledge my compulsion to manipulate people and situations, to lie and deceive, in order to achieve a short-term gain. I also had to acknowledge that those acts resulted in harm to other people: my kids, Jane, Mara, all of my friends and associates.

I could admit that I had a problem with manipulation. I could also accept that I suffered from a great many other defects. Prison makes you open to such thoughts. The DAP program pushes you through the door of acceptance. You do it because you can see it's the right thing, but also because of the reward—a reduced sentence—that waits at the end. Besides the goal of early release, which was a wonderful motivator, I actually benefited from the distance between Milan and Los Angeles. West Coast friends had to take a long, expensive flight to see me. As a result, even Mara and Robert came less frequently. That gave me more time to focus on my program, to make sure I would graduate.

As my time in the Drug and Alcohol Program dwindled, I became almost superstitious about not messing up. All of us in the cadre felt that way, and we kept an eye on each other. I also began to reflect on what I had learned, how I had changed in prison. Though I wasn't actually a substance abuser, I had learned that I had become hooked on certain experiences—achieving wealth, public adulation, setting records in business and sports. I had set myself up for the fall that brought me to Milan by training people to need me in an almost childlike way, and then feeding my ego with their dependency. I was the big father figure, and I loved the rewards—the respect, wealth, love—that came to me as a result of playing that role.

On the day I graduated from the program and they handed me my certificate, I could say that I had gotten control of my ego habit. But it wasn't all gone. Like a drunk who has to live in a world of bars and liquors, I knew there would be temptations everywhere. However, I understood my problems. And if I could stay honest with myself, I could avoid a return to my old ways. I no longer needed to grab attention at any cost or to be the center of attention in every room I entered. I wanted, instead, to make a life based on connections with people who loved me for the person I was, rather than what I could do for them.

. . .

Two people who related to me simply because they cared—Mara and Robert—would be the first people I met when I left the prison on March 7, 2001. On the night before my release I packed everything I wanted to take with me in a single bag. The rest I gave away. Rollo got my radio. I distributed commissary stuff and shoes to whoever asked for them. Then I laid out the clothes that Mara had sent for me to wear—simple sweats and a jacket.

The departure process would require quite a bit of paperwork. I got to the unit where they released you at 5 A.M. There were already half a dozen men there. The staff wouldn't show up for another hour. I felt a certain excitement, but I was also calm. I didn't want anything to go wrong.

When they told us to put on our civilian clothes, I discovered that I had the plainest outfit of all. The poorest inmates, those who had to accept charity from the prison, had been given garish mismatched stuff that looked like it came from a donation box at some supermarket. Other guys wore flashy suits and gold chains. One man put on a leather suit with matching shoes.

I received the cash left in my commissary account—about $200. And we all got travel cards to serve as identification. I would need that at the airport. Those were red cards with the words INMATE TRAVEL written across them. For a moment, I imagined what the airline check-in agent would think when I handed it over. Then I realized I didn't care. I was being released.

At about 8 A.M., one of the guards called out to the group, "Okay everybody. Your folks are out there." Cars were lined up on the road in front of the prison. The routine called for an officer outside to allow the cars to drive up to the gate, one at a time. When a car stopped, the man they were there to retrieve would be allowed through the door. Once they pulled away, the next car would be signaled forward.

When my turn came, I went through the gate and saw Robert behind the wheel of a rented car, and Mara in the seat beside him. I hurriedly opened the back door, behind Mara, and got in. She turned to kiss me, and we were off. Words cannot describe how it felt to be with them in a regular car, driving down an open road, for the first time in five years.

Though we had a little extra time, I refused Robert's offers to stop for coffee or breakfast. I wanted to get to the airport and on the plane that would take us to Los Angeles. At the airport, I was struck by the bustle of life in the terminal. Then we stopped at a newsstand and I was overwhelmed. They had so many magazines and paperback books for sale. For five years a paperback book had been like gold to me. Now I felt like I was standing in King Solomon's mine. I grabbed as many as I could hold, forgetting that I was no longer restrained from reading whatever I chose.

On the way to our gate I saw a Starbucks and said, "Oh, my God, a latte. That's what I really want." I listened as the man who took my order used steam to heat the milk and make froth on the top. I was nervous, happy, excited, even afraid that what I was experiencing was not real. It was not until I was in my seat on the airplane and we roared into the sky that I began to truly accept that I was no longer in prison. Looking out the window, at the sunlit clouds and the expanse of Earth below, I suddenly experienced a feeling I had forgotten for five years: optimism. This is how it feels to be starting over, I thought to myself. It felt good.

POSTSCRIPT

~

TO SAY THAT MY GREAT run through the coin business, movies, and sports was "fun while it lasted" may sound flippant, given how I ended up. But if you have come this far with me, and read the whole story, you understand that I cannot deny how much I enjoyed it. Setting records in coin sales, winning horse races against the world's best, making movies, grabbing Gretzky, reaching the Stanley Cup finals: Anyone would be satisfied by one of those experiences. I had had them all.

Perhaps the fact that I chased so many dreams, and felt driven to grab them all, explains why I ultimately fell from grace. The hunger that was my need to please, achieve, and impress began when I was a boy with a silent, often rejecting father who could not recognize me as a good and worthwhile child. That original, deep-seated need to get his approval came to define my life. Because I failed to recognize what it truly was—a need to be loved—that desire was never satisfied. Instead, it drove me to achieve at impossible levels. And it is when we try to achieve the impossible that we start cutting corners, breaking rules, breaking laws.

I like to remind people, and myself, that the frauds I perpetrated were against institutions, not individuals. This is true. I didn't bilk little old ladies out of their savings. (If there were any who had invested in the Athena Funds, Merrill Lynch had repaid them.) I took money from faceless, nameless banks, and given how most people feel about banks, a lot of you might take some secret pleasure in what I did. But the deeper truth is that I did hurt a lot of people, especially my children; my ex-wife, Jane; Mara; and the people who worked for me. I believe that there are even millions of hockey fans who lost something when I could no longer devote myself to the game.

The character flaws I identified in myself with the help of DAP counselors in Milan and five years of personal reflection are real. But they are also universal. If there is a lesson in my story, it is that it is human to want love, attention, and security. And under the right circumstances, any one of us might fall into a cycle of manipulation, self-delusion, that can lead to crime. It all depends on both our character and our environment.

Just as nature and nurture compete to influence our physical and intellectual growth, I would argue that they also affect how we conduct our lives. In my case, I was born with a craving for love and attention that was not satisfied. That was my nature. As an adult I was nurtured in an environment—the Storytown that is Los Angeles—that encouraged me to use whatever means necessary, including fabrications and falsehoods, to get what I wanted, what I needed. I was like a compulsive gambler set down on the Vegas Strip.

Upon my release from prison, I was assigned to a halfway house, a dreary converted motel on the corner of Sunset and Western, one of L.A.'s worst neighborhoods. A few months later I was permitted to live on my own. However, I will be on probation until 2006, and the restitution I owe to my creditors—millions upon millions of dollars—will be garnished from every paycheck I receive, probably for the rest of my life.

As much as Mara and I both hoped that our partnership would resume and thrive, it didn't. Our years of separation, and the wounds that I inflicted upon the relationship, were too much. After living together for a short time, we split up. We remain close friends. I don't think that will ever change.

However, I have changed, for the better. At least that's what my children report. They are just about grown now, and can tell me how they feel. Overall, I would say that we have become closer as a result of the ordeal. I know I have learned to value them more than ever, and I try hard to stay in touch with them.

Today I do value the people I love above the money and achievements that come with a career. I have discovered that a great many of my friends and associates feel the same way. The Gretzkys, Frank Gehry, Michael Eisner, Kurt Russell and Goldie Hawn, Alan Thicke, the Robitailles, Emmanuel de Seroux, Burt Sugarman, and Mary Hart—there really are too many good souls to name. Their support for Bruce McNall, the flawed and humbled man, has been greater than it was for Bruce McNall, the toast of Los Angeles.

Of course, my new life will require meaningful work so that I can pay my way and, as much as possible, repay my debts. I have become a business partner to Robert Geringer, who showed unwavering support when I was in prison. We're going into the entertainment business, but this time at a modest, manageable level. We are discovering that as much as it is a land of illusion, Hollywood can also be a place of forgiveness and generosity. There are a great many people in town who understand what happened to me, recognize that I retain valuable talents, and want to do business with me again.

The irony in my return to the real world, and the community where I went so wrong before, lies in the fact that what I always wanted—love and acceptance for who I was—is there for me. I have even begun to enjoy a better relationship with my father. I suspect it was always there. I just needed to take an incredible journey, from fame and fortune to ultimate failure, before I could recognize it.

INDEX

~